Boston Confucianism

SUNY series in Chinese Philosophy and Culture
David L. Hall and Roger T. Ames, editors

Boston Confucianism

PORTABLE TRADITION IN THE
LATE-MODERN WORLD

Robert Cummings Neville

STATE UNIVERSITY OF NEW YORK PRESS

Published by
State University of New York Press

For information, address State University of New York Press,
90 State Street, Suite 700, Albany, NY 12207

Production by Marilyn P. Semerad
Marketing by Anne M. Valentine
Cover concept, photos, and drawings by Beth Neville

Library of Congress Cataloging-in-Publication Data

Neville, Robert C.
    Boston Confucianism : portable tradition in the late-modern world / Robert
Cummings Neville.
        p. cm. — (SUNY series in Chinese philosophy and culture)
    Includes bibliographical references and index.
    ISBN 0-7914-4717-0 (alk. paper) — ISBN 0-7914-4718-9 (pbk. : alk paper)
    1. Confucianism.   2. Philosophy, Comparative.   3. East and West.   4. Tu,
Wei-ming—Views on Confucianism.   I. Title.   II. Series.

BL1852.N48 2000
181'.112—dc21   00-020624
                          10 9 8 7 6 5 4 3 2 1

Dedicated to Thomas Berry
Mentor in World Philosophy

Contents

Foreword by Tu Weiming   xi

Preface   xxi

1. The Short Happy Life of Boston Confucianism   1
    1.1. Portable Confucianism: Roots and Branches   1
    1.2. Ritual Propriety   8
    1.3. Pragmatism   11
    1.4. Confucian Critique for Boston   15
    1.5. Bostonian Modifications of Confucianism   21

2. Confucianism on Culture   25
    2.1. Philosophy of Culture   25
    2.2. An Elementary Theory of Culture and
         Nature in Xunzi   27
    2.3. Chinese Orientations to Culture: Confucian,
         Daoist, Legalist, Moist, and Buddhist   29
    2.4. Confucius, Mencius, and Xunzi Compared   33
    2.5. Confucian Contributions to a Contemporary
         Philosophy of Culture   38

3. Confucianism in the Contemporary Situation   41
    3.1. Historical Background   41
    3.2. Interpretive, Bridging, and Normative Philosophers   43
    3.3. Roger T. Ames and David L. Hall   47
    3.4. Cheng Chungying   50
    3.5. Wu Kuangming   52

4. Confucian Spirituality   57

   4.1. Philosophy and Religion   57

   4.2. Spirituality and Ultimate Reality:
       Defining Hypotheses   62

   4.3. Self, Truth, and Transformation   69

   4.4. Confucian Spirituality in a Scientific Society   74

   4.5. Confucian Spirituality in a Global
       Moral Democracy and Ecology   79

5. Tu Weiming's Confucianism   83

   5.1. Conversation and Existential Choice:
       Way of the Sage   83

   5.2. The Question of Conversion   88

   5.3. The Question of Ritual   92

   5.4. The Question of Love (Ren)   96

   5.5. The Question of Evil   102

6. Motif Analysis East and West   107

   6.1. Motif Analysis   107

   6.2. Comparison   111

   6.3. Ancient Cultural Motifs and Their Development   115

   6.4. Relations of Motifs to Deeper Imaginative Artifacts 121

   6.5. Motifs and Their Sequelae   124

7. Motifs of Being   129

   7.1. The Trouble with Being   129

   7.2. Philosophy as Engagement   131

   7.3. Western Motifs for Being   134

   7.4. The Dialectic of Being   135

   7.5. South and East Asian Motifs for Being   139

8. Motifs of Transcendence   147

   8.1. Transcendence as a Category   147

   8.2. Transcendence in Ancient Confucianism   151

   8.3. Transcendence in Neo-Confucianism   154

   8.4. God and the Imago Dei   158

   8.5. John Wesley and the Image of God   161

9. Resources for a Conception of Selfhood   167
     9.1. Problems with the Self   167
     9.2. The Self as Contradictory and Self-Deceived in
         Western Thought   169
     9.3. The Self in Confucian Thought   175
     9.4. Self-Deception in Confucian Thought   179
     9.5. The Self as Orientation and Poise   186

10. Confucianism, Christianity, and Multiple Religious Identity   193
     10.1. Engaging Problematic Cases   193
     10.2. Filial Piety as Holy Duty   194
     10.3. Ritual Propriety   201
     10.4. Jesus as Model   204
     10.5. Multiple Religious Identity   206

Notes   211

Bibliography   223

Index   237

Foreword

Tu Weiming

The first time the idea of "Boston Confucians" came into being, not simply as a casual reference but as a well-conceived designation, was when Robert Neville entitled his contribution "A Short Happy Life of Boston Confucians" for the 1994 *Daedalus* authors' conference for the special issue on China in Transformation. Although the editors then felt that the idea was too novel and too idiosyncratic for Sinologists, I was deeply impressed by its conceptual clarity and its predictive power. While I agreed with my colleagues in Chinese studies that Neville's idea did not quite fit the pattern of the China in Transformation issue, I strongly sensed that, in the long run, "Boston Confucians" would outlast in relevance and significance most of our contemporary, if not journalistic, observations of Whither China. Indeed, Neville has single-handedly identified a vibrant intellectual activity, and by so doing, he virtually created a discourse community with all the fruitful ambiguities that a potent symbolic force engenders.

It would be grossly inaccurate to assume that Neville actually "manufactured" Boston Confucianism. His own involvement in the Confucian discourse was a precondition for his ability to recognize the phenomenon and to give it a proper name. Without his own philosophical odyssey, which included strenuous scholarly journeys to Hong Kong, Seoul, and Beijing, he would not have been prepared to strike a sympathetic resonance with fellow Boston Confucians, let alone fellow Confucians in East Asia. Furthermore, through his long and concerted effort to actively engage himself in Confucian-Christian dialogues, not only as a theological exercise but also as a spiritual discipline, he has become so musical to Confucian motifs that the sympathetic resonance he evokes in his conversation partners is a reflection of his own personal knowledge as well. His inner mental attentiveness acquired through self-cultivation enables him to listen

xi

well to the subtle activation of the feeble "Confucian" voices around him with an attuned ear. Surely, Neville never claims to be a Sinologist, but his grasp of the Confucian *Problematik* and his sensitivity to the contemporary relevance of the Confucian project have made him not only a worthy colleague but also a seasoned internal critic of the Confucian tradition and its modern transformation. For many of us, he is a truly exceptional teacher-friend.

One of the most challenging tasks in studying Confucianism as a living tradition in a comparative cultural perspective is translation. To me, thinking in English from Confucian roots is a daunting hermeneutic praxis. Leaving aside all the technical issues of translating classical Chinese characters into meaningful English words, the fundamental question of whether or not Confucian ethics could be taught in languages other than classical Chinese is still unresolved in Sinological circles. However, I fully agree with Neville that as those who have not mastered ancient Greek or Hebrew can still make original contributions to Greek philosophy or Christian religion in English, even without direct access to the classical texts, enlightening and insightful observations about the Confucian tradition and its modern transformation are possible and practicable. Of course, some forms of scholarship such as that which require philological competence, cannot be done by Neville or, for that matter, David Hall or Herbert Fingarette. Yet it is obvious that, without their generous participation, Confucian studies as a field would have been significantly impoverished.

Since I do teach and write in Chinese, I am acutely aware of the inevitable loss or distillation of the "original flavor" as potent Confucian ideas of *ren, yi, li, zhi* and *xin* are translated as humanity (benevolence), rightness (righteousness), ritual propriety, wisdom and trust. Yet if Confucianism as a living tradition is to continue to evolve, it cannot afford to remain linguistically forever inscribed in a Sinitic mode. Surely the tradition is so much intertwined with Chinese culture that once it is detached from its Sinitic origins, its inner identity, its authenticity becomes problematical. One may point to the fact that before the Western impact in the mid-nineteenth century, even though Confucianism had spread to Vietnam, Korea, and Japan (and thus assumed several distinctly non-Sinic forms), classical Chinese was always the medium of communication among educated Confucian scholars throughout East and Southeast Asia. Although, unlike the relationship between Islam and Arabic, a theological argument for expressing Confucian ideas solely in classical Chinese has never been made, it was not even a rejected possibility for traditional Confucians to entertain alternative media of communication. Understandably, when

Neville began to talk about ritual propriety (*li*) as a Boston Confucian, he raised challenging questions about the nature of the Confucian discourse that he envisions and the prospects of the Confucian tradition becoming an integral part of American intellectual self-reflexivity.

I have been intrigued by these questions. When I first encountered the issue of teaching Confucian ethics in English as part of a primary and secondary school curriculum in Singapore in the 1980s, I strongly felt that the Confucian discourse as I understood it was entering a new threshold and that, for its own well-being, it could not recoil into its Sinitic or East Asian safety net. The danger of losing its original flavor, decentering its inner identity and problematizing its authenticity notwithstanding, the creative possibility, not to mention the intellectual excitement, of thinking philosophically and religiously about Confucianism in terms of humanity, rightness, ritual propriety, wisdom, and trust was too important and exciting to resist. This awareness helped me to put my career in Confucian studies in North America in a new perspective. In retrospect, without sustained effort to broaden and deepen my understanding of the Confucian tradition by discussing its core values in English with colleagues at Princeton, Columbia, Berkeley, and Harvard, I would not have been prepared to offer a course on Confucian philosophy in Chinese at Beijing University in 1985. Nor would I have had the courage and the resources to invite colleagues in mainland China to take part in a joint venture to revitalize the Confucian discourse as a cross-cultural hermeneutic enterprise.

What Neville has offered, however, is more than a way of philosophizing from Confucian roots in English. Intent on making the Confucian discourse relevant to modern America, he suggests a method of doing comparative philosophy with profound implications for reconfiguring Confucianism as a contemporary philosophy of culture. As a philosopher and the dean of a major school of theology, Neville's self-definition as a Boston Confucian is fitting in the sense that what he aspires to is the Confucian principle of the unity of knowledge and action, rather than the separation of the contemplative and active modes of life. As a Confucian, Neville is politically concerned, socially engaged and culturally obliged. The idea of the scholar-official may not serve as a standard of inspiration for him working in the academic community, but as a scholar-administrator, since his administrative responsibility forms an integral part of his commitment to the life of the mind, he is inevitably involved in the practical living that the Confucians take for granted. In this particular sense, the idea of the public intellectual, a functional equivalent of the Confucian literatus in modern America, is more appropriate as a model for him than the Greek philosopher, the Hebrew prophet, the Christian priest, or the Hindu guru.

As an exemplification of the public intellectual, Neville is impressed by the relevance of the Confucian classics, the Confucian praxis of ritual propriety and the Confucian idea of selfhood for contemporary American education, especially education for the sake of "cultivating humanity." Specifically, he recommends that the Four Books (*The Great Learning, The Analects, Mencius,* and *The Doctrine of the Mean*) and Xunzi, together with selected writings and sayings of the Neo-Confucian masters (notably Zhu Xi and Wang Yangming), be incorporated into the curricula of American colleges. The assumption is that the core values in Confucian moral self-cultivation are of profound significance for educating future generations of American leaders. Furthermore, the introduction of the praxis of ritual propriety in the lifeworld of university campuses can enhance the development of ethical intelligence, as well as cognitive intelligence, in liberal arts education. Indeed, the idea of the self as a center of relationships, informed by classical learning and ritual practice, can serve as a wholesome reference for the strong individualistic habits of the heart in modern American youth culture.

However, it is misleading to interpret Neville's fascination with Confucian ethics as merely a heuristic corrective to what is happening in the United States today. Although as a pragmatist he is seasoned in the language of expediency and practicality, his philosophy of culture transcends any narrowly utilitarian conceptions of usefulness. Rather, his intellectual commitment to and existential engagement in the Confucian project is predicated on an ecumenical vision of the human condition in which dialogue among civilizations is inevitable and inspirational. The exclusive dichotomy of "the West and the rest" must be replaced by a holistic notion of the emerging world culture. As the West is present in virtually all corners of the globe, often not by invitation, the rest has also made its presence in the West, especially in North America, sometimes through immigration. The coexistence of many religiophilosophical currents on the American spiritual scene may not automatically lead to the desirable fusion of horizons, but it presents an unprecedented challenge to the contemporary American philosophical self-reflexivity.

Neville's response to this challenge is to develop a world culture of philosophy through a creative reconstruction of American philosophy. By incorporating Confucianism, among other world philosophic cultures, into this intellectual endeavor, he intends to show to his col-

leagues (professional philosophers, theologians, comparative religion-
ists, and other theory-minded scholars in the humanities and social
sciences) that the complexity of late-modernity demands that serious
thinkers everywhere make a concerted effort "to embrace all the traditions within the world culture of philosophy." This inclusive vision
may be seen as his articulation of faith: "the world society will never
be civilized until a genuine world culture is developed that respects
the diverse cultures and harmonizes them to make crucial responses
to such issues as care for the environment, distributive justice, and the
meaning of human life in the cosmos." Boston Confucianism so conceived is a step toward the transformation of seemingly highly specific
local knowledge into a globally significant philosophical task.

For more than 150 years, East Asian thinkers have been devoted
students of Western learning. They have appropriated Dutch, British,
French, German, and American learning as a necessary path for their
own intellectual maturation in the modern world. Nowadays, knowledge about the West has become a defining characteristic of being a
public intellectual in China, Japan, Korea, and Vietnam. Three generations of New Confucians since the 1919 Chinese May Fourth Movement have fully incorporated Western ideas into their reconstruction
of the Confucian tradition. An important focus of their communal
critical self-consciousness has been the authentic possibility of a creative response to the Enlightenment mentality of the modern West
without totally deconstructing the comprehensive humanistic vision
central to Confucian cultural identity for centuries. There are rays of
hope, but the dawning of a new era of world philosophy, acknowledging the positive contribution of the Confucian discourse, requires patient
watchfulness.

Ironically, since Hegel, the belief that all non-Western axial-age
civilizations ought to be relegated to the sunrise stage is still firm in
the academy East and West. In the People's Republic of China, the
decoupling of the Confucian tradition from the feudal past has only
begun to gather momentum. The practice of measuring Confucian
thought and practice according to the yardsticks of science and democracy is still common. The teacher-disciple relationship between
Dewey and Hu Shi and Feng Youlan in the beginning of the twentieth
century has been so much ingrained in the collective memory of modern
Chinese intellectuals that a leap of faith is required for them to imagine
the possibility that Confucianism (China's past) may be heuristically
relevant to America's present. The matter is compounded by the fact
that since the end of the Second World War, the United States has
assumed the role of a teaching civilization for East Asia. This asymmetry

in Sino-American scholarly communication makes it painfully difficult for American society to transform itself into a learning culture in reference to East Asia. In this connection, Neville's story about Boston Confucianism is truly exceptional, if not unique.

Although implicit in Neville's chapter "The Short Happy Life of Boston Confucianism" is a move from the politics of domination to the politics of inclusion, his project, far from a strategy in the politics of recognition, transcends politics and, for that matter, ideology. It is intrinsically a hermeneutic praxis within the Confucian discourse itself. His distinction between Boston Confucianism on the two sides of the Charles River clearly indicates that he is not satisfied with the "axiological thinking" centered around Mencius and that he underscores the importance of Xunzi as a major contributor to the contemporary significance of ritual propriety. In so doing he self-consciously defines his own Confucian genealogy, both departing from and returning to the classical Confucian insights in the Mencian tradition. Furthermore, by linking the Confucian *Problematik* with Dewey's pragmatism and Charles S. Peirce's semiotics, he strongly suggests a collaborative line of inquiry for mutual elucidation and enrichment. Surely Neville philosophizes as a Confucian thinker, but as a Christian theologian and a comparative religionist, he primarily frames his ideas in the context of world philosophy of culture with particular emphasis on the American scene. Against the backdrop of this kind of ecumenism, despite his deep sympathy with and personal knowledge of the New Confucians, Neville meditates on the Confucian project in a critical spirit. This critical spirit can also be construed as an invitation, an encouragement to offer Confucian perspectives on major American thinkers such as Jonathan Edwards, Ralph Emerson, William James, and Alfred North Whitehead.

Actually, Neville's methodology—motif analysis in a comparative cultural perspective—does not at all privilege any particular tradition. As far as Confucianism is concerned, the demands of motif analysis, as a form of modern scholarship, are rigorous. The reinterpretation of core Confucian texts and the reconstruction of their practical implications for the world of late-modern global culture require that "the background assumptions and social situational factors [be] made much more explicit than traditional intracultural scholarship has been wont to do." As a result, the philosophically minded New Confucians must be willing to engage themselves in a mode of thinking unprecedented and unimaginable within the safe haven of their own symbolic universe. Neville's "motifs of being" and "motifs of transcendence" have opened up new space for resourceful reinterpretation and set a new agenda for creative reconstruction of the Confucian project.

Neville's warning that "it would be disastrous for contemporary Confucian spirituality to retreat to 'mere humanism' in order to avoid the challenge of modern science" is thought-provoking. Yet he observes:

> The dimension of Confucian spirituality that relates to the ultimate as grounding value and human value-discernment is simply impossible for contemporary persons whose sensibilities are deeply formed by the fact-value dichotomy suppositions of the theory of knowledge usually associated with modern science.

His wise counsel, then, is that "contemporary Confucianism needs to develop a comprehensive conception of knowledge expressive of its core motifs of value and valuation, a kind of axiology of thinking" which must address "four families of thinking, imagination, interpretation, theory, and practical reason." His trilogy, *Reconstruction of Thinking* (1981), *Recovery of the Measure* (1989), and *Normative Cultures* (1995), offers a coherent picture of how these seminal ideas are profoundly meaningful for reconstructing "the valuable elements of the Confucian tradition's symbols, from Mencius' Four Beginnings to Mou Zongsan's moral metaphysics."

I fully agree with Neville that we need to go beyond "existential Confucianism" and develop a theory of ritual as constitutive of humanity so that the New Confucian approach to norms can be made more effective in an age of pluralism, social disintegration, and conflict. I greatly appreciate Neville's calling our attention to the authentic possibility of formulating "the ritual theory of normative cultures" from Confucian resources in the Xunzian tradition, but if we are mindful of the fluidity and dynamism of meaning-making in live conventions, we need to avoid the danger of essentializing, if not museumizing, ritual as a static structure. Neville's idea of the self as "maintaining poise in balancing all together" rather than as "a fixed pattern of harmonization" is instructive. By emphasizing "(1) the relational character of personal existence in orientation, (2) the harmonizing character of individual life in poise, and (3) the particular character of individuality in actions, he offers a persuasive reading of the Confucian conception of the ritual life.

However, the matter is complicated by his insistence on the fourth condition: "the derivative character of all three from the principle or God who makes harmonious things possible and real." The need of the fourth proposition for making the Confucian tradition "spiritual" rather than "merely human" is obvious. Yet I am still hesitant to accept Neville's strong thesis that the creation myth and, by implication, the transcendent God are necessary conditions for Confucian spirituality. While I am deeply indebted to him for posing the question concerning "the seriousness of the alienation from heavenly principle or divinity at one's heart and the correlative question of the role of heavenly principle or divinity as a necessary means of grace for the recovery from alienation," I prefer at this juncture to consider, in the spirit of the philosophy of change and transformation, the cosmic process as the unfolding of creativity in-itself. Principle or God as creativity, rather than as a creator outside the cosmos, enables human beings to cultivate a form of life that aspires to fruitful interaction between the individual and community, sustained harmony between the human species and nature, and mutual responsiveness between the Way of Heaven and the human heart-and-mind. The sense of self as being constituted by self-reflexivity containing contradiction does not invalidate the hope that "forming one body with heaven, earth, and the myriad things" is a human responsibility ontologically grounded and aesthetically articulated.

To me, personally, the most intriguing issue is Neville's challenge to the Mencian interpretation of the Confucian project concerning positive evil. His powerful example from Saint Augustine clearly illustrates that the human psyche, for lack of a more apt description, possesses an urge to do evil, something like the destructive will. How do we recognize such an obvious fact of life, if we do not accord any ontological status to evil? Whether or not Augustine himself, in the last analysis, defined evil in terms of the absence of good, his example of the destructive will need not lead to the conclusion that human nature is endowed with aggression as a sort of psychophysiological reality. On the contrary, the aggressive behavior that does not seem to have any element of goodness in it may result from a desire which, in itself, does not necessarily lead to antisocial or inhuman consequences. Imagine the desire of an adolescent to show off. It may simply take the form of trying to impress others with what one is capable of doing (climbing up a tree, picking a fruit, and hitting a target with it). This inappropriate act seems innocuous at first glance, but upon reflection, its inadequacy becomes obvious. The problem with that particular desire is that it was allowed to be expressed perhaps because of youthful ignorance. The proper response is to recognize its potential destructiveness and learn to displace or transform it by moral training or self-cultivation.

After all, this is how the examined life in accordance with ritual purports to be. Either Confucian or Aristotelian ethics encourages the cultivation of ethical intelligence rooted in the desire for human flourishing. Augustine's answer to "What is man that thou art mindful of him?" seems in perfect accord with the Mencian faith in self-realization. If we are made in the image of God, our ability to overcome alienation is deeply rooted in our human nature. The Pauline assertion that it is the "devil" in me that has seduced me into sin is problematical precisely because, as an illocutionary utterance, the speaker who has acknowledged that uneasiness must have already transformed that unhappy situation through reflection and deliberation. It is in the same spirit that I cannot accept Kierkegaard's characterization of Abraham as the "knight of faith," let alone the idea of "absurdity" as a defining characteristic of total commitment to the wholly other. For the true voice of human conscience, tantamount to God's command, is not to sacrifice one's own son for the glory of an unknowable creator but to create and procreate as a way of participating in the cosmic joint venture: "Heaven engenders, human completes!"

It is not without fear and trembling that I allow myself to articulate a possible link between the Confucian idea of the "great transformation" (*dahua*) as the unfolding of creativity in-itself and the Christian vision of the omnipresent and omniscient God. To avoid the predicament of theodicy, we may venture to imagine that God's love for humanity is so profound and complete that, by granting us freedom, omnipotence, in practicality, is no longer an unquestioned divine attribute. There is structural limitation to grace, despite God's unlimited compassion. Therefore, human self-destructiveness is real and the continuous well-being of the cosmos requires human stewardship. Such is the magnitude and awesomeness of our human responsibility, not only to ourselves but also to heaven, earth, and the myriad things. My veil of ignorance on theological matters is so thick that only in appreciation of Neville's most inspiring and generous overture do I dare share my tentative thoughts with the anticipation that the dialogue will continue.

Preface

Ernest Hemingway's short story, "The Short Happy Life of Francis Macomber," has long seemed to me an exquisite evocation of the value of a life achieved and fulfilled in a brief moment. So it was that I adapted Hemingway's title for the first chapter in this book, convinced that at a particular moment the Confucian tradition had achieved the status of a world philosophy, in the sense that it could be claimed by those of non–East Asian origin just as Plato and Aristotle can be claimed by non-Greeks. After the moment passed, I thought, it would be only ordinary for anyone to be able to be a Confucian.

At the Second Confucian-Christian Dialogue Conference, held in Berkeley, California, in 1991, three participants, John H. Berthrong, Chung Chai-sik, and I, attended from Boston. At the First Confucian-Christian Dialogue Conference, in Hong Kong in 1988, we three had also been in attendance, but then only I was from Boston; Tu Weiming from Boston attended the first conference and helped plan the second. So as the conference opened in Berkeley, many joking remarks were made about the growing school of "Boston Confucianism." Part of the joke had to do with people moving from Korea (Chung) and Canada (Berthrong) to Boston. But the funnier part was that the phrase "Boston Confucianism" is oxymoronic: Bostonians might be brahmins but only East Asians can be Confucians.

As the conference progressed a major theme dividing the participants was whether Confucianism indeed is so intimately related to and expressive of Chinese ethnic culture that it can be transplanted to other lands only through the massive infusion of Chinese influence. Is Confucianism rooted and rootable only in East Asian culture? To those who argued that one cannot understand Confucianism without being born into or adopting an East Asian culture preformed by Confucian-

xxi

ism, I answered that these conditions do not obtain even within parallel Western traditions of philosophy. Very few American philosophers have a Greek ethnic heritage, and few have a working knowledge of the classical Greek language. Yet nearly every American philosopher identifies herself or himself as a Platonist or an Aristotelian. And every American philosopher without exception who holds a Ph.D. in the field can discuss ideas attributed to Plato and Aristotle. Plato and Aristotle are world philosophers to Westerners who are not Greek; they are also world philosophers in the curricula of most contemporary philosophical academies in East Asia and India. Now the Chinese philosophies should also be world philosophies in all philosophic academies, I urged with support from my Boston colleagues.

East Asian Confucian philosophers have been responding to Western philosophies for well over a century.[1] They have asked how Chinese traditions can learn from and also criticize Western thought. The wholesale adoption in this century of Marxist philosophy by at least one large segment of Chinese scholar-officials is an extraordinary chapter in the world history of cross-cultural borrowings. But there is a difference between relating Western philosophy to the East Asian situation and what I am talking about. My point concerns living as a Confucian outside the East Asian situation. My own Confucianism grows not by responding to Western influences but by being used for living philosophically in the Western situation, or rather in a world situation with mixed cultural heritages.

Some of us at the Berkeley conference argued that Confucianism and Daoism from the beginning have been critical philosophies that have existed in serious dialectical tensions with their indigenous cultures. Confucius, Mencius, and Xunzi complained that in their day the ancient practices that constitute harmonious civilization had been corrupted so that people no longer by habit were filial, capable of true friendship, or socially responsible. Laozi and Zhuangzi complained that the human assertion of artificial forms obscured the natural connections with the dao. The ancient Moists and Legalists were also reformers. Over the centuries East Asian cultures became deeply influenced and shaped by these philosophies. At various times one or another of these philosophies, and others, had official sanction at court. Although both Confucianism and Daoism sometimes argued by appealing to lost virtues of the past, and therefore presented themselves as appearing conservative (see *Analects* 7.1, 19), they in fact called for change, often for radical change.[2] Sometimes the change itself was conservative. Because of the centuries of dialectical interaction, it is impossible to understand East Asian culture except as reflecting *changes* wrought by Confucianism and Daoism.

Might it also be possible to transport the ancient Chinese traditions of philosophy into the context of non–East Asian cultures and learn from their critical and speculative perspectives? Although I *read about* Confucianism in the context of East Asian culture in order to understand its critical and speculative perspectives, philosophically I *think with* Confucianism in relation to my own mainly Western culture and in relation to the various problems of world cultures. Confucianism today faces problems of multicultural embodiments and indigenization analogous to those faced by Christianity, Islam, and Buddhism. "Boston Confucianism" became identified with this view at the Berkeley conference because those of us from Boston defended it, and the oxymoronic sound of the name emphasized the point.

Then an extraordinary thing happened. Partway through the conference, two feminist participants attacked Confucianism for its patriarchal oppression of women in East Asia. There were several interesting responses to the attack. One was to admit its validity and reject Confucianism, an unpopular response at a conference of Confucian scholars. Another was to admit the validity of the claim but to say that Confucianism was right to subordinate women; this position was argued meekly and only during coffee breaks out of the earshot of women. A third response was to say that the claims about patriarchal oppression are exaggerated; no women responded this way.

The fourth and most interesting response was to draw a sharp distinction between primary or "primal" East Asian culture, which is admittedly patriarchal, and the Confucian movement that offers a critical lever in favor of harmony and against any oppression that fails to honor "principle" in each person. "Principle" is the Neo-Confucian category for the ground of definiteness and the drive toward harmonization in process. Identified with the Boston Confucians, this fourth response can admit that, although Confucianism often became male-oriented and forced women into servile roles, this is not the fault of Confucianism as a living philosophy but of the primal culture over which Confucianism never fully prevailed. Like Daoism, Confucianism in its early and late basic texts emphasizes reciprocity rather than oppressive subordination, and like Daoism Confucianism waged a critical and often losing war against primal patriarchalism. That Confucianism more often than Daoism became the social vehicle of patriarchal customs in East Asia speaks only to its success in becoming powerful and corrupted by power, not to its basic commitments.

The "primal culture" of Boston is the rationalist egalitarianism of the European Enlightenment mixed with vigorous ethnic and minority communities from all over the world. Has Confucianism anything to say to this? Perhaps it can rework its criticism of Moism and emphasize "love with distinctions" so as to humanize abstract egalitarianism and respect conflicting cultural differences. I shall argue below that the way to do this is with a new ritualization of Boston (Western) modes of social discourse and interaction. An analysis of the dialectical and critical relation Confucianism should have to American culture might very well cast retrospective light on its dialectical and critical relation to primal East Asian culture. It was observed at the conference, for instance, that one major reshaping of Confucianism in the American context is that it places relatively more emphasis on the virtues of public life than on the virtues of filiality, although both are still important. Of those at the conference who identified with the position of Boston Confucianism, a significant number (Judith Berling, John Berthrong, William Theodore de Bary, and Rodney Taylor, as well as myself) were or had been academic deans or provosts, consciously identifying ourselves as scholar-officials.

The result of the conference discussion, especially after the feminist critique, was that a significant number of persons, East Asian as well as Western, identified themselves with the Boston Confucian position. Those of us in the religion business know that the enthusiasm of the Christian altar call often does not endure long after. Furthermore, Confucians in New York, Boulder, Berkeley, Hong Kong, Taipei, and Seoul might not want to identify themselves for very long by the proud name of Boston. So Boston Confucianism as a school might have had a short but happy life at that conference.

Nevertheless, a large number of scholars for years have attempted to develop Confucianism into a world philosophy rather than one limited to a specific historical culture.[3] The short happy life of Boston Confucianism provides an opportunity for an important rite of passage. Until now, self-professed East Asian Confucians have had to worry about their ethnic heritage, even in diaspora, and about how Confucianism responds to the modernization of East Asian societies. Non-Asians have had to think of themselves as scholars *of* Confucianism and sympathizers rather than as Confucians in and from non–East Asian cultures. But with the short happy life of Boston Confucianism, it is possible for ethnic East Asians to see Confucianism as a tradition with many cultural embodiments and identities. The first-generation people in diaspora have lived through at least two. Second, third, and fourth-generation citizens of Western countries whose ethnic heritage is East Asian have lived in only Western Confucian contexts. Those of us with no ethnic connection to East Asia, who attempt to shape our personal and social lives by Confucian standards in Boston and elsewhere, can now acknowledge that we are Confucians of non–East Asian varieties. Moreover, under the brilliant leadership of Tu Weiming, a working group of Confucians has indeed been organized in Boston with that name. So, Boston Confucianism has achieved a real life that is happy but not as short as I had anticipated.

In its brief existence the school of Boston Confucianism has developed an internal structure, namely, a division of emphases between its proponents north of the Charles (Tu Weiming and his Harvard colleagues) and those south of the Charles (those of us centered at Boston University). North of the Charles River, which separates Cambridge from Boston City proper, they emphasize the Mencian tradition of *ren* ("humaneness"), and South of the Charles we emphasize Xunzi's concern for *li* ("ritual propriety"), and its potential connections with pragmatic semiotics. Each branch appreciatively recognizes the other's concerns, but maintains its emphasis. These issues are discussed briefly in Tu's foreword above and more extensively in the chapters below. The issues of emphasis are so delicate that I suspect that neither branch would affirm its own without the confidence that the other branch would make the other case. There is one school, for this reason.

II.

The reasons for public interest in Confucianism go far beyond the concerns of professional philosophers, Chinese intellectuals in diaspora, and persons involved in interfaith dialogue. Surely Geoffrey Barraclough (1964) was right to say that the important events of the first third of the nineteenth century were not those of the European settlement of boundaries and regimes in the aftermath of the Napoleonic wars but the extensions of the United States and Russia to the Pacific Ocean, the development of the China-India-West trade cycle, and the factors that vastly increased Asian populations. Now we are witnessing the rise of Asian powers to great importance in global politics and culture, equal to that of Europe and North America. Within a year of this writing (June 1998) economic turmoil in East and Southeast Asia has unsettled the global economy, and India and Pakistan have exploded nuclear bombs to show they could do it. What could be more important for understanding the world's fragile interlocked initiatives of power than a grasp of the philosophic assumptions defining the perspectives of each of those initiatives?

Confucianism is the philosophic ground of much of the culture in East and Southeast Asia.

Western readers might think that this is a case of the need to understand the "others." What naivete! How can we distinguish "us" from the "others?" No Asian country has failed to be influenced deeply by European and North American science, technology, and economic models; with these have come Western motives and definitions of what is important for life and civil society. Few European countries have failed to be enriched by significant Asian immigration and the cultures that come with that; Asian immigration in the United States is vast and influential. Very few people indeed live under the influence of only Western culture, or only some Asian one. Before the Internet it might have been possible to distinguish "us" from "others" on a sheerly geographic basis, but now even that is impossible.

The worldwide society is such that the outgrowths of the cultural roots of all the world's living ancient traditions are interacting nearly everywhere. Every contemporary person or group lives within a tangle of branches arising from many roots. We are defined by and define ourselves within the contemporary tangle, and sophistication includes sorting out the roots of the many branches within which we live. Samuel Huntington (1996) is 180 degrees wrong when he says we live in a time of the "clash of civilizations." On the contrary, we live in a time of the entanglement of civilizations. Sometimes groups attempt to disentangle certain roots with which they identify and to make them dominant; this is especially tragic when the roots are supposed to be ethnic and the effort involves ethnic cleansing or the establishment of an ethnic state. But the sheer pervasiveness of modernization, not to speak of all the other interactions of world cultures, makes that nostalgia mere whistling in the dark, regardless of what armies assemble at the whistle. Military victory would be no more advantageous than military defeat for keeping traditions true to their roots in the age of email.

The proper address to Confucianism, then, is to make it part of our culture in critical and sophisticated ways. The same could be said for the traditions of Islam, South Asia (religiously marked by Hinduisms and Buddhisms), the other traditions of East and Southeast Asia, and for Africa, South America, and various "traditional" or "indigenous" cultures. The Western tradition too has to be appropriated in critical and sophisticated ways. Indeed, each of these "traditions" is a family of traditions not to be understood in homogenized ways. Careful and respectful distinction for the sake of deferential appropriation increases our sense of the multifariousness of world cultures and makes the us-versus-them mentality utterly unrealistic. My own interest takes a special focus on Confucianism, however, because it seems peculiarly fruitful for what I believe to be the most important philosophic and cultural questions of our time, as discussed in the chapters below.

III.

For the first time in history it is possible for any self-conscious participant in a worldwide philosophical culture to speak of Confucianism in the same breath with Platonism and Aristotelianism, phenomenology and analytic philosophy, as a philosophy from which to learn and perhaps to inhabit and extend. Indeed, until recently the little worldwide philosophic culture that existed was almost exclusively Western in inspiration, spread abroad by modern European imperialism and implanted in universities everywhere with such vigor as to outlast the retreat of imperialism.[4] Confucianism is one of the most ancient philosophic traditions, older than any of those mentioned, and it has been perhaps the dominant intellectual influence in East Asian cultures. But until our time it did not play significantly in a worldwide philosophic culture.

Confucianism has entered the philosophic mainstream for many reasons. Surely among the most important reasons is personnel. Confucian philosophy in the twentieth century has enjoyed a most remarkably fertile relation between two generations. The extraordinary transformations of China after the May Fourth Movement of 1919 produced two kinds of reaction among the mature Chinese thinkers of that time. On the one hand were the Westernizers who treated Confucianism as the straitjacket of China; these included Marxists such as Mao Zedong and scientistic thinkers such as Hu Shi. On the other side were thinkers ready to learn from the West but devoted to reconstructing Confucianism for the modern world with a Confucian appropriation and criticism of Western culture and thought. Among these people were Hsiung Shih-li, Liang Shu-ming, Ma I-fu, Chang Tung-sun, Ch'ien Mu, Fang Tung-mei, Chang Chun-mai (Carson Chang), T'ang Chun-i, Hsu Fu-kuan, and Mou Zong-san. This last group endured the Communist revolution that rejected them as much as they rejected it, often, though not always, in exile in Taiwan or Hong Kong. They were avid students of Western philosophy but were convinced of the value, importance, and truth (not to put too fine a point on it) of Chinese philosophy. In diverse ways they developed careful and critical Confucian responses to the Western traditions of philosophy, interpreting Western philosophy in Chinese terms and sometimes interpreting Chinese philosophy to the West.

This group was succeeded by a truly remarkable generation of Chinese thinkers who were educated partly in East Asia but also in Western universities, who write in English primarily, but also in Chinese, and whose audience is as much the Western philosophical world as the East Asian. Several of these thinkers are discussed in chapter 3. What is most remarkable about this group is that each of them has made colleagues of non–East Asians. Some of these colleagues are professional Sinologists such as Roger T. Ames, William Theodore de Bary, Judith Berling, John H. Berthrong, Anne Birdwhistell, Irene Bloom, P. J. Ivanhoe, Rodney Taylor, and Mary Evelyn Tucker. Others, such as Herbert Fingarette, David L. Hall, Lee Yearley, and myself, are professional philosophers or what Tu Weiming calls "religiophilosophical thinkers" whose Sinology is a bit secondhand but for whom the Chinese philosophical traditions are major resources for thinking. This is the group, or group of overlapping groups, of East Asians and non–East Asians, of Sinologists and non-Sinologists that has entered the world culture of philosophy as "Confucians," "New Confucians," or "Boston Confucians."

Of course, many other conditions have been involved in creating our situation. Among the most important is the development by Western and East Asian Sinologists of a vast literature in Western languages, especially English, that makes Chinese philosophy accessible to non-Sinologists. One thinks of the outstanding works of translation. Then there are the scholarly institutions for carrying on the Confucian conversation in the larger world context, including the *Journal for Chinese Philosophy* and the International Society for Chinese Philosophy, both founded by Cheng Chungying; the philosophical programs at the American Association of Asian Studies; the Chinese philosophy programs at the American Philosophical Association; the Chinese Religions Section and the Confucianism Group in the American Academy of Religion; *Philosophy East and West,* now edited by Roger Ames; and the publication programs of several scholarly publishers, especially the University of Hawaii Press and the State University of New York Press.

Although many scholarly impulses have gone into the creation of this situation, among the most important is that the second-generation Chinese philosophers invited all the rest of us in and legitimated us in taking Confucianism to heart. They told the Sinologists that they could come out as philosophers on their own, and they assured the Western educated philosophers who read little Chinese that they could function critically with the Chinese ideas in the late-modern world. The result is a diverse group, much larger than the few representative thinkers cited here and in chapter 3, that addresses the philosophical issues of the contemporary world, not just the West, nor just East Asia, but the world, with the heritage of Confucianism as well as Platonism and the rest. That so many academic American philosophers do not recognize any non-Western philosophy as philosophy is no criticism of this group of New Confucians but only of the fact that much American academic philosophy has not itself entered the world philosophic culture and does not address the world's issues.

For obvious utilitarian reasons, the world culture of philosophy needs and benefits from Confucianism and other philosophic traditions outside the West. The philosophic issues of late-modernity are so deep, so perplexing, and so far from the cultural traditions of the Axial Age that gave rise to the great traditions and their elementary motifs, that we need any good ideas we can get, any perspectives that can open up new angles of vision.

There is a nonutilitarian reason, however, to embrace all the traditions within the world culture of philosophy. Philosophy is not only a practice by professionals. It is the self-conscious interpretation and guidance system of a society, shaping the way people live, tend their institutions, and understand their lives, for which the professionals are the representative and creative thinkers. Although we have a world society now, knit together by economic, political, military, and informational causal connections, we do not have a well-knit world culture. Rather, we have an entanglement of many cultures with different ancient roots, often with a history of mutual hostility as well as borrowing. Leaders from all the world's cultures know that the world society will never be civilized until a genuine world culture is developed that respects the diverse cultures and harmonizes them to make crucial responses to such issues as environmentalism, distributive justice, and the meaning of human life in the cosmos.

All the world's philosophic cultures have been dynamic, building upon ancient motifs but changing and developing through more than two millennia. Each generation reconstructs its history in order to appropriate its past. Often the reconstructions are radical, involving large rejections, distortions, or shifts in what the past represented as important. Our own generation's task of developing a world culture of philosophy requires much reconstruction, for no tradition brings relevant ready-made answers to the problems of late-modernity and the diverse traditions cannot be simply synthesized into a good solution. Harmonization of world traditions leaves none unchanged.

Nevertheless, all need to be present for each of the world's cultures to find itself represented in the world culture of philosophy. If some culture is left out, the societies it has formed cannot appropriate the world culture. Its own history needs to be involved and subjected to the reconstructive process that takes place whenever ideas are put into play.

And so there can be no world culture of philosophy, owned by all the world's cultures, without Confucianism, and that in its Chinese, Korean, Japanese, and Vietnamese forms. The same could be said for the other philosophic traditions of China (only abstractly separable from Confucianism) as well as those of India and the Islamic world and, indeed, for the less literate traditions of traditional peoples. Given the size and importance of East Asian societies, the entry of Confucianism into the world culture of philosophy is a historic moment.

IV.

The present volume attempts to advance the cause of Boston Confucianism from several different directions. The first and longest chapter lays out my principal claims for Confucianism as a world philosophy, directly addressing issues as to its portability to the West and concerns for what is lost in that translation, as well as suggesting programatically what it might contribute to philosophical understanding in the world situation. The second chapter steps back to examine some classic Chinese, especially Confucian, philosophies of culture, a crucial issue for the question of Confucianism's portability. The third discusses the current state of Confucian philosophy as the context for Boston Confucianism. The fourth chapter develops a theory of spirituality, shows that Confucianism is a form of spirituality, and discusses how that spirituality is compatible or not with others; the existential issue here is that of multiple religious identities—I am a serious practicing Christian, indeed, the dean of a Christian theological school, as well as a Confucian. Although the issue of Confucianism within multiple religious identities is an old one in China—the Three Schools movement (Confucianism, Buddhism, and Daoism) dates from the Song dynasty—it needs to be addressed anew with regard to the religions that have been definitive within "Boston" culture.[5] The concluding section in this book in chapter 10 summarizes the theme of multiple religious identity. The fifth chapter reviews the themes of the earlier ones by a concentrated discussion of Tu Weiming, one of the signal leaders of the contemporary Confucian discussion.

Chapter 6 steps back for a methodological look at the kinds of issues of comparison involved in connecting Confucianism with other forms of philosophy in the world's public conversation. It sketches a theory of comparison and then details the form of that used most often in this book, motif analysis. The remaining four chapters illustrate motif analysis in various ways. Chapter 7 does a comparative study of the motifs of being; chapter 8, the motifs of transcendence that have so exercised David L. Hall and Roger T. Ames (see their 1987, 1996, and 1998 works); chapter 9, the motifs of selfhood; and chapter 10, those motifs by which Confucianism and Christianity are most often contrasted in the religious realm. These all are among the hardest issues to compare because their articulation seems so dependent on Western motifs, a problem with which our method must deal. Beyond mere comparison, however, these last four chapters argue crucial points to develop the viability of Boston Confucianism as a living philosophy. Chapter 7 analyzes the context for engaging the crucial problem of being at the most profound ontological level but in ways that draw Confucianism and Western philosophy into a common discussion. Chapter 8 has two purposes: One is to rebut the charge of Roger Ames and David Hall that Chinese and Western cultures are too dissimilar to have common topics, such as transcendence; the other is to construct a comparative analysis of transcendence as it relates to the human self. Chapter 9 then develops a conception of the self drawing on both Western and Confucian motifs. Chapter 10 frames the issue of multiple cultural identity, which must characterize Boston Confucianism, in terms of its most severe religious forms.

Each of the chapters here began as a lecture or popular presentation. Like most scholarly authors, my heart and soul are invested in the technical monographs that are impenetrable to all but a few devoted readers. So it is with a bit of wistful hope that I offer here another book of essays consisting of talks heavily rewritten to go together as a quasi-monograph on a theme, thankful that they are readable even if judged to be not worth reading.[6] In each case the chapters have indeed been rewritten heavily, often with material that began in some other talk and may bear only nostalgic reference to the original presentation. This preface and chapter 1 include material from a paper presented to the American Academy of Arts and Sciences called "The Short Happy Life of Boston Confucianism" and from my presidential address, "Confucianism as a World Philosophy," for the Eighth International Conference on Chinese Philosophy in Beijing in 1993, published in the *Journal of Chinese Philosophy,* volume 21 (1994, 5–25). Chapter 2 began as an article written for the *Encyclopedia of Chinese*

ism, I answered that these conditions do not obtain even within parallel Western traditions of philosophy. Very few American philosophers have a Greek ethnic heritage, and few have a working knowledge
of the classical Greek language. Yet nearly every American philosopher identifies herself or himself as a Platonist or an Aristotelian. And
every American philosopher without exception who holds a Ph.D. in
the field can discuss ideas attributed to Plato and Aristotle. Plato and
Aristotle are world philosophers to Westerners who are not Greek;
they are also world philosophers in the curricula of most contemporary philosophical academies in East Asia and India. Now the Chinese
philosophies should also be world philosophies in all philosophic
academies, I urged with support from my Boston colleagues.

East Asian Confucian philosophers have been responding to
Western philosophies for well over a century.[1] They have asked how
Chinese traditions can learn from and also criticize Western thought.
The wholesale adoption in this century of Marxist philosophy by at
least one large segment of Chinese scholar-officials is an extraordinary
chapter in the world history of cross-cultural borrowings. But there is
a difference between relating Western philosophy to the East Asian
situation and what I am talking about. My point concerns living as a
Confucian outside the East Asian situation. My own Confucianism
grows not by responding to Western influences but by being used for
living philosophically in the Western situation, or rather in a world
situation with mixed cultural heritages.

Some of us at the Berkeley conference argued that Confucianism
and Daoism from the beginning have been critical philosophies that
have existed in serious dialectical tensions with their indigenous cultures. Confucius, Mencius, and Xunzi complained that in their day the
ancient practices that constitute harmonious civilization had been
corrupted so that people no longer by habit were filial, capable of true
friendship, or socially responsible. Laozi and Zhuangzi complained
that the human assertion of artificial forms obscured the natural connections with the dao. The ancient Moists and Legalists were also
reformers. Over the centuries East Asian cultures became deeply
influenced and shaped by these philosophies. At various times one or
another of these philosophies, and others, had official sanction at court.
Although both Confucianism and Daoism sometimes argued by appealing to lost virtues of the past, and therefore presented themselves
as appearing conservative (see *Analects* 7.1, 19), they in fact called for
change, often for radical change.[2] Sometimes the change itself was
conservative. Because of the centuries of dialectical interaction, it is

impossible to understand East Asian culture except as reflecting *changes* wrought by Confucianism and Daoism.

Might it also be possible to transport the ancient Chinese traditions of philosophy into the context of non–East Asian cultures and learn from their critical and speculative perspectives? Although I *read about* Confucianism in the context of East Asian culture in order to understand its critical and speculative perspectives, philosophically I *think with* Confucianism in relation to my own mainly Western culture and in relation to the various problems of world cultures. Confucianism today faces problems of multicultural embodiments and indigenization analogous to those faced by Christianity, Islam, and Buddhism. "Boston Confucianism" became identified with this view at the Berkeley conference because those of us from Boston defended it, and the oxymoronic sound of the name emphasized the point.

Then an extraordinary thing happened. Partway through the conference, two feminist participants attacked Confucianism for its patriarchal oppression of women in East Asia. There were several interesting responses to the attack. One was to admit its validity and reject Confucianism, an unpopular response at a conference of Confucian scholars. Another was to admit the validity of the claim but to say that Confucianism was right to subordinate women; this position was argued meekly and only during coffee breaks out of the earshot of women. A third response was to say that the claims about patriarchal oppression are exaggerated; no women responded this way.

The fourth and most interesting response was to draw a sharp distinction between primary or "primal" East Asian culture, which is admittedly patriarchal, and the Confucian movement that offers a critical lever in favor of harmony and against any oppression that fails to honor "principle" in each person. "Principle" is the Neo-Confucian category for the ground of definiteness and the drive toward harmonization in process. Identified with the Boston Confucians, this fourth response can admit that, although Confucianism often became male-oriented and forced women into servile roles, this is not the fault of Confucianism as a living philosophy but of the primal culture over which Confucianism never fully prevailed. Like Daoism, Confucianism in its early and late basic texts emphasizes reciprocity rather than oppressive subordination, and like Daoism Confucianism waged a critical and often losing war against primal patriarchalism. That Confucianism more often than Daoism became the social vehicle of patriarchal customs in East Asia speaks only to its success in becoming powerful and corrupted by power, not to its basic commitments.

well as friends. Ames and Hall (1995) cite my household as an example of Confucian balance amid change, and so I thank my wife, Beth Neville, and my children Naomi Neville and Leonora Neville, all of whom, however, might prefer apologies to thanks if my case for Confucianism here is not persuasive. Beth is the creator of the photos on the cover and the art on the inside, and is to be thanked for that. I thank Wesley Wildman for the most exacting challenges to my arguments as well as for his deep friendship. As usual, Jay Schulkin has thought and worried with me over all the issues here as well as the rest of the issues of my life, a true friend. I give special thanks to Mark H. Grear Mann, my assistant, for careful commentary, editing, and criticism of this volume; he has improved it greatly. Nancy Ellegate, my editor at SUNY Press, and once again my fine production editor, Marilyn Semerad, are thanked for bringing this book into existence.

Of this group, two need to be singled out for special comment here.

John H. Berthrong has been my closest partner in Confucian enterprises for over a decade. A Sinologist and historian of religions, it was he who, at the 1988 Confucian-Christian dialogue in Hong Kong, convinced me by the example of his own person that it is possible and admirable to be at once a bureaucrat and a thinker with integrity (he had been a bureaucrat for the United Church of Canada for a decade). Inspired by him, I made the Confucian resolve to live as a scholar-official and accepted the deanship of the School of Theology at Boston University. I had always been chair, director, or even a kind of sub-dean at the institutions in which I worked: but none of those offices assumed responsibility for the *destiny* of the institution as a seminary deanship does. Intermingling of personal and institutional destiny is at the heart of the life of a Confucian scholar-official. John Berthrong soon came to be academic dean at the School of Theology, and our destinies have been together with the school ever since. His first major book at Boston University, *All under Heaven*, thematized the problematic of multiple religious identities discussed below, an obvious issue for Confucians who are also Christians and Christian seminary deans. His second, *Transformations of the Confucian Way*, is now a standard historical introduction to Confucianism for the English-speaking world. This is an essential and brilliant contribution to the project defended here, the integration of Confucianism into the world philosophic and religious conversation. His third book, *Concerning Creativity*, is perhaps our best paradigm so far for retrieval of Confucian (actually Neo-Confucian) resources for resolving a contemporary debate, namely, that between process theologians and myself (Berthrong defends the process side). His most recent book, *The Divine Deli,* is an analysis of religious pluralism. Among Boston Confucians, Berthrong is the Sinologically responsible scholar in the south-of-the-Charles branch of the school and is the only one of us who perhaps rivals Tu Weiming as an irenic ritual master. I celebrate his achievements and am grateful to work with him.

Tu Weiming is one of the most original Confucian thinkers of our time, and chapter 5 is an expansive response to much of his creative thought. I want here to thank him with greatest sincerity for the gracious foreword he has written for this volume. In part, that foreword continues our long-standing dialogue, responding to some of the issues raised in chapter 5 and also to the foreword I wrote with some of the same material to the new edition of his *Humanity and Self-Cultivation.* His response both reaffirms the importance of the north-of-the-Charles emphasis on Mencian humaneness and expresses with new subtlety the Confucian worry that the Christian creation myth has some objectionable literal commitments to God as a being separate from the world. In larger part, however, his foreword embodies Boston Confucianism in action, building a flexible and vital conversation through deeply appreciative reformulations and extending the conversation through rigorous criticism. The effect of this is to give the enterprise symbolized by Boston Confucianism a serious authority. I have argued elsewhere (1987a) that neither Confucianism nor Christianity so far has solved the problem of authority for a multicultural world. Tu's ministering efforts to create a world political and philosophical discourse, illustrated in his foreword and discussed in chapter 5, are perhaps the best hope we have to remedy that lack. I am both personally and institutionally grateful for his foreword and what it represents.

This book is dedicated with deep gratitude to Thomas Berry who, many years ago, asked why I thought I was a philosopher without relating to Chinese and Indian thought and, when I could give no good answer, set me about engaging those cultures. He insisted I learn to teach Indian and Chinese philosophy, arranged for me to study Chinese, and himself directed my study of Sanskrit. Boston Confucianism is barely catching up with his long practice of world philosophy.

Biblical quotations are from the *New Revised Standard Version* (1989), copyrighted by the Division of Christian Education of the National Council of the Churches of Christ in the United States of America.

1

The Short Happy Life of Boston Confucianism

1.1. Portable Confucianism: Roots and Branches

"Boston Confucianism" means two things, according to the account of the name given in the preface. The first is the general project of bringing the Confucian tradition into play with the other great civilized traditions in the creation of a world civilization. Part of this is bringing Confucian philosophy into the world philosophic conversation, the main focus of Boston Confucianism. Two things need to be done to make Confucianism a full participant in world philosophy, one negative and the other positive. The negative task is to show that Confucianism is not limited to East Asian ethnic application and can in fact be transported to a larger non–East Asian environment, for instance, Boston. The argument for this requires facing several important philosophic problems about the relation of a philosophy to its context and the nature of continuity in a philosophy or religious culture when moving from one context or time to another. The positive task is to demonstrate that Confucianism has something genuinely interesting and helpful to bring to contemporary philosophical discussions. These discussions are not defined by professional philosophers alone, but also, and perhaps in larger part, by society's needs for philosophic guidance. This chapter lays out the structure of arguments addressing both the negative and positive needs in the Boston Confucian project; subsequent chapters fill in the arguments from more angles.

The second meaning of "Boston Confucianism" is the work of the group of Confucian thinkers gathered in and around Boston under the leadership of Professor Tu Weiming, Director of the Harvard-

1

Yenching Institute. Boston Confucianism in this sense is a particular microcosm of the former sense, naming a philosophical cultural project and, indeed, lending its name to that project, as recounted in the preface. Local Boston Confucians are preoccupied with the issues of the larger movement of Confucian development. Our discussions exhibit many of the positions and strategies of the larger movement, and the distinctions among us epitomize distinctions with broader significance. Of course, much of the activity of the local Boston Confucians is to engage those abroad by drawing them to Boston and visiting them in their own contexts. The Boston conversation spreads far beyond Boston. The humorous irony in the name "Boston Confucianism," should not be forgotten, even when it gets serious.

There are Confucians who are not East Asians, just as there are Platonists who are not Greek or even Western. But the idea of a Western Confucian seems more problematic to some than the idea of a non-Greek Platonist. Confucianism, of course, was not limited to China, spreading to Korea, Japan, Vietnam, and elsewhere in East Asia, and to diaspora communities of these nationals outside of East Asia. But it took with it, according to the common belief, a rich East Asian primary culture of family life and authority structures that was distinctive to Confucianism and yet is alien or irrelevant to the primary cultures of non–East Asian societies. Confucianism is thought by many to be unable to flourish outside of an East Asian family culture. This chapter examines the conditions under which Confucianism might be transported to cultures outside the East Asian type, understanding that this transition in Confucianism may be effected in part by the rise, temporary and ironic as it might be, of its Boston school.

First the chapter will present a formal hypothesis about the portable roots of Confucianism, with a discussion of ways of understanding the relation of those roots to the cultures in which they might be planted and the branches into which they might grow. This discussion has theoretical implications for the notion of cross-cultural transition and introduces problems to be discussed further in chapter 6. Second, the discussion will present the programmatic point that Boston Confucianism calls for the recovery and uniquely American development of the ancient emphasis on *li* as ritual propriety. The heart of the program is the defense of the thesis that American pragmatism offers a Western philosophic language for expressing the relevance of Confucian ritual theory for the modern world, the topic of the third section. Fourth, several practical applications of Confucian principles to the Boston cultural situation will be laid out as projects for further development. Fifth, a quasi-ironic reflection will be offered on several changes in our usual views of Confucianism that are occasioned by the transitions effected by the Boston School.

Although it would be fruitless to attempt to discover an "essence" for Confucianism, as if that were an historically neutral abstraction, it is imperative in any questioning of cross-cultural transfer of influence to state the core of the influence. Chapter 6 below will argue in detail that the best way to identify a tradition is to trace the variegated history of its core texts and motifs rather than to specify essential practices or doctrines. The identifying core of any tradition is itself the locus of ongoing controversy. Zhu Xi in the twelfth century made an extraordinarily influential modification of what constitutes the core texts of Confucianism when he chose the Four Books rather than the larger list of "classics" that had been standard or other ancient texts (Tillman 1992). The argument here is to offer an hypothesis fit for our own situation. The hypothesis attempts a minimalist statement—if leisure exists to transport more than this, so much the better. Because "core" does not mean a universal essence, it should be stressed that what follows is an hypothesis about the core that ought to be carried over into the contemporary situation with respect to Boston (and the rest of the West); cores for other transportations, such as to India or Africa, might be different.

The proposed core of any transported philosophical or religious culture consists of three elements: primary scriptures, secondary scriptures, and an interpretive context. In the case of Confucianism, the hypothesis is that the primary scriptures are the Four Books, selected by Zhu Xi in the Song dynasty as classics, i.e., *The Analects*, *The Doctrine of the Mean*, *The Great Learning*, and *The Book of Mencius*, plus *The Book of Xunzi*. That the Four Books make the list is not surprising; the inclusion of Xunzi will be justified later.[1] The secondary scriptures for Confucianism are the major Neo-Confucian texts of the Song, Yuan, Ming, and Qing, including (among many others) the important writings of Zhou Dunyi, Zhang Zai, Shao Yung, Cheng Hao, Cheng Yi, Lu Xiangshan, Zhu Xi, Wang Yangming, Wang Fuzhi, and Dai Zhen. The interpretive context involves both the historical setting and surrounding texts required to understand how the primary and secondary scriptures took the shape they have; in addition to understanding some Chinese, Korean, and Japanese history, the interpretive context includes texts such as the *I Ching*, the writings of the Daoists, Mohists, and Legalists, and the texts as well as the spiritual practices and social organizations of the Chinese Buddhists.

In discussing each of these briefly it will be possible to indicate both something of the meaning of the rubrics of primary and secondary scriptures and of interpretive context, as well as reasons for these specific choices for Confucianism as identified for its Boston school.

Primary Scriptures

Primary scriptures are those texts, or songs or rituals, that the entire tradition, "generally and for the most part" (as Aristotle would say), accepts as providing its normative principles and motifs of self-understanding. Part of claiming that one's own reconstruction of what is worthwhile in a tradition is correct is the demonstration that one's reconstruction provides a legitimate appropriation of the primary scriptures.[2] Primary scriptures are differently interpreted, of course, with different points emphasized by different schools, some elements suppressed and others exaggerated; the interpretations of primary scriptures can be plainly contradictory to one another, and it is always to be recognized that the role that the primary scriptures play in one school or another is as much a function of the school as of the scriptures themselves. Good test cases for the "canon" of primary scriptures are cases in which a new movement within a tradition acknowledges itself to be partially heterodox because of something it excludes from the canon or seeks to innovate into the canon.

The Confucian *Analects* are primary scriptures not only because of their founding role in what came to be called "Confucianism" but for two other principal reasons. First, they provide the major themes and motifs of Confucianism, elements developed by nearly every other major thinker. These include humanity, ritual propriety, righteousness, filiality, learning, reciprocity, the importance of developing personal relations that acknowledge differences as well as the equalities of friendship, and a commitment to public life and service; these are usually associated in *The Analects* with incidents or characters that particularize them.

Second, *The Analects* provide a particular orientation to the life of the sage, namely, to criticize intellectually and seek to amend practically the current social habits in light of a better way. For Confucius, this took the form of laments about the loss of public and personal virtues compared with the golden age of ritual propriety, and a campaign to restore those virtues through a sensible recovery of ritual propriety.

Because of the centrality of this point for Boston Confucianism, it is worthwhile to note that Confucius' project has an analogue in Plato's. Plato wrote during a period in which the classic values of Greece, for instance as expressed by Pericles, had been undermined.

The wars with Persia and the ease of travel to Egypt had shown that there are other ways to have high culture than the Greek. The Sophists had developed a serious philosophy of cultural relativism. And the rise of democracy meant in some quarters that anyone's opinion is as worthy of respect as anyone else's, regardless of education, experience, public spiritedness, or thoughtfulness. Plato's philosophic project is to be read in light of this situation. He invented a subtle metaphysical scheme for describing the nature of real values and showing how they are easily relativized and misunderstood; he demonstrated again and again the dialectical process of discerning what is worthwhile in situations; he developed theories and practical procedures for both educating people to discern the true amid relativities and bringing the true to bear upon politics. Most importantly, he raised the question of what a just person could do in an unjust world, where even the best political efforts would be perverted to unjust ends, and answered that just people need to go into education. Plato invented the Western university just as Confucius invented or at least popularized the style of the Confucian teacher. When Confucianism is brought to a culture that has been prepared by Plato, the frustrated sense of Confucius' life and his failure to win at big-time politics may be understood in terms of his extraordinarily successful alternate strategy.[3]

The Doctrine of the Mean is a primary scripture of Confucianism because it provides the classical expression of the Confucian model of the self as a polar structure stretching between the inner heart of centered readiness to respond to all things according to their value and the ten thousand things of the world (see section 9.3). All persons are identical with regard to the readiness to respond in the center, a point identified later in the tradition as universal principle, but each person is uniquely located in perspective on the ten thousand things, needing to respond differentially. The structures of psyche, knowledge, sensibilities, and skills connecting the two poles constitute the self. The Confucian lesson is that these need to be made sincere and subtly transparent so that the centered heart can see the ten thousand things without distortion and act upon them appropriately without perversion. The customary structure of the self in psyche, knowledge, sensibilities and skills is selfish, however, both distorting vision and perverting action, and the Confucian Way is to remedy this selfishness.[4]

The Great Learning is a primary scripture because it shows that the task of education is not limited to the privacy of the soul or even personal life but runs with appropriate shifts in nature through personal social roles, through family structures, community life, and even to the most universal and remote structures of political office. Indeed, true education is based in cosmic realities: the self as described above which should be clear with regard to the manifestation of character, the highest good which is the true home for human nature, and the human community needing renovation, which is the true scale of human nature. The juxtaposition of self and society, mediated by cosmic goodness, such that a continuity of obligation exists between personal and public life, are themes surprisingly congenial to Plato, though expressed in unique ways by the Confucian classics.

The Book of Mencius is a primary scripture because of its elaboration of the nature of the centered readiness to respond to the true worths of things, described by Mencius in his discussion of the Four Beginnings (*Mencius* 2A: 6, in Chan 1963, 65). Throughout the book he elaborates the themes of the original goodness of human nature and its perpetual frustration and perversion. He identified miseducation and inadequate social structures as the sources of the failure of the original goodness to be manifest and properly cultivated. His point focuses the direction of the Confucian project of education.

The writings of Xunzi were not included by Zhu Xi in his canon of primary scriptures, and so I must admit that there is a risk here of heterodoxy; nevertheless, nothing is more orthodox in the Confucian tradition than disputes about the canon. Xunzi has always been deeply honored, and his contribution consists in a theory about nature, convention, and corruption. If human nature is originally good, why are people ever selfish? His answer is that people are formed by ritual propriety, or by its distorted and perverted forms, or they fail to be formed humanly at all because of a lack of the normative but conventional forms of propriety. Therefore, the content of the Confucian project is to amend, rectify, and inculcate the forms of ritual propriety. From an educational standpoint, this concern with propriety is far more important than celebration of the original goodness of human nature or attention to the stern stuff of obligation, which are preoccupations of Mencius. Rather, the Confucian focus is best directed, says Xunzi, toward the stylized or conventional social forms that mediate people's relations with one another, with nature, and with institutions such as family, community order, government, and the arts and letters.

By the time of the Song revival of Confucianism, the philosophical stress on ritual piety had diminished, though Zhu Xi (1991 translation) published a massively influential book on household ritual. Certain stylized habits of life were by then firmly associated with Confucianism as such, either rightly or because Confucianism had given in to some of the social forms expressive of other cultures, perhaps primal ones, that are not in accord with the spirit of Confucianism as expressed in the Four Books and Xunzi. The Neo-Confucian thinkers did not need to stress what they thought they already had, and besides, it is embarrassingly easy for stylized forms of ritual propriety to become hollow forms, so one might do well not to call too much attention to them. The Neo-Confucian stress in this period was rather on sincerity, on perfection of personal knowledge, and purity of will. Perhaps something of the Daoists' ridicule of Confucian ritual manners as empty pomposity was taken to heart. Nevertheless, even in stressing sincerity and humaneness, Song and later Confucians were ready to acknowledge the point made by Confucius' and Xunzi's stress on ritual propriety.

A major emphasis of Boston Confucianism is precisely its revival of the call for ritual propriety within Confucianism. To be sure, the humanizing conventions of the American situation are vastly different from those of ancient or Ming China, deriving from the Western tradition, especially from the Enlightenment. The point of Boston Confucianism is not to reinstate some older set of personal manners—that would be Boston brahminism. The point rather is to focus ethical life on the development of social forms and styles that properly humanize people, where humanization is seen within the context of self, society, and goodness as expressed by both the Confucian and Western classics. The long-run argument for the orthodoxy of Boston Confucianism has to be that the inclusion of Xunzi as a portable root for planting in America brings out the best in Confucianism for this situation.

Secondary Scriptures

In contrast to the portable primary scriptures, the portable secondary scriptures do not constitute a body of writings that needs to be appropriated and given some positive interpretation. But they do constitute writings that exhibit a complex dialogue with reference to which subsequent Confucians must locate themselves. We do not need to side with Zhu Xi or with Wang Yangming; nor do we need to agree with Zhou Dunyi on exactly what is vacuous. Yet we do need to be aware of the issues that shaped that discussion and have a stance toward them. This is similar to a contemporary Western philosopher having to treat the great thinkers of early modernity such as Descartes, Hobbes, Locke, Hume, Spinoza, Leibniz, and Kant as secondary scriptures; one need not agree with any against the others, but one does need to have a stance toward them. Perhaps contemporary Confucians have to "get over" the Neo-Confucians just as postmodern Western philosophers are supposed to get over modernity; still, that would be shaping their current work with a stance toward those secondary scriptures. Of course, not all practicing Boston Confucians need to be philosophers or scholars, and so they might have little direct knowledge of the Song, Yuan, Ming, and Qing debates; yet their practice would be shaped by those debates and by how they are relevant or not to the present.

Portable Interpretive Context

The portable interpretive context for Confucianism has to be enough knowledge of Chinese culture and history to be able to situate the primary and secondary scriptures, especially the former. Obviously, there never is enough background knowledge, and scholars will continue to provide hermeneutic readings of the ancient Confucian texts regardless of their transportation beyond the bounds of East Asia and the East Asian diaspora. But it is not too much to expect liberally educated Westerners to learn about the East Asian background so as to be able to situate the Confucian texts. In fact, given the decline in historical knowledge of the Western tradition in Western cultures, there is hardly any greater difficulty in making Confucian texts live with college students than with making the ancient Greeks or medieval Christians accessible.

This section has expressed elements of Confucianism that need to be portable from East Asian to other cultural grounds, such as the American or even Bostonian. These are roots that need to be planted and to grow for a new and non–East Asian flowering of Confucianism to take place. The theme of roots and branches from *The Great Learning* is a fruitful way to conceive the relation of a fully rooted and flowering culture in Asia to a new vineyard in different cultural soil.

1.2. Ritual Propriety

Although the basic Confucian texts were excellently translated into English thirty-five years ago by Wing-tsit Chan (1963), Confucianism came to the attention of the broad American philosophic public with Herbert Fingarette's (1972) *Confucius: The Secular as Sacred*. Fingarette's thesis was that Confucius' philosophy elaborated two essential principles, humanity (*ren*) and propriety (*li*). The lever of his interpretive argument was the concept of performance in symbolic action, as contrasted with the mere meaning of the symbols. He showed that those things that constitute the human qualities of life—for instance, filiality rather than biological connection, community rather than power relations, friendship rather than pragmatic cooperation—all consist in the performance of symbolic acts. The acts do not symbolize something else, as a sign means an object, but in their performance indeed are the humanizing elements of life. Friendship is not described or signified by friendly behavior but consists in it. In this and the next section these ideas shall be developed in other language, first in terms of Xunzi's theory of ritual, and then in terms of Charles Peirce's pragmatism.

Humanity (*ren*), the first of Fingarette's pair, has seemed close to a range of Western philosophical notions, from Christian love to Heideggerian authenticity (see section 5.4). Its Confucian forms have been applied to the Western situation by several thinkers.[5] Chapter 5 will examine Tu Weiming's account of humanity in detail.

Propriety or ceremony, however, has been a more difficult notion for Americans than humanity. Although Confucian propriety has been presented to the West as akin to good manners and polite behavior, there is a deep-seated hostility in North Atlantic cultures since the late eighteenth century to the stylized manners of courtliness. European Enlightenment egalitarianism distrusts manners that have to be learned from others through imitation (Confucius admitted this takes a life-time). Rather, peasants and poor people are just as excellent as culti-vated people if their heart is sincere, according to the typical American.[6] To a Confucian this is to assert that humanity by itself is sufficient without propriety.

But propriety has had a far deeper meaning in the Chinese tra-dition, and its Western parallels are not merely good manners. Three aspects of its deeper meaning will be elaborated throughout this book: that propriety creates culture, is conventional, and is a peculiar kind of harmony. These three will be sketched here and drawn more fully in subsequent chapters.

Perhaps the most important insight of Confucius and Xunzi, with almost no parallel in the West, is that the higher institutions of culture consist in the exercise of ritual propriety, broadly considered. With little culture, people can be ruled by a strongman, but cannot enjoy good government. With little culture people can cooperate, but they cannot be friends without the elaborate learned ways of behaving that make up mutual interest, respect, sharing of enjoyment and sorrow, and delighting in one another with faithfulness. With little culture people can have children and receive life from their own parents, but without the learned ritualized behaviors they cannot bring up their children in virtue or honor their parents in a filial manner. The Con-fucian problem with barbarians was not that they had the wrong culture but that they hardly had culture at all, and the reason was that they had no or inadequate behaviors of ritual propriety by means of which to embody the higher excellences of civilization.

Ritual behaviors are conventional. It does not really matter what forms are practiced so long as they work to give existence to the cultural virtue in question. Confucius pointed out that regarding ritual hats it makes little or no difference whether they are linen or silk, whichever is most convenient. But in showing deference with regard to the temple, a quick bow while going in the door is a diminishment or routinizing of respect, so it is far better to make a full obeisence before ascending the temple steps (*Analects* 9.3). When Confucian propriety is properly generalized, language itself appears as a learned, conventional ritualized behavior. Being conventional, languages differ from one another, but the normative question is whether the language in question can convey what is needed. Those languages able to support deep civilization are good; those that are impoverished so that friendship, family relations, and good government cannot be expressed and exercised linguistically are not so good.

The third trait of the Confucian notion of propriety is that it produces a special kind of harmony. "Produces" is not quite the right word, however, for the harmony is not a consequent effect of propriety. Rather, the harmony consists in the practice of the rituals at the right occasions by the right people. This was Confucius' most important moral point about propriety: when ritual propriety is observed, people are brought into cooperative action that respects the place, needs, and merits of each. Where ritual propriety is not observed, or where a society lacks the rituals that articulate the diverse positions, needs, and merits of its citizens, morality falls back to dependence on the following of moral rules and the happenchance exercise of good will. Unlike moral rules and good will, propriety is lodged in the habits of bones and muscles and in the deepest schemes of imagination. Propriety, of course, is no substitute for the deliberative parts of moral reasoning, nor for sincerity of the heart, just as having an eloquent language and habits of speech does not tell one what to say or how to intend. But propriety, especially an eloquent and nuanced language, brings the special harmony that can elude even moral correctness and the good heart.[7]

Propriety is the particular part of the Confucian tradition to be related here to American pragmatism, although there are other elements that are equally interesting to relate. When pragmatism's theory of signs, its semiotic, is used to interpret propriety, a vastly more sophisticated analysis is available to Confucianism than the tradition itself has developed, one that bring Confucianism into intimate connection with the wealth of the Western philosophic tradition without compromising its own heritage. Thus Confucianism as a philosophy for the Western as well as East Asian world can incorporate significant elements of pragmatism while rejecting other parts, just as the Daoxue movement of Neo-Confucianism did with Daoism and Buddhism.

1.3. Pragmatism

Pragmatism here means the philosophy of Charles S. Peirce and his followers.[8] William James, who popularized the term "pragmatism," did not have a theory of signs and missed Peirce's whole point. Moreover, James popularized the view that pragmatism is the philosophy of "what works," a desperately mistaken distortion of Peirce's original insights.[9] The tradition of pragmatism in America has grown through John Dewey in several directions. The most popular is the Neo-Pragmatism of Richard Rorty (1982), which rejects the speculative side of the philosophy and emphasizes its connections with rhetoric and sophistry. The line of development that embraces the speculative side of Peirce and Dewey and learns from Alfred North Whitehead (1929) and Paul Weiss (1974) is far more interesting for relating to the Confucian approach to ritual.[10]

Peirce invented pragmatism as a corrective to a line of Western philosophy from Descartes to Kant. Descartes had said that mind and body are distinct substances with the consequence that mental representations are of a mysteriously different stuff from the corporeal things they might represent. Kant had said that the only way to know that mental representations accurately and certainly represent the material world is by a transcendental argument about what that knowledge would be if it were possible. Peirce said, to the contrary of both, that representations are just as much part of nature as anything else, except that they exist in interpreters. Interpreters such as human beings are natural things whose interactions with the world and one another are guided by their representations. With well-guided interactions the interpreters construe the world accurately and do not miss the distinctions that are important for the interpreters' welfare and purposes. For Peirce, the point is that the relation between representations and their objects is a special kind of causal relation that has to do with guiding interactions in discerning ways. Rather than focus on the mental property of intentionality, which makes the causal connections between minds and external things unintelligible, pragmatism analyzes intentionality as a special kind (or kinds) of causation having to do with purposive interaction. Peirce's major point about pragmatism as a test for ideas is that the realities of the things with which interpreters interact will correct their representations. For Peirce and Dewey, knowing as having a mental picture is subordinated to learning as the correction of the representations that guide interaction (see John E. Smith 1978 and Neville 1989).

Another important contribution of pragmatism is to argue that representations are not mental entities but habits of the behavior of interpreters.[11] The habits have two main connections. On the one hand, the pragmatic theory shows how habits are connected with the things with which interpreters interact, including physical nature, social structures, and other interpreters. The realities of these other things are correctives to habits that do not anticipate them accurately. On the other hand, habits are connected with the human purposes from which interactions take their guidance. Interpretations have many functions. On rare occasions, their purpose might be simply and only to know. On most occasions, however, they play performative functions, serving some other purpose that cannot be carried out without some construal of the world and of how to accomplish things. Sometimes purposes are passive and interpretations function to enable sheer enjoyment. Like the Confucians, pragmatists recognize the primacy of the performative or illocutionary functions of interpretation.[12]

The interpretations in any interpreter or community are intricately interwoven and nested the way habits jointly make up a complex life. Semiotics, or the theory of signs, is the analysis of the structures of interconnected interpretations. Interpretations are made up of signs that interpret, signs as objects interpreted, and signs as the habits of interpreting. Whereas European semiotics (deriving from Saussure, 1959) focuses on signs as interdefined in codes, pragmatic semiotics focuses on how signs come to be in this or that context, on how they become determinate or fade into vagueness, on how systems of signs presuppose one another and how changes in one system of signs affects other more or less general systems.

Three particular traits of the pragmatic theory of signs should be lifted up for notice. The first is that it sees any particular interpretation as resting in a vast background of other interpretations, systems within systems; every interpretation has a context and every environment of interpretations can contain an indefinitely large number of focal points.[13] The second is that interpretations are appreciative of the value, worth, and appeal of things, as well as their dignity and place. These value-elements are all part of the reality of things, and pragmatism does not have to accept any fact-value distinction that associates objects with form or structure and value with mental projections. Thus pragmatism treats experience as fundamentally appreciative, with the values of objects interacting with the purposes of interpreters. Third, the pragmatic theory of signs recognizes that appreciative interpretation spreads across the whole breadth of interpretations from circumambient feelings of the world and its moods to specific purposes and enjoyments, all in continuity. Thus the pragmatic theory resonates with the sense of continuity, spontaneity, and aesthetic experience Chang Chungyuan (1963) ascribes to Daoism but that applies equally well to the Confucian sensibilities.

The continuity from background to foreground interpretations in the pragmatic theory is supplemented by an even more important continuity, namely, in the range of interpretive habits. At the fundamental level are the animal habits of organic nature. In English, the ordinary language of interpretation is stretched to say that the heart interprets exertion by beating faster, that the stomach interprets hunger by growling, or that an animal interprets sudden large movement by fleeing; nevertheless, these organic habits are low-level interpretations that construe the situation to be a certain way and respond a certain way. The human range of interpretive habits becomes distinctive within the animal world with elementary cooperation, gestures, basic language, and expressive semiotic modes. Together the organic range of interpretations and those involved in elementary human cooperation and society constitute a kind of biopsychic dance, attuned to and structured by nature's rhythms, but reflecting purpose. At this point, conventional signs begin to develop over and above, or as modifying, the natural signs of interpretation. With the more elaborate development of conventional signs, social discourse becomes possible with complex languages, cultures, and social organizations. Even though the signs and the habits they structure become more subtle and sophisticated, with conventional elements that may be artful and abstruse, they still are modifications and enrichments of the organic and elementary habits. When societies develop the elaborate sign systems of high civilization, they have those elements of ritual propriety about which Confucius and Xunzi wrote, the elements that modify cooperation so that it becomes respectful friendship, sex so that it becomes profound love and caring, procreation so that it becomes family life with filiality, and so forth. As the ancient Confucians knew, it does not matter exactly which sign system carries the functions of ritual propriety, only that a culture have some sign system that does. This account of the pragmatic approach to signs shows, first, how signs create culture out of and over and above nature; second, how signs are conventional; third, how the signs of high culture constitute the harmonious interactions of which the virtues of high culture consist. In this way, pragmatism picks up on three of the most important elements of the Confucian notion of propriety.

The Confucian theory of ritual propriety can be generalized to include the entire pyramid of signs or of organic and social habits, the higher modifying the lower, the lower undergirding and making possible the higher. The ancient Confucians did not believe, as the Daoists suggested, that the higher signs of ritual behavior can be imposed carelessly on baser habits. On the contrary, the uses of ritual propriety are precisely to fulfill the potential excellence of more elementary natural habits by turning power into government, cooperation into friendship, and so forth. The Confucians recognized that the proper uses of propriety require the acknowledgment of and care for the entire range of humanly meaningful nature. They have been optimistic about the power of carefully observed propriety to bring us closer to nature and obviate its distortions.

In this sense, for Confucianism humanity fulfills heaven and earth, and forms a trinity with it not through being a distinct substance but through shaping interpretively the structured behaviors that constitute a new human reality in civilization. The pragmatic theory of signs offers a rapprochement between the Confucian top-down view of propriety as properly containing all nature and Heaven, and the Daoist bottom-up view of nature's habits as the touchstone for the authenticity of human culture. The truth lies in recognizing the integrity of the continuum, as expressed in the pragmatic theory.

The moral significance of propriety, or a fully civilized system of signs, is that it makes possible the existence of high culture as harmonies of habits. The achievements of culture have life only in the exercise of the habits whose sign structures define the culture. Unless there are signs for friendship, family, good government, and so forth, it simply is not possible to have friendship, family, or good government. The moral significance of propriety or a civilized sign system is its culture-building function.

As already noted, the sign system by itself does not solve the problems of moral deliberation, though it makes that deliberation possible at a sophisticated level. Propriety does not tell us what purposes to have except in the negative sense of setting limits to purposes that would be destructive of the practice of civilized behavior. Nor does the fact that a society has a civilized sign system and practices propriety mean that it is also humane: The rituals can be employed hypocritically and interpretation can be humanly empty. Nevertheless, without a sign system, high civilization itself is impossible.[14]

What pragmatism learns from Confucianism at this point is that much of the moral critique required by our society consists in the analysis of the signs shaping our social habits. More than deliberation about purposes and policies, although those also are to be considered, Confucianism calls attention to the strengths and weakness of the sign-systems that define our civilization itself, our society's practices of propriety. This leads the discussion to a few brief reflections on the moral contributions of Boston Confucianism, that is, on Confucianism enlarged by the pragmatic theory of signs reflecting on the sign-shaped social habits characterizing Boston and analogous areas of Western civilization.

1.4. Confucian Critique for Boston

What follows are intended to be brief suggestive remarks for developing a Confucian critique of a largely non–East Asian culture. Three major Confucian themes will be defined as problems of both propriety and humaneness and then considered regarding how they might apply to the social situation in Boston and its analogues. The first theme is how individuals relate to their community and play official and semiofficial roles in the community. Although Confucians call this the relations among ministers and the emperor, here it shall be called the theme of civility, where civility recalls its roots in the Latin word for city. The second theme is how friendship might be constituted in late-modern societies such as Boston's. The third theme is how families should be organized in such societies. In this way at least certain important elements of the "five relations" (*Doctrine of the Mean*, chapter 20; *Mencius* 3A:4; for both, see Chan 1963) will have been translated to the modern Western context. Each of these themes will be developed further in later chapters.

A Confucian approach to civility in Boston must recognize and acknowledge the elementary cultural and social habits that a civilizing propriety needs to modify. The first and most important social fact about Boston and most modern cultures is that they are racially, ethnically, and religiously diverse. When ancient Confucians thought of their own group, their fellows were generally racially, ethnically, and religiously homogeneous. For most Americans, although acutely conscious of their racial, ethnic, and religious character because of the always visible alternatives, "we Bostonians" means all the groups that live in Boston, not merely "we Irish-American Bostonians" or "we Chinese-American Bostonians" or "we African-American Bostonians." This sense of diverse groups belonging together and needing to work for the good of all is one of the great achievements of Western culture, and some of the milestones in its development were in fact traversed in Boston. Boston Confucians thus need to point out that the "in principle" commitment to cultural diversity requires concrete positive social habits of deference to the diverse cultures.

Boston's current social habits do not include harmonious ways of deferring to the appropriate cultures, and ethnic tensions are rife. Ironically, nearly everyone would like an inclusive and diverse society respecting all the groups together, but Boston's actual social habits frustrate this desire and lead to alienation and sometimes violence. Boston Confucians need to invent rituals for everyday life and government that foster inclusive cultural diversity, for without that, the respect required for humaneness cannot be expressed or exercised.

Another social fact with which Confucianism must deal is the Enlightenment tradition of egalitarianism. Egalitarianism is a rich ideal, beginning with the equal dignity of all persons as such and including equalities of opportunity, of standing before the law, and of rights of expression and political participation. Although morally sensitive Bostonians are conscious of the fact that egalitarinism is habituated in our expectations far more than in actual practice, compared with many cultures, including those of most East Asian societies, the habits of actual practice often do give equality to women, ethnic minorities, and persons from lower classes and unconnected with powerful families. Racial inequalities seem almost intractable but still there is greater opportunity for racial minorities in Boston and like places than in places unaffected by the European Enlightenment. Confucians would point out that even where egalitarian ideals are institutionalized fairly well in social habits, people still need to be recognized as individuals with unique positions and values. The abstractness of equality is a dehumanizing burden, treating people as mere tokens occupying a position in a system, if the social habits of equality are not also framed with the rituals that recognize persons in their different and unique qualities. By itself, abstract Enlightenment equality is inhumane. The Confucian task in an egalitarian society is to develop social habits that recognize and reinforce equality while also addressing the unique persons playing egalitarian roles.

That Boston's late-modern society is egalitarian, at least in the habits of expectation, does not mean that it does not need a hierarchy of roles in government, business, and other systems such as education. But the late-modern Enlightenment hierarchy aims to be functional in structure and meritocratic in terms of qualification to office. Tradition has little weight in American culture for defining offices; offices and roles are constantly being modified, rearranged, invented, or phased out. The meritocracy of qualifications for office is similar in many respects to the ideal of the Chinese Confucian examination system but extends throughout society, for instance, to business. Seniority has to do not with age but with length of time and experience in a position. Although the functional hierarchies and meritocratic placement of position holders are always imperfect, even if it were perfect, the Confucian should ask further critical questions: Do the civilizing habits of the society adequately recognize the whole person in the office, and are the offices defined so as to be held by whole people? For instance, a person in a low position at work might be a high official in church or in the family. A person in high responsibility in government or business might be extremely needy in the context of family and a very poor athlete in recreational sports. The civil rituals by which we relate to ourselves and to others in various hierarchical offices need to acknowledge that holding those offices is not the entirety of the person's life. Business relations need not invade privacy, but they ought not deny it either. Confucians in Boston should work for the social rituals that allow people to relate to others in official or semiofficial positions as complex human beings.

Let's turn from the Confucian theme of civility to that of friendship. The conditions for friendship in Boston reflect the social conditions mentioned above, namely, inclusive cultural diversity in race, ethnicity, and religion, egalitarianism, and a social system with functional hierarchies and a meritocracy. Whereas Chinese Confucianism as well as Western Aristotelianism have emphasized equality as a condition for true friendship, that condition cannot obtain in a society with the late-modern conditions of Boston. Even egalitarianism means that people are to be treated with equal respect who are vastly different in age, talent, interests, and background. With rare exceptions, true friendships in the Boston situation will have to be possible among "unequals," among people of different gender, different ages, different talents and intelligence, and different positions in social hierarchies.

Boston Confucians then need to point out that at the heart of true friendship are the social habits or rituals for enduring through a long time. Friendships are formed only through long endurance of changes in relations among the friends; gender roles change as people age, social positions change with age, talents and responsibilities change, as well as offices in hierarchies. Friends are those who learn to love, respect, and defer to one another through a long period of changes. In this way, they come to relate heart to heart to one another as whole persons. Friendships can begin with the infatuation of a common interest, a shared attitude, or a reciprocal wit, but they need to develop so as to create a subculture of interpersonal habits that arises through participating in one another's lives over time. Confucian ritual strategies need to be developed to sustain friendships through changes in inequalities over time. Confucians rightly warn against the fake rituals of instant familiarity that we associate with sales representatives; the manners of "instant informality" are a crass similacrum of friendship when applied to people who do not really know one another well.

Boston Confucianism needs also to distinguish true friendship from two other relations with which it is easily confused in late-modern Western culture. One is the civil relations of functional interaction within society discussed above, where the social habits with true propriety allow us to recognize people in their wholeness while relating to them according to their functions. Thus we need rituals for dealing with shopkeepers, bureaucrats, and politicians, but these are not the rituals that necessarily foster true friendship. The second relation to be distinguished from true friendship is collegiality, which is much closer to friendship than civil relations and often its source. Collegiality is the type of relation developed through close proximity, perhaps in working conditions or through living in the same neighborhood. Colleagues relate not only functionally but in sharing much of the rest of their social and personal lives. The rituals of collegiality properly insist that colleagues help one another when in trouble and rejoice and grieve with one another; in traditional societies collegiality is what is meant by "community." But collegiality is a function of the circumstances of proximity. When one changes jobs or moves to a different neighborhood, one can change colleagues with no serious loss. New people enter into one's life to share events, to help, with whom to rejoice and grieve. In such a mobile society as has developed in late-modernity, proper Confucian rituals of collegiality are extremely important, but they are not true friendship, which endures the changes of circumstances and proximity. True friends stay together through change and separation.

The final Confucian theme to which I would like to relate Boston's circumstances is the family, under which the themes of husband-wife relations, filiality, and sibling relations are comprised. The general Confucian civilizing reality sought in the propriety of family relations is that each member be prized, supported, and cared for with respect to the ongoing tasks of integrating with excellence the appropriate roles the person has within the family with those the person plays outside the family. This is to say, the family is the matrix within which people find the home to become fully human in all the dimensions of their life, and the care and affection appropriate for the family should consist in the social habits fostering this.

The differences between traditional East Asian and modern American families have often been emphasized by those who claim that Confucianism requires the East Asian structure. Among the differences are these: the traditional East Asian family more sharply distinguishes the sex roles, women tend more to be confined to the home and domestic activities whereas men are more likely to play public roles, seniority is granted greater authority, separate responsibilities are more likely to be given children on the basis of birth order, and sharper separations are made between family members and those who are not kinfolk. Although these differences are real, they still are a matter of degree; families in contemporary China may not be as close to the traditional stereotype as to the modern American stereotype.

Confucianism for a modern American family, especially of the middle class, must cope with the fact that the family is intricately integrated into other public institutions that in traditional East Asia would be internal to the family. Children, for instance, must relate to the school systems and often receive very little formal education by family members, but where the school system fails, the family in America must make up the difference. Instead of a typical Chinese family business in which people are secure in a position and attain seniority that can be exercised as long as desired, Americans often shift companies, working their way to management responsibilities of some sort and then retiring to a life of expected leisure supported by retirement plans. American family proprieties or rituals need to accommodate their treatment of each individual according to the shifting roles they play in school and work. A youngish person might be junior in the family but the owner of his business and the boss of older people, including perhaps older relatives. A student might be a failure as a scholar but a helpful and responsible family member. Confucian family propriety cannot address primarily the person as defined by the family role, as perhaps is typical in the traditional Chinese family, but must also address the person as integrating the familial with the public roles.

About the time of the Moist egalitarian critique of Confucian ideas in China (Chan 1963, chapter 9; Graham 1989, section II: 2), the prophetic tradition of Israel, followed by the rabbinic institutions and especially by Jesus, attacked the tight kinship system of Jewish life as unjust because of its neglect and persecution of those lacking family. The early Christian concern for widows, orphans, and strangers led Jesus to denigrate his personal kinship connections and to appropriate kinship language for universal relations (*Mark* 3:31–35): we are all brothers and sisters, children of the one divine father (see sections 5.4 and 10.2). In both the Jewish and Christian traditions membership in a synagogue or church has taken over many of the senses of interpersonal identification typical of kinship families but extended to include those without families. For many people communal religious identification is as important as their family identification. Confucianism for American Judaism and Christianity needs to recognize in family ritual propriety the identifications members might have with religious communities that exercise some family-like functions.

Having stressed the differences in family conditions between traditional East Asian Confucianism and Boston Confucianism, let me now stress the need for a positive Boston Confucian contribution. American families by and large do not have the civilizing rituals they need to integrate school and home life, to acknowledge women with careers who also are mothers and homemakers, to cope with mature men who can be consumed by job responsibilities or out of work completely, to mediate the passing on of family traditions with what children learn at school and work, to dignify retirement while keeping family ties, and so forth. American families still need to cope with the fact that so many family members live alone, separated from the family. The modern American family enjoys many advantages of opportunity and, in certain circumstances, has obvious problems to be addressed by more and better jobs or better housing arrangements. But even if the advantages were celebrated and the problems overcome, there are insufficient rituals of family life for it to be the home in which people can be supported in working out the issues of wholeness in their lives. Confucianism in Boston and the modern West has both critical and creative philosophical work to do, in continuity with two and a half millenia of work in East Asia.

In this chapter so far I have argued that Confucianism (and by extension other traditions of Chinese thought) is now a world philosophy with all the intellectual responsibilites this entails. Confucianism can learn from and extend the Western tradition of pragmatism and therefore enter into internal dialectical relations with the Western traditions of philosophy so as to form in part a world tradition of philosophy inclusive of East Asia and the West. Boston Confucianism properly focuses on the moral implications of the pragmatic theory of signs in its emphasis on ritual propriety. I have surveyed cases in which Confucianism in its Boston school can relate to modern American society as critic and cultural creator through ritual propriety, just as it has done for millennia to East Asian societies. Incomplete though this argument is, it indicates how Confucianism can make a contemporary contribution to a cosmopolitan culture such as Boston's. But what does this do to Confucianism?

1.5. Bostonian Modifications of Confucianism

One must take this discussion of Boston Confucianism with a large sense of humor. The fact that Charles Peirce and Tu Weiming are Bostonians is sheerly accidental, and I mean to be speaking for a wide range of people in America and Asia who approach Confucianism as a portable world philosophy.[15] But if, with humor, we take Boston Confucianism as a symbol for a larger development, there are at least four novelties or modifications to be introduced into the Confucian tradition in the current discussion of its Boston extension.

First, the self-conscious development of a non–East Asian form of Confucianism requires internalizing a historical self-consciousness to a degree unprecedented in the Confucian tradition. Beginning with Confucius, of course, the tradition has been aware of historical distance and change, even when conceptions of the past were mainly legendary. The importation of the primary scriptures of Confucianism to a living tradition in the West, however, requires that the interpretive context be not only the *Yijing* but also Plato's *Republic*. Just as Neo-Confucianism in the Song and Ming dynasties learned from the Buddhists and Daoists, Boston Confucianism learns from the pragmatists and must interpret itself to the Kantians, phenomenologists, and Western logicians. The scale of historical transformation, the degree of change, and the jeopardy of connecting roots with branches is increased now.

Second, to the extent Confucianism flourishes in new forms in the West, there will be people identifying with it, living according to its primary texts and programs, and speaking for it, *who are not serious scholars*. Only a few Confucians in East Asia are serious scholars— ordinary Confucians there imbibe the philosophy with their culture. But in the West until very recently, the few and only people who had any connection with Confucianism at all were diaspora East Asians and serious scholars. Like any religious philosophy, Confucianism looks far better when represented only by its learned leaders. But from now on, Confucianism will be represented sometimes by people such as myself who have no pretense at Sinological scholarship and who read the texts in translation. The price of vigorous success is popularization, in this case by some who are Westerners.

Third, success in the West will make multiple religious identity a forced option for Confucians. The nature of religious affiliation is a complex problem that has not been addressed yet, though it will surface in the preface. Nor has the question been discussed whether Confucianism is a religion, although it surely is with respect to defining a way of life and shaping "ultimate concern" (see section 4.1).[16] In East Asia at various times, Confucianism has been affiliated with Buddhism, Daoism, Shintoism, and Shamanism according to diverse models, with some equivocation regarding the meaning of affiliation.[17] In the West, the question will arise whether Confucianism is compatible with Christianity, Judaism, and perhaps eventually Islam. Regarding the first encounter of Confucianism with Christianity, the "Rites" controversy ended in a negative answer to that question.[18] In the present work, several chapters will argue that the answer is different.

Fourth and finally, the importance of the virtues of public life for Boston Confucians is made more evident by the emphasis on the recovery of ritual propriety. The Confucian way is to attend to the improvement of all those meaningful social and significatory forms that shape personal and social habits for it is through these habits and through the signs that shape them that all human relations are mediated, even relations to oneself. What is public office but the care of social structures? What is a scholar-official but a holder of public office who sees that the principal instrument of administration or care is education, particularly education in ritual propriety? By no means is all exercise of public office merely a process of education. But education is perhaps the most effective way of exercising office because it consists in helping people take on signs guiding their habits that they lacked previously or practiced badly. Human beings are hard-wired to be responsive to changes in signs. All other exercise of public office involves force, which is inefficient and counter productive to free human life.

Is Confucianism inordinantly attractive to deans? Deans, of course, attempt to administer by a combination of broadcasts of vision and rewards for good practice; they have little other power. Is Confucianism merely the view that the world is a somewhat loosely run school? Not in its Boston branch. War is an evil shaped by the ritual signs of enmity, greed, and bitter memory. Poverty is shaped by the ritual signs that define ownership and exchange. Psychic and sexual abuse are behaviors shaped by signs feeding needs and passions. Hopelessness, despair, acting out, neighborhood violence, and self-destructiveness turned into a subculture are all functions of the signs shaping the realities of our culture. The signs, the ritual behaviors, are not about something other than themselves in context: they in their exercise are the very realities of human life. The Confucians have indeed identified the hard realities of life and offer a way to reform them so that self and society are united in goodness.

This chapter has offered an overview of most of the themes to be discussed at greater length in the chapters that follow. At the heart of its claims about the dialectical and critical relation of Confucianism to culture is a set of issues about culture itself. The arguments about Confucianism as critical and portable will be strengthened if they can be shown to reflect a Confucian philosophy of culture, or at least a Chinese philosophy of culture. That is the next topic.

2

Confucianism on Culture

2.1. Philosophy of Culture

Philosophy of culture is a Western category that has no exact Chinese counterpart. Chinese philosophical traditions, often far more finely than Western ones, discriminate kinds and conditions of cultural elements including: the development of the virtues such as humanity, righteousness, propriety, and wisdom (see, e.g., *Mencius* 2A: 6, in Chan 1963, 65); cultivating the Five Relations (between parents and children, ruler and minister, husband and wife, older and younger, and friends) (see, e.g., *Mencius* 3A: 4); the elaboration of the arts and philosophic life; the honing of skills such as calligraphy, sewing and sericulture, archery, cooking, music, and dance; the maintenance of economic practices such as agriculture, pottery, and trade; and the practices of public life from the village to the empire. How do all these things, and others, add up to culture as such? With what is culture to be contrasted? What are the particularly Chinese philosophies about culture?

The standard Western anthropological notion is that culture is what has to be learned from other people and can be passed on. Its contrast is with nature and what comes naturally to people. The contrast is complex because most natural human dispositions need also to be specified and shaped by culture, as the disposition to eat is culturally shaped by specific ways of finding and preparing food, or the disposition to procreate is culturally shaped by social habits of family life. Most elements of culture not only need to be learned but should be learned well, that is, cultivated: *good* cuisine and *healthy and nurturing* families. So most elements of culture can be assessed as to their appropriateness and degree of excellent development. Societies acknowledge not only distinctions between high and low culture but

25

also those between degrees of appropriate acculturation. All these elements are present in the Chinese appreciation of culture.

The specific elementary Chinese approach to philosophy of culture, however, is reflected in the trinity of heaven, earth, and the human. The classic *Doctrine of the Mean* says:

> Only those who are absolutely sincere can fully develop their nature. If they can fully develop their nature, they can then fully develop the nature of others. If they can fully develop the nature of others, they can then fully develop the nature of things. If they can fully develop the nature of things, they can then assist in the transforming and nourishing process of Heaven and Earth. If they can assist in the transforming and nourishing process of Heaven and Earth, they can thus form a trinity with Heaven and Earth. (Chapter 22, in Chan 1963)

The Chinese philosophy of culture has to do with the human contribution over and above what is given by heaven and earth, a contribution that fulfills heaven and earth but is not reducible to their natural principles and processes. *The Doctrine of the Mean* cites the development of the nature of the self, other people, and things as the content of the human contribution. Chinese philosophers differ widely in their interpretations of these elements and in the attitudes they advocate toward their development.

Two Chinese words are especially associated with the idea of culture, although that idea is more complex than a match for any single English word. The most common association is with *wen*, which usually means high culture, the arts, especially language and literature; its roots go back to the idea of pattern. The other is *li*, which is translated variously as ritual, ritual propriety, or manners of civility. As we saw in the previous chapter, however, its basic root meaning is learned, conventional, semiotically shaped behavior (see also Neville 1995, chapter 7). In this broad sense of symbolic behavior, ritual encompasses artistic culture and language, and is the orienting locus for a discussion of Chinese philosophy of culture.

The Chinese philosophy of culture can be analyzed under the following heads: (1) an elementary theory of culture relative to nature in Xunzi; (2) a schematic contrast of Confucian, Daoist, Legalist, Moist, and Chinese Buddhist approaches to culture; (3) ancient Confucianism in Confucius, Mencius, and Xunzi; and (4) the enduring contribution of Chinese philosophy of culture to the contemporary world philosophic situation. This discussion, except in the final section, restricts itself to ancient sources; the motifs there have been elaborated in extremely diverse ways for two milennia.

2.2. An Elementary Theory of Culture and Nature in Xunzi

Xunzi (c. 310 to c. 210 BCE) was an extraordinarily careful and responsible thinker who explicitly defended Confucianism in relation to Daoism, Moism, and incipient Legalism. But in his essay, "Tian Lun" (Knoblock, volume 3, book 17; also in Chan, 1963, 116-24; Machle 1993, chapter 7) he analyzed the relation of the human sphere to heaven and earth in a way that articulated what the other schools pretty much presupposed. Even the other Confucians, however, did not agree with all the conclusions Xunzi drew from this analysis. His elementary analysis, suspending judgment about the conclusions, is a good introduction to the Chinese philosophy of culture.

For Xunzi and his predecessors nature was a binary, not a single notion. On the one hand are the natural processes of things, extensive in time and space, the "stuff" of nature ranging from gross material processes to spiritual impulses and historical forces; these were called earth, and in various ways were identified with *qi* (or *ch^{c}i*, "material force"). On the other hand are the principles that order or harmonize the natural processes, that define regularity and integration, that are the source of goodness in contrast to chaos, and that in some spheres can fail to be fully actualized in which cases there is disaster, failure, or for human beings, the obligation to make the principles effective; these principles were called heaven and in deep antiquity were personalized in the form of a High God (*Shang Di*), though by the time of Confucius and especially Xunzi, they were not personalized. Frequently heaven and earth were spoken of together as a rough equivalent to the Western range of meanings for nature. Heaven was often paired with the human sphere in discussing obligation, especially the self-cultivation of what is the best in human beings. Heaven and earth were subsequently given extensive metaphysical interpretations as Principle and material force by the Neo-Confucians.

Xunzi, in the "Tian Lun" (Machle 1994, 95ff) pointed out that human beings are born with four kinds of natural endowments—heavenly orderings of biological processes. One is *feelings* such as desire, aversion, delight, anger, grief, and joy. Another is *sensibilities* such as the ear, eye, nose, mouth, and body, each of which has an appropriate object such that the objects should not be interchanged. A third natural endowment, which Xunzi called the "ruler," is the *mind* that can order the five sensibilities and that can use things other than mind to nurture its own intrinsic fulfillment, that is, the mind can use nonmental things as instruments by ordering human activity. The fourth natural endowment is *government*, namely, the capacity to harmonize with the things that fulfill the human sphere, which is a blessed capacity. To be at odds with what is fulfilling is human disaster. Government, in Xunzi's conception, refers to personal and familial as well as social governance.

"Fulfillment," in these remarks, refers to the supposition in Xunzi and others that each thing has its own dao, an intrinsic way of playing itself out with excellence. Dao has some connotations of unfolding, although not in the Aristotelian sense of actualizing potentialities given at the beginning or in early stages; a thing's dao needs to relate to and harmonize with other things and is not a function of the thing's essence. Dao also has some connotations of achieving an end, of purposive behavior in the human and higher animal cases, although again not in the Aristotelian sense of an end or purpose defined in the thing. Rather the end of the dao has to do with the appropriate contribution the thing might make to a larger harmony. The daos of natural things are intricately interrelated and also dependent on the dao of heaven and the dao of earth; they relate as well to more cosmic conceptions of the universal dao.

Human feelings, sensibilities, mind, and government are all natural (biologically based) capacities. But unlike most if not all other natural things, those human endowments cannot fulfill themselves by nature alone, not by any combination of heaven and earth. The human dao requires culture in order for feelings, sensibilities, mind, and government to exercise their daos and fulfill themselves. That we have capacities for desire, aversion, delight, anger, grief, and joy does not mean we direct them at the right things. We need culture to define their direction, and then those cultural elements themselves are appropriate objects of desire, aversion, and so forth. Moreover, high culture gives us extraordinarily excellent things to desire, and extraordinary evils to avoid, far beyond what nature might provide without culture. The sensibilities have their objects but their responses cannot be integrated without culture; and with their integrating culture, such as dance, more complicated and excellent harmonies of sensibilities are possible. The mind has the natural capacity to act instrumentally but needs cultural knowledge of what to do to accomplish its ends, namely, the fulfillment of the human dao. It especially needs to know what the dao is. Government, which at the natural level is the capacity to control self and others relative to the fulfillment of the daos involved, needs culture to give it shape so that the exercise of control does not destroy the fulfillment but nourishes it to flourishing.

What then is culture? It is the sum of the conventions that shape the natural endowments so that they can be fulfilled and together fulfill the human. The body can move in countless different ways but needs a culture to teach it a way of moving for walking, for eating, for making eye contact, for gesturing, and for expressing meaning through body language. The body can make many sorts of different sounds but needs a culture to teach it ways of communicating and speaking through systems of verbal symbols. People can interact in a great many ways, but every interaction, to be understood so that people assume roles within it, needs to have some ritualized parameters, such as greeting and feasting rituals. With minimal conventions people can copulate and reproduce, but only with the rituals of high civilization can there be family life with love and nurturing. With minimal conventions people can cooperate in the hunt and economic production, but only with the rituals of high civilization can there be public life and effective just government. With minimal rituals people can be colleagues, but only with the rituals of high civilization can people be genuine friends. The problem with the barbarians, thought the ancient Chinese, is not that they have the wrong customs but that they have customs and conventions inadequate to the actual exercise of high civilization. All the rituals of high civilization need to be coordinated with each other and with the larger environment. Seasonal rituals of family and public life, up to the imperial court, are intended to set the rhythms and choreograph the dance of social interaction and of human interaction with heaven and earth. For Xunzi and the other early Confucians, all these learned conventions, from styles of movement to court rituals, were encompassed under the notion of ritual propriety (*li*). All of them, with extraordinarily complex connections, constitute culture, that which the human sphere adds to the original endowments of heaven and earth to bring those biological and other natural daos to their fulfillment. Something like this complicated sense of culture was understood by all the early schools, although they took different stances toward it.[1] Culture in this sense is a semiotic system of the sort associated with Peirce's pragmatism and connected in the previous chapter to Confucianism in the West.

2.3. Chinese Orientations to Culture: Confucian, Daoist, Legalist, Moist, and Buddhist

Xunzi himself represented the generally positive Confucian approach to culture. The Confucians affirmed the assertion quoted in 2.1 from *The Doctrine of the Mean* that the cultural human sphere fulfills heaven and earth and adds a positive ontological reality. The ancient Confucians differed among themselves as to how to attain to high culture and the character of the obstacles to it, a point addressed in the next section.

The Daoists by contrast emphasized the fact that culture is artificial and therefore can interfere with the natural daos of nature. They saw high culture as an ambiguous good, if not a plain evil, and advocated the deconstruction of ritual behavior and cultivation of more naive, spontaneous behavior. It is hard to know just how serious they were in their advocacy of the back-to-nature theme because they lived within a highly ritualized and cultured society, even when the culture was in trouble. The *Daodejing* by Laozi, chapter 80, says:

> Let there be a small country with few people.
> Let there be ten times and a hundred times as many
>   utensils
> But let them not be used.
> Let the people value their lives highly and not migrate far.
> Even if there are ships and carriages, none will ride in
>   them.
> Even if there are armor and weapons, none will display
>   them.
> Let the people again knot cords and use them (in place of
>   writing).
> Let them relish their food, beautify their clothing, be
>   content with their homes, and delight in their
>   customs.
> Though neighboring communities overlook one another and
>   the crowing of cocks and barking of dogs can be
>   heard,
> Yet the people there may grow old and die without ever
>   visiting one another. (in Chan 1963, 175)[2]

Much of the *Daodejing* and the writings of Zhuangzi are about government and social administration. But at the very least, the classical Daoist attitude toward culture, especially high culture, was suspicion.

The Daoists and Confucians shared an image of human life as a kind of hierarchy of organized functions. Toward the bottom are physiological processes such as heartbeat and metabolism that have a natural rhythm and are deeply embedded in environing natural rhythms, say, of the ecosystem. Moving up, these physiological processes are organized into behaviors such as moving, working, eating, and primitive cooperation; the forms for these organization are learned and are the rudiments of culture. Then the processes are organized into speech, family life, and political cooperation and finally into the arts of high civilization. The most harmonious and sophisticated civilized flourishing of the dao requires beating hearts and a food system, but we understand it mainly in terms of the high cultural levels of organization shaping the natural processes.

The Confucians were convinced that the higher levels of cultural organization are necessary for the flourishing of the lower levels and the merely natural processes; without those higher levels, the lower levels will not be able to fulfill their human dao and might even be self-destructive. The Daoists, by contrast, even though they admitted the higher levels, and excelled at the most sophisticated virtues, were fearful that the higher levels would distort and pervert the rhythms of the lower levels; if the higher levels could not be seen as natural and spontaneous outgrowths of the lower, they are to be distrusted. Moreover, as Zhuangzi so often argued, the higher levels are ambiguous with regard to how they build upon the lower; language is deceptive about intentions, and even the discrimination of waking and sleeping is ambiguous about simply being.

Another element in the Daoist approach to culture consists in its peculiar focus on cultivated insight. Like the Confucians, the ancient Daoists advocated meditation and the cultivation of subtle perception. But whereas the Confucians focused on the human sphere and the setting of the human within the cosmic, the Daoists focused more on the cosmic first, on what Western philosophy would call the metaphysical or ontological. The *Daodejing* opens with a reflection on the dao that cannot be named. Zhuanzi speculates about reality and appearance. Perhaps the most metaphysical of the philosophical Daoists was Wang Bi who wrote at length about being and nonbeing and developed the distinction between substance and function, influenced by Buddhism (Chan 1963, chapter 19). Processes of meditation and philosophical speculation are as much part of culture as the institutions of family life and government; for many, especially in the West, the Daoist sage of contemplation, rather than the Confucian sage of human action, is the epitome of Chinese culture (Hansen 1992).

The Legalist philosophy, say, of Han Feizi, focused on a different aspect of culture as ritual. The Confucians had argued that moral and holy behavior to a large extent consists in shaping life by the conventions of high culture and believed that when people widely practiced or exercised these conventions proper justice, deference, and distribution would happen as a matter of course. The authority for the rituals of high culture was attributed to the ancient sage kings by the

Confucians, but they thought the merits of high civilization were apparent on their own. The Legalists observed that, however good and just the conventions of high culture might be, people do not take to them naturally. The authority of the sage kings is irrelevant and not easily knowable. Moreover, many of the policies of good governments are not of the form of general habitual behavior but rather of making specific changes. Therefore, the Legalists said that laws and policies should be explicit and that people do good when they are shaped, perhaps even coerced, to do so by a clear regimen of rewards and punishments. The Legalists rejected the efficacy of the rather aesthetic appeal of both Confucian cultural practices and Daoist spontaneous naturalism and said that high culture should be built by the clear statement of laws and their strict enforcement by rewards and punishments. Concommitant with demystifying the aesthetic and antiquarian authority of social convention and ritual, Legalism had the effect of promoting social equality and also a pragmatic rationalization of culture (Graham 1989, 267–92). Although the Legalists were influential in the authoritarian Qin dynasty (221 to 206 BCE), they were soon rejected as deeply insensitive to high civilization for such policies as their advocacy of book burning.

The Moists took an even more utilitarian approach to the conventions of high culture. They developed a rather straightforward conception of social benefit and universal respect or love and judged conventions by the extent to which they promoted social benefits. In this they did not deem the fairly esoteric matters of ritual practice of high civilization, accessible only by the elite, to be much benefit and thus attacked elaborate funerals and mourning customs, displays of music, and the like. Whereas the Confucians saw mourning customs, for instance, as part of the very reality of respect for persons, and the performance of music and dance as the very stuff of what makes life worth living, the Moists saw these kinds of things as likely impediments to economic progress and fair distribution. Wing-tsit Chan (1963, 212) speculates that, whereas the Confucians aimed to draw people from all walks of life to take on an elite life of ritual propriety, the Moists represented peasants for whom high civilization meant little.

Early Buddhism in China did not develop a distinctive attitude toward culture as such except to see it as having only instrumental value for the liberation or enlightenment of sentient beings.[3] The Buddhists did not see much importance to completing the trinity of heaven, earth, and the human when the real human task is enlightenment. Nevertheless, an enlightened person still lives in the world, dealing with the issues of samsara, and in these capacities can contribute as much as anyone to the building of a high civilization. The Buddhist contributions to Chinese art are of extraordinary importance. Although there have been many forms of Buddhism in China beginning in the first century of the Common Era or earlier, in practice they share a middle path between the Confucian pressure to create ever more sophisticated and elite conventions and the Daoist pressure to deconstruct these in favor of natural immediacy with the dao. It should be noted that by the time Buddhism began to flourish in China, Daoism had evolved, even in its mystical forms, to a ritualized religion with temples and a priesthood (Kohn 1991, 1992; Lagerwey 1987).

This schematic survey of Chinese attitudes toward culture is of course too selective and broadly generalized. The ancient Confucian movement will be investigated here in more detail.

2.4. Confucius, Mencius, and Xunzi Compared

Although the historical figure of Confucius has been overdetermined by the legendary roles to which subsequent interpreters have subjected him, it is clear that he, by his activities and force of personality, formed a school (perhaps also a model for a widely imitated type of school) for the cultivation of ritual competence (Eno 1990). His recorded sayings (*The Analects*) express the suppositions, motivations, and goals of his movement. Three points are important with respect to Confucius' philosophy of culture.

First and probably most important was his interpretation of the social situation. He lived in the declining years of the Spring and Autumn period as it was degenerating into the worse political chaos of the period of the Warring States. The imperial government had relatively little power, the various states warred against one another, and none kept the peace very well. Groups were desperate to enhance their own power and the quality of life declined, at least according to their way of thinking. This is the kind of social chaos Thomas Hobbes (1950 [1651], 104) described, in discussing the English revolution, when he called the quality of human life "solitary, poor, nasty, brutish, and short." But whereas Hobbes thought the problem was a lack of governmental power to enforce civil order (a point to which the Legalists would have been sympathetic), Confucius' analysis was quite different. The evils of his day consisted in the operative failure of rituals and conventional forms of social behavior to keep the peace automatically, to distribute goods fairly, and to facilitate the fulfillment of people of varying stations and conditions. So instead of good family life, political competence, and friendship, there was barely more than procreation, strong-man politics, and exploitation. Even if there were a powerful enough government to bring a cessation of violence by authorized force (Hobbes's solution), without civilized ritual according to which people could behave, the government would have nothing to do with lasting good. And with civilized ritual, the need for governmental force would be minimal. Confucius thus argued that the key to social life is the inculcation of properly ritualized habits of life, beginning with the students in his school.

Confucius thought that the rituals he advocated were recoveries of the high civilization of the legendary sage kings, and he claimed that he himself was no innovator, only passing on what he had learned. A logical problem lies behind this stance: if humanizing conventions are in addition to heaven and earth, where do they come from and with what authority? A past golden age answers that question, at least on the surface. Because of Confucius' denial of originality, he has often been regarded merely as a reformer. But as mentioned previously, he was in fact a radical revolutionary, radical in the sense of going to the root of the trouble—lack of operative civilizing rituals—and revolutionary in the sense of calling for a total transformation of his society and a reversal of the power-political directions in which it was moving. The genre of Western literature to which *The Analects* is most like is the Hebrew prophets, especially *Jeremiah*: professions of highly purified ideals are juxtaposed to bitter complaints about the current state of affairs, with strident calls to amend our ways before it is too late.

The second element of Confucius' philosophy of culture is the conception of high civilization to be made possible by ritual. Fundamentally, civilization is to enable people to live harmoniously with themselves, their fellows, and the cosmos. The rituals and conventional social habits are to orient people so that the daos of nature, social institutions, and themselves are caused to flourish in harmony. Moreover, all the personal and social activities that exist in their exercise are themselves players in the harmony, so that harmonization is recursive: The rituals that orient us harmoniously are themselves the object of harmonious orientation. The result is an extraordinarily rich conception of the texture of things that should be brought into harmonious balance, and things are understood in terms of the correlations and connections that highlight issues of harmony and balance (Hall and Ames 1987, 1995). Confucius did not have as exalted and metaphysically expressed notion of the cosmic dao as was prevalent in Daoism, but he saw the human project as requiring harmony with the cosmos. He did not have (or was not recorded as having) as detailed a conception of ritual as Xunzi, or as elaborate a theory of pedagogy as Mencius. But he knew and taught about those things and was extraordinarily effective as a teacher. The rest of the Confucian tradition can be understood as a development and elaboration of Confucius' ideals for civilization as made possible through ritualized conventions.

The third element of Confucius' philosophy of culture was his conception of the sage or properly educated person (*zhunzi*, or *chun-tse*). The most obvious element in the sage is competence at ritual and the habits of practicing it in all circumstances. Less obvious but perhaps as important was Confucius' requirement of humaneness (*ren*). Humaneness for Confucius seemed to have three aspects: toward objects, toward personal constitution, and toward practical effects. Regarding objects, the sage should be properly deferential, acknowledging and prizing each thing for what it is and comporting himself or herself appropriately. Rituals provide the forms for deferential comportment, but they can be practiced without real deference in the heart. Regarding personal constitution, the humane sage should be pure in the sense of clarity of heart through activities and dispositions; the sage should not be muddied by selfish desires but able to perceive the nature and worths of things without distortion and respond appropriately; the sage's heart should be open and perspicuous, and privacy is a fault. Regarding practical effects, the sage should not only live a moral and politically beneficial life but should do so in such a way that others conform in emulation. Force is not so important in government, Confucius thought, because the exemplary power of sages, especially a sage emperor, moves people's hearts so as to bring them into humaneness and civilized ritual practice. The ritual practice by itself might not be powerfully commanding, but the humane heart of a sage is hard to resist. The love between parents and children is the seed from which humaneness grows (Tu 1976b).

Culture, for Confucius, is thus not merely the rituals and conventions laid on top of nature but the way of life that connects the human heart in resonance and harmony with all the things in the universe, including the rituals, symbols, and institutions that facilitate that harmony. All of these themes have been stressed in one way or another by subsequent Confucians.

Mencius focused primarily on humaneness and emphasized how natural it is to human beings, epitomized in the slogan that "human nature is good." Western philosophies have often conceived the distinction between the natural and conventional to be a sharp one; under the influence of substance philosophies, Western thinkers have sometimes represented the natural to be one kind of thing and the conventional another. For the Confucians, it is the dao innate to human being that itself develops the conventions of civilized life. *The Doctrine of the Mean* begins:

> What Heaven (*T'ien*, Nature) imparts to man is called human nature. To follow our nature is called the Way (Tao). Cultivating the Way is called education. The Way cannot be separated from us for a moment. What can be separated from us is not the Way. (in Chan 1963, 98)

Mencius elaborated this point with his theory of the Four Beginnings (*Mencius* 2A: 6, in Chan 1963, 65), which are the innate feelings of commiseration, shame and dislike, deference and compliance, and right and wrong. Illustrated in the famous parable of the instant feeling of alarm people feel when sighting a child about to fall into a well, these Four Beginnings are incipient sensitivities, readinesses to respond. When cultivated through civilized education, they lead to the sophisticated virtues of humanity, righteousness, propriety (ritual observance), and wisdom.

If the development of these civilized virtues springs from natural endowment, how does Mencius conceive that we ever go wrong? Like any Confucian he was convinced that children need to be surrounded by an educational environment to shape growth, beginning with the family and including communal ritual (*Mencius* 3A: 3, in Chan, 66–67). In some instances, that environment might be lacking. But he was more troubled by the destructive forces of society that would teach selfishness, bad habits, and barbaric conventions. Somewhat like the Daoists, therefore, but with no diminution of the Confucian stress on effort, he thought the larger social task is to remove destructive social elements and get out of the way of the natural exfoliation of the virtues, especially humanity. Thus he did not stress as much as some others the importance of ritual learning because ritual can be learned without humanity, and it can be bad ritual in the first place. But no matter how misguided and depraved a person might become, the root of virtue remains and is ready to sprout if given half a chance.

Mencius had much to say about the social conditions that allow humanity naturally to flourish. They include a commanding humanity on the part of the emperor, and a just and cooperative local social structure in which people bear one another's burdens and make sure everyone has enough to eat and good work to do. When the emperor fails of virtue, his authority is lost and the people have the right of rebellion. Mencius' emphases on personal virtue and social justice have been major themes of the Confucian tradition ever since.

Xunzi was less impressed with the readiness of human nature to flower into virtue than he was with the fact that, without fairly explicit social cultivation, people would not grow into the explicitly human dao at all. Human beings start out selfish, and from this he concluded that human nature is bad. Virtue comes not from a given nature but from activity that develops this nature (Xunzi, chapter 23 in Chan, 128–35; Knoblock, III: 150–62). Xunzi thus stressed the importance of culture that elicits humane activity:

> In antiquity the sage kings took man's nature to be evil, to be inclined to prejudice and prone to error, to be perverse and rebellious, and not to be upright or orderly. For this reason they invented ritual principles and precepts of moral duty. They instituted the regulations that are contained in laws and standards. Through these actions they intended to "straighten out" and develop man's essential nature and to set his inborn nature aright. They sought to tame and transform his essential nature and to guide his inborn nature with the Way. They caused both his essential and inborn natures to develop with good order and be consistent with the true Way. . . . It is the environment that is critical! It is the environment that is critical! (*Xunzi* 1994, 151–62).

Like nearly all good philosophers, Xunzi developed his position by a subtle criticism of neighboring conceptions.[4]

The main line of the Confucian tradition, especially in the Neo-Confucians and down to our own time in the work of Mou Zongsan and Tu Weiming, has followed Mencius rather than Xunzi in stressing the continuity of innate human nature with the development of civilized forms. But the difference between them has been overstressed. If one considers a situation in which the social forms are actually degenerate and helpful ritual lacking, the result will be the development of greedy and power-seeking people, as Xunzi said. However ready human nature might be to learn right action in the presence of civilizing conditions, a matter Xunzi would not dispute, when those conditions are absent, people will not develop in any way except defensively and selfishly. Xunzi was perhaps closer than Mencius to Confucius' concern about what to do with degenerate social conditions, although his rhetoric runs counter to that of classics such as *The Doctrine of the Mean*.[5]

The subsequent developments of Confucianism and Neo-Confucianism are extremely various and will not be summarized here. During the Neo-Confucian period the personal cultivation of sagehood became a dominant theme, though never without a political concern.

The school of Zhu Xi in the Southern Song dynasty was explicit about its political involvement in both foreign policy and with respect to the education of persons for the literati class and the government bureaucracy (Tillman 1992). Others such as Wang Anshi, who are not customarily thought of as philosophers, were deeply involved in the shaping of Song culture.

The explicit emphasis on ritual dropped back from prominence in Neo-Confucian discourse in favor of an emphasis on personal cultivation and humanity. This was not because the Neo-Confucians did not share the logical point of the ancients about the ritual constitution of civilization but because Confucianism had largely won. From the Han through the Song dynasties, China had become a highly ritualized society, and the point of ritual's importance no longer had to be made. The concern was rather with the cultivation of genuine sagehood and the performance of the proper rituals (Zhu Xi 1991 translation).

The advent of Western thought in China in the nineteenth century, especially Marxism more recently, has been devastating to the authentic appreciation of the ritualized aspects of culture, however much many of the rituals have been carried on. The utilitarianism of the Western influence has been a delegitimating force on the Chinese philosophy of culture as much as it has on the pretechnological aspects of that culture itself. Even John Dewey (1963 [1939]), whose own theory of the social construction of culture as part of human nature is remarkably similar to many ancient Confucian themes, filtered that down to a crass scientism in his 1919–20 lectures in China (Dewey 1973). Perhaps before the genius of the ancient Chinese philosophy of culture can be appreciated in China today, its contribution to world philosophy needs to be made manifest. In contrast to the effort to revitalize the Chinese philosophical tradition characteristic of the previous generation of Chinese philosophers, the contemporary generation focuses its effort on reconstructing Chinese philosophy, especially Chinese philosophy of culture, for the world conversation.[6]

2.5. Confucian Contributions to a Contemporary Philosophy of Culture

There are at least four distinctive contributions from the ancient Chinese philosophy of culture that are important for contemporary world philosophy and that reinforce the approach to Confucianism as a world philosophy, as expressed in chapter 1. They can be called the semiotics of ethics, the aesthetics of culture, the personal competence of civilization, and the irony of convention.

As argued in section 1.4, the contemporary expression of much of what the ancient Chinese meant by ritual is in the semiotics of pragmatism (Neville 1995, chapters 3, 6–7). A pragmatic semiotic reconstruction of Chinese ritual theory gives the Chinese tradition thick access to the Western philosophies leading to semiotics. But the Chinese tradition has shown how rituals make possible all layers of civilization in ways far more subtle than Western semiotics, which has tended to identify sign systems with mere languages, not with the institutions and behaviors whose exercise constitutes civilization. This vastly enriches the discussion of signs. Moreover, it contributes even more to contemporary ethics. The Western ethical traditions generally have focused on actions, decisions, and goals or values, missing the Confucian point that social activities are not possible without the significant ritualized behaviors whose exercise constitutes their existence; how can one decide to be good or do the right if there is no behavioral vocabulary for good and bad, right and wrong, behavior? The Chinese philosophy of culture allows for the critical examination of the social habits and rituals of a society, and for the invention of good ones where they are lacking, a topic almost entirely obscured by the Western preoccupation with decisions, actions, and goals. The specific ancient rituals of China might be entirely inappropriate for egalitarian and meritocratic societies, but something like them needs to be developed for the civilizing of societies formed by the technologies and economies of late modernity.

The aesthetics of culture to be gleaned from the Chinese tradition, both Daoist and Confucian, stands to supplement and correct the modern Western preoccupation with the instrumentalities of culture (Hall 1982a, 1982b). The Western Enlightenment has focused on the development of cultural elements that foster progress, and great progress has been made in matters of health, security, farming, economic production, and social justice.[7] But as the demand to die with dignity shows, for instance, progress can be dehumanizing. The aesthetic contribution of Chinese culture is not just in fine arts or appreciative contrast to instrumentalism but rather in a reconceiving of the problem of instrumentalism itself. The Chinese contribution is to insist that the purpose of culture is to harmonize human life with the dao in the cosmos, in society, and in other people. Moreover, because of its recursive quality, the institutions of civilization have daos of their own with which everything else should be brought into harmony. Progress itself should be conceived as the enhancement of harmony, properly understood according to the causal connections among natural and conventionally constituted processes. The Chinese aesthetics of culture need not deprecate technology and the Western impulse to progress, only put it in an appropriate context of harmonization.

The personal competence of civilization is a definition of the human project that recognizes that people are not born civilized. They need to undertake to become civilized by appropriating their culture's civilizing forms. Personal life has the task of becoming civilized. This ideal stands in some contrast with the Western emphasis on the fitness of the ordinary and the glorification of popular culture (Charles Taylor 1989). But it also stands in contrast with heroic ideals requiring extraordinary effort open only to a few: sagehood is open to everyone, both Confucians and Daoists would agree. This theme is not absent from Western culture; it was in fact a centerpiece of Dewey's philosophy. But it has often been associated with the aristocracy. The Chinese can bring the theme into the world discussion without the associations of aristocracy (though modern Confucianism often had that association). The theme resonates with Christian ideals of holiness.

The irony of convention is a consciousness that comes from China's long preoccupation with ritual and its obvious temptations to abuse. Crudely put, Daoist humor punctures Confucian pomposities when ritual is glorified without humaneness. Of course, the situation is more complicated than this crude statement; religious Daoism is highly ritualistic, and Confucians long appreciated the need to make ritual humane. But the Chinese tradition with these checks and balances has been able to recognize from very early on that conventions are conventions, not natural processes or singularly authoritative like natural law, and yet very important for civilization, indeed. It does not matter in the Chinese tradition what conventions a society has so long as they serve to make possible the practice of high civilization. The West has tended to vacillate between taking its conventions to be singularly and exclusively normative or treating them as merely relative and therefore not important, perhaps even unnatural. The Chinese contribution of the irony of convention is particularly important in a situation where the great world civilizations are in commerce, if not conflict, with one another.

The contributions of Chinese philosophy of culture to the contemporary situation therefore are potent for ethics, philosophy of technology, personal cultivation, and the encounter of civilizations. Moreover, they reinforce the importance of Chinese philosophy, especially Confucianism, for the contemporary world conversation in philosophy. The argument of this book now turns to examine the contemporary situation with regard to the Confucian contribution.

3

Confucianism in the Contemporary Situation

3.1. Historical Background

Confucian studies are now undergoing a revival in China, just as they are coming to prominence within the English-speaking world. Because of the interest of this book in the transportation of Confucianism to the late-modern West, however, this chapter will concentrate on the latter. Although most academic philosophy departments in Great Britain and the United States at the present time do not consider Chinese philosophy to be part of the mainstream curriculum, there is a growing recognition among the broader community of philosophers that the traditions of China (and also of India, Islam, and Orthodox Christianity) are necessary components of the contemporary public discussion of philosophy.[1] Chinese philosophy is indeed part of the mainstream curriculum in English-speaking philosophical studies in Hong Kong and Singapore, as well as at the University of Hawaii; many American philosophy departments have at least token representation of Chinese philosophy. And although academic philosophy in the United States and Great Britain has become narrow in its self-definition of method and topic, the broader philosophical issues important in Chinese philosophy are frequently and rather thoroughly addressed in American departments of religious studies.

The influence of Chinese philosophy on the West is not recent. It began in early modern times with the reports of Marco Polo and Christian missionaries to China that were read by European philosophers such as Leibniz. Leibniz was fascinated with China from his youth, corresponded and visited with missionaries, and edited a book of missionary reports; he also wrote essays or long letters on Chinese theology, Neo-Confucian metaphysics, Chinese morality, and on the Chinese approach to mathematics in the *Yijing* and the writings of *Shao Yung*.[2] Joseph Needham (1956, 291–93) cites the influence of Leibniz's interpretation of Chinese (especially Zhu Xi's) theories of natural law and organicism on Whitehead's organic process philosophy, although his interpretation is not universally accepted.

The widespread knowledge and use of Chinese philosophy in the English-speaking philosophical world has been made possible by the achievement of a critical mass of translations and scholarship in intellectual history. Perhaps the single most important event for Chinese philosophy in the West was the publication in 1963 of Wing-tsit Chan's (1963) *A Source Book in Chinese Philosophy*. That volume, over 850 pages long, contains sober scholarly translations, with straightforward explanatory notes, of the whole or large selections of *The Analects, Mencius, The Great Learning, The Doctrine of the Mean*, Xunxi (Hsun-tzu in the Wade-Giles transliteration Chan used), Laozi (Lao-tzu), Zhuangzi (Chuang-tzu), Mozi (Mo-tzu), the School of Names, the Yin-Yang school, Legalism, Dung Zhungxu (Tung Chung-shu), Yang Xiong (Yang Hsiung), Wang Chung (Wang Ch'ung), Huainanzi (Huai-nan Tzu), Liezi (Lieh Tzu), Wang Bi (Wang Pi), Ho Yen, Guo Xiang (Kuo Hsiang), early Buddhism, Sengzhao (Seng-chao), Zhizang (Chi-tsang), Xuanzang (Hsuan-tsang), Huisi (Hui-ssu), Fazang (Fa-tsang), *The Platform Scripture of the Sixth Patriarch*, Shenhui (Shen-hui), Yixuan (I-Hsuan), Han Yu, Li Ao, Zhou Dunyi (Chou Tun-I), Shao Yong (Shao Yung), Zhang Zai (Chang Tsai), Cheng Hao (Ch'eng Hao), Cheng Yi (Ch'eng I), Lu Xiangshan (Lu Hsiang-shan), Zhu Xi (Chu Hsi), Wang Yangming (Wang Yang-ming), Wang Fuzhi (Wang Fu-chih), Yen Yuan, Dai Zhen (Tai Chen), Kang Yuwei (K'ang Yu-wei), Tan Situng (T'an Ssu-t'ung), Zhang Dungsun (Chang Tung-sun), Feng Yulan (Fung Yu-lan), and Xiong Shili (Hsiung Shih-li). This volume put before the English-reading public a serious representation of the vast array of philosophic thinking in China's history. With this volume alone, British and American trained philosophers could come to engage major ideas of the Chinese philosophic tradition in critical fashion. Meanwhile, for decades departments of history or East Asian languages and cultures in universities such as Cambridge and Oxford in Britain and Columbia, Yale, Harvard, Princeton, Chicago, Wisconsin, Berkeley, and Stanford in the United States and Toronto in Canada, have been producing graduates whose typical dissertation is the translation of some important Chinese text in a critical edition with an historical commentary. In the last decade or so, these graduates have replicated the translation-historical-philosophic studies programs at many universities and colleges of hitherto lesser reputation for Chinese studies. The result is an ever-increasing flood of good translations and increasingly sophisticated historical studies of Chinese philosophy in English so that non-Chinese reading philosophers can engage Chinese philosophical ideas and movements just the way they can European ones. Of course, philosophers in Britain and America who cannot read Chinese cannot be *scholars* of Chinese philosophy, just as they cannot be scholars of Plato, Aristotle, Epictetus, or Augustine without reading them in the Greek or Latin originals. But just as most English-speaking philosophers engage the ancient Western philosophers in translation, so can they now engage the Chinese. The question is how they engage it.

The recent history of the influence of Chinese philosophy in English-speaking philosophy can be studied under three rubrics. The first is the work of interpretive philosophers, often translators, whose aim is to make Chinese thought accessible to Westerners. The second is the work of bridging philosophers who do explicit comparisons of Chinese and Western philosophical ideas, often advocating the former as improvements upon, or at least helpful supplements to, the latter. These will be treated in section 3.2. The third is the work of philosophers who identify some Chinese school such as Confucianism or Daoism as central to their own heritage but whose main philosophic intent is neither interpretation nor comparison but the normative engagement of contemporary philosophic problems within our own discourse or conversation. In this category the projects of Roger T. Ames and David Hall, of Cheng Chungying, and of Wu Kuangming will be discussed, each in a section of its own. The entire discussion of Tu Weiming in chapter 5 falls under the third rubric of "normative philosophers," that is, those developing theories about the truth of the issues, not merely writing about philosophers.

3.2. Interpretive, Bridging, and Normative Philosophers

The work of Wing-tsit Chan has already been mentioned, and it includes far more than his *Source Book in Chinese Philosophy*. Under his inspiration and editorship, a number of major scholars published *Chu Hsi and Neo-Confucianism*, and his own *Chu Hsi: New Studies* has helped supplant the earlier commentary by J. Percy Bruce. Chan has a translation of Zhu Xi's *Reflections on Things at Hand* and also a full translation of Wang Yangming's *Instructions for Practical Living*.[3] In all these translations Chan has copious historical and philosophical commentary. A new generation of historians writing in English, such as Hoyt Cleveland Tillman (1992) and Peter K. Bol (1992), suggests that Chan and his followers overemphasize philosophy in the Neo-Confucian project to the detriment of their social involvement. But that does not detract from Chan's contribution to the philosophers' understanding of the Neo-Confucian tradition.

As important as Chan has been, William Theodore de Bary, who for many years was professor of East Asian thought at Columbia University, has trained a great many of the scholars of Chinese philosophy now working in the United States and Canada who have made and are making the translations of important works. He was for much of the same time the Provost of the University, exemplifying the life of the Confucian scholar-official. For many years he has led the Columbia University Seminar on Neo-Confucianism, which has been an intellectual meeting ground to discuss Chinese philosophy for many persons of a scholarly and/or philosophical bent. He has edited the *Sources of Chinese Tradition* (1960) and then edited and contributed significantly to a number of conference volumes, among which the most important are *Self and Society in Ming Thought* (1970) and *The Unfolding of Neo-Confucianism* (1975). His recent work, for instance, *The Liberal Tradition in China* (1983), has focused on historical backgrounds in philosophy for contemporary philosophic debates in China, such as human rights.

Although Confucians by temperament, like Aristotelians, might be more prone to translation, scholarly editions, and interpretive commentary, the Daoist traditions have had their representatives in interpretive work. The *Daodejing* has been translated into English more times than any other Chinese classic, and there are many beautiful editions of translations of the *Zhuangzi*. Herrlee G. Creel's (1970) *What Is Taoism* is a classic study, and the early works of Wu Kuangming, *Chuang Tzu: World Philosopher at Play* (1982) and *The Butterfly as Companion: Meditations on the First Three Chapters of the Chuang Tzu* (1990), are deep interpretations oriented to the Western problematics of philosophy. Daoism, of course, is not only a philosophy in the Western sense, although Laozi and Zhuangzi are usually interpreted that way. The religious dimensions of Daoism have received brilliant interpretive attention from Norman Girardot (1983) in *Myth and Meaning in Early Taoism*, from Isabelle Robinet's (1993) *Taoist Meditation*, from John Lagerwey (1987) in *Taoist Ritual in Chinese Society and History*, and from the extraordinary translations and interpretations of Livia Kohn—*Early Chinese Mysticism* (1992), *Taoist Mystical Philosophy* (1991), *Taoist Meditation and Longevity Techniques* (1989) and *The Taoist Experience* (1993). All of these scholars are primarily interpreters of the Chinese traditions.

Interpreting, though moving beyond that to do direct comparisons, are thinkers who can be called "bridging" scholars. Far and away the most important recent book on Chinese philosophy for Western philosophers is Herbert Fingarette's (1972) *Confucius: The Secular as Sacred*. Fingarette is a distinguished philosopher in the analytic tradition who has written on many topics within the Western problematic. Whereas Western philosophy since the European Enlightenment has taken quite a dim view of ritual as associated with religious superstition, authoritarian court etiquette, and an evasion of plain-speaking, as pointed out earlier, Fingarette drew upon notions associated with John Searle to show how ritual is a performative act. Suddenly, Confucianism, and Daoism too for that matter with its emphasis on ritual, became intelligible to Western philosophers as philosophically significant beyond moralistic commendations of virtue. The significance of Fingarette's thesis is that it showed the Confucian notion of ritual to make social relations possible and to be the medium of ethics. It made sense finally to Western philosophers for Confucius to have responded to the lawless anarchy of his time with a call to retrieve civilizing rituals. Fingarette is perhaps the most effective bridging philosopher so far.

David S. Nivison is another analytic philosopher who has entered into detailed sinological studies of the history of Chinese philosophy but who has also made explicit expositions of thinkers in that tradition as contributing to the solution of contemporary Western philosophical problems. His principal interest has been in ethical questions, and he mines the Chinese tradition from the most ancient times to the Ming, as in his most recent book, *The Ways of Confucianism: Investigations in Chinese Philosophy* (1996). Another analytical philosopher who has dealt extensively with Chinese philosophy as a source for contemporary thinking is Antonio Cua. His *Dimensions of Moral Creativity* (1978) involves an extensive treatment of Confucius. *The Unity of Knowledge and Action* (1982) is a brilliant interpretation of Wang Yangming as a moral psychologist and ethical thinker with contributions for the contemporary debate. *Ethical Argumentation* (1985) is a study of Xunzi as a moral thinker, equally apt for the contemporary discussion.

Philip J. Ivanhoe is a scholar who also relates Confucian thought to contemporary philosophical problems, again mainly ethics but not entirely so. His view of Western philosophy is somewhat broader than the analytic tradition, but he writes with the clarity about particular arguments often association with analytic thought. His *Confucian Moral Self Cultivation* (1993) studies six thinkers, Confucius, Mencius, Xunzi, Zhu Xi, Wang Yangming, and Dai Zhen, showing the contemporary relevance of their thought; this volume is not technical sinology, which might be daunting to Western philosophers, yet it rests upon very exact sinological research. His *Ethics in the Confucian Tradition* (1990) is a careful study of Mencius and Wang Yangming; after this book there is no reason for Western philosophers not to respect those thinkers as they do Plato and Descartes.

Perhaps the most explicit bridging interpreter is Lee H. Yearley whose *Mencius and Aquinas* (1990) sets the standard for careful comparison. His topics are theories of virtue and courage in those two thinkers, and he handles masterfully the issues of bringing together thinkers from separate traditions and vastly different epochs of time.[4]

Most of the bridging interpreters of Chinese philosophy pick up on the Confucian side. One of the earliest and most inventive, however, relates primarily to Daoism, Chang Chungyuan, long a professor of philosophy at the University of Hawaii. His *Tao: A New Way of Thinking* (1975) is a translation of the *Daodejing* with extensive commentaries on each chapter. He explicates the meaning of that book in connection with Western philosophy, though he hardly mentions analytic philosophy and his major dialogue partners are Heidegger and Whitehead. His *Creativity and Taoism: A Study of Chinese Philosophy, Art, and Poetry* (1963), is a genuinely creative philosophical essay in which he retrieves major Daoist themes for what is essentially a study of the Western problematic of imagination. Although Chang's work is fundamentally a kind of bridging interpretation of China to the West and vice versa, its originality as a philosophical synthesis anticipates the later work of Wu Kuangming.

There is no sharp line between interpreting and bridging philosophers, on the one hand, and normative ones, on the other. That distinction is more a matter of emphasis than anything else. It might be the case that the primarily interpreting thinkers were trained most often as historians and textual critics, whereas normative thinkers were trained most often as philosophers, with the bridging philosophers mixed in the middle. But even that distinction does not hold for those whose training has a strong East Asian component because those disciplinary distinctions do not hold well for universities themselves shaped by the East Asian traditions.

Any number of contemporary philosophers could be cited for their normative engagement of current philosophical issues with the resources of Chinese philosophy. As argued above, for most practical purposes, the Chinese tradition of philosophy is as available to Western thinkers as the Greek and European, even if the cultural context is understood less well. And in matters of understanding cultural contexts, recent critics such as Michel Foucault have made even the Western tradition unfamiliar to Westerners and thus more objectively understandable. Important work has been done by Charles Weishun Fu, Liu Shuhsien, and Lik Kuen Tong, and many of the thinkers discussed earlier for their interpretive and bridging work could be reconsidered for their own philosophical thought, especially Chang Chungyuan. But in recognition of influence and of the distinct type of their contributions, three positions or thinkers will be examined in detail here: Roger T. Ames and David L. Hall as a collaborative team, Cheng Chungying, and Wu Kuangming. Tu Weiming shall be discussed in greater detail in chapter 5, continuing the analysis begun here. All are North Americans of European or Chinese ancestry and have had the major part of their teaching careers at American universities.

3.3. Roger T. Ames and David L. Hall

Roger T. Ames and David L. Hall have collaborated on three extremely influential volumes: *Thinking through Confucius* (1987), *Anticipating China* (1995), and *Thinking from the Han* (1998). A new book on human rights in contemporary China, *The Democracy of the Dead* appeared in 1999. Ames is professor of philosophy at the University of Hawaii and edits the major comparative journal *Philosophy East and West*. The sinologist of the pair, Ames is expert in ancient Chinese political philosophy and is the author of *The Art of Rulership* (1983) and *Sun-tzu: The Art of Warfare* (1993). He also has edited or coedited a number of volumes using both Chinese and Western philosophy to deal with current problems. David L. Hall, a professor of philosophy at the University of Texas at El Paso, is a classically trained (Yale) Western philosopher whose topic is philosophy of culture and whose bent is to lift up the aesthetic dimension over Western preoccupations with ethics and classificatory metaphysics and epistemology. This was the burden of his first book, *The Civilization of Experience: A Whiteheadian Theory of Culture* (1973), and he deeply mined the resources of Chinese Daoism in the aesthetic philosophy of culture in *The Uncertain Phoenix* (1982a) and *Eros and Irony: A Prelude to Philosophical Anarchism* (1982b). *Eros and Irony* contains an extraordinary critique of conceptions of regular order, which he attributes to European thought, from the perspective of aesthetic order that he finds in Daoism. His preference for the aesthetic stance over the assertive or foundationalist prompts an appreciation of Richard Rorty's conversational neopragmatism, expressed in Hall's *Richard Rorty: Prophet and Poet of the New Pragmatism* (1994).

The collaborative work of Ames and Hall in *Thinking through Confucius* (1987), *Anticipating China* (1995), and *Thinking from the Han*

(1998), is the first full-blown philosophy of culture in the West to be undertaken primarily from a Chinese perspective. To be sure, Western thinkers such as Ralph Waldo Emerson, Max Weber, Friedrich Nietzsche, and Ernst Cassirer had some knowledge of Chinese culture and often brilliant insights. Chang Chungyuan began a Chinese-based philosophy of culture, as mentioned above. But Hall and Ames bring that project to brilliant, if controversial, fruition.

Their central idea is to contrast Western and Chinese cultures more or less as wholes, generalizing each to certain essential characteristics. No summary can do justice to their detailed and learned argument, but roughly stated the contrast is this. Western culture, in its Greek and Semitic roots and European flowering, is based fundamentally on ordering principles that transcend what is ordered. The West finds meaning in the asymmetrical relations between God and the world, for instance, or between metaphysical or scientific explanatory principles and what is explained. In ethics, the West searches for transcending grounding principles, and in science it explains things by antecedent causes and universal laws. Western culture thinks in terms of linear ordering going from ground to consequent, from earlier to later in narrative. This leads to the cultural instincts that take the abstract to be more real and perhaps better than the concrete and valorizes orders of dominance and submission.

The Chinese cultural assumptions, by contrast, are based on what Ames and Hall call, following A. C. Graham (1989, 320ff), "correlative thinking." They point to reciprocal notions such as yin and yang, to the explanatory habits of identifying the classifications in which things fall, and to the classifications themselves arranged in correlative orders, such as the eight directions plus center, the cyclic interactions of the five elements (fire, earth, metal, water, wood), and their directional orientations (water/north, wood/east, fire/south, metal/west, and earth/center). Chinese science, medicine, cuisine, politics, and philosophy all exhibit correlative thinking. Moreover, they do not exhibit transcendent or asymmetrically linear thinking of the sort characterizing Western culture. As a consequence, the Chinese sensibility is primarily aesthetic, concerned with wholeness and patterns, and interprets difficulties as matters of attaining or restoring harmony. This contrasts with the primary Western sensibility which is to see what follows from what and to set things straight according to transcendent norms. In *Thinking from the Han* they argue that Western notions of truth and transcendence just do not have Chinese equivalences.

This rough sketch of Hall and Ames' philosophy neglects their subtle qualifications. Of course, there are many nontranscendent and aesthetically oriented elements in the West, and many unidirectional, transcendent, and morally authoritarian elements in China. They are particularly careful in *Thinking through Confucius* (1987) to limit their claims to Confucius himself, admitting that later developments introduced more transcendent and less correlative matters. In *Anticipating China* (1995) they provide narratives of how Western and Chinese cultures developed the ways they did to their general characteristics. But in the end, their project is to cause philosophers to become aware of the general traits of the two cultures, overriding special exceptions, and providing differing contexts of cultural assumptions. Awareness of the difference reduces false familiarity, both about the other and about one's sense of one's own tradition. Above all, Ames and Hall argue subtly for the superiority of the Chinese cultural tradition as a resource for philosophy of culture.

A certain irony perfumes their procedure.[5] One of their most telling points is that the aesthetic order in Chinese culture emerges from within concrete experience and is not imposed from the outside, as they accuse Western culture of doing. Wu Kuangming (1997) in *On Chinese Body Thinking* makes a similar point about concrete interior order. Yet their method of contrasting cultures by generalizing to basic principles and trivializing exceptions follows the Western Aristotelian strategy of developing a grid of categories, for instance, the Four Causes in Aristotle's case, and locating thinkers and cultures within them. Their recent exemplars of this method are Richard McKeon, F.S.C. Northrop, Walter Watson, and David Dilworth. Those aspects of a thinker's thought or of cultural traits that do not register in the categories of the scheme are ignored, and what is most important is not the concrete textures of a thinkers' ideas but the abstract ways in which those ideas or cultures are transcendence-oriented, on the one hand, or correlative-oriented, on the other. This is surely an imposition of categories from without to the neglect of the concrete, a matter they ironically would consign to the West. Even in the West, however, that strategy is typical only of the Aristotelian strain: the Platonic tradition has been far subtler in its dialectical relations of the concrete with abstractions that allow for discriminations within the concrete. The work of Hall and Ames will be discussed at various places throughout this volume, especially in chapter 8 on transcendence.

The chief contribution of Hall and Ames's collaboration is not to do interpretive or bridging work, although of course their work does that too. Rather it is to move all philosophy into a sensibility of culturally constructed assumptions in which there are real and pervasive differences between traditions that can be known and adjudicated.

Moreover, even if their method and intent are classificatory in an Aristotelian sense, their cultural resources and sensibilities are most favorably Chinese. Or to put the matter more plainly, after their work no philosopher in China or the West can innocently assume his or her own cultural assumptions. Rather, those assumptions relative to the others constitute a philosophic problem.

3.4. Cheng Chungying

Cheng Chungying, by contrast, is not a philosopher of culture, except incidentally; his project is to develop a contemporary speculative metaphysics and ethics funded primarily from the Chinese tradition. He is a good Confucian, of the generation of Tu Weiming and with many of the same teachers and influences, including a Harvard Ph.D. But whereas Tu's doctoral work was on Wang Yangming, Cheng's was on Charles Peirce, the founder of American pragmatism, as well as on Dai Zhen, the great thinker of China in the modern Jing dynasty and the contemporary of David Hume.[6] Rather than displaying the differences and incommensurabilities of Chinese and Western philosophies, or attempting as Tu does to create a public global conversation in which Chinese philosophy plays a large part (see section 5.1), Cheng's project from very early days has been to reconstruct Chinese philosophy in order to make it part of the world philosophic conversation in league with Western philosophy. His topics thus have been easily recognizable by Western philosophers, for instance, conceptions of being, causation, explanation, mind, morality, knowledge, art, and the like.

Cheng has been tireless in his work to bring together the institutions of Chinese and Western philosophy. He was the founding editor of the *Journal of Chinese Philosophy* and the founding president of the International Society for Chinese Philosophy. Although there are many venues in which Chinese and Western philosophers now interact, including conferences of many sorts and a variety of philosophical journals including *Philosophy East and West*, his journal and society are the most focused. He too is a Confucian scholar-official who has founded and cared for institutions.

Cheng's primary philosophical work, however, has been the construction of a philosophical system using key elements of Chinese philosophy. The major locus for this is his *New Dimensions of Confucian and Neo-Confucian Philosophy* (1991), as well as many book chapters and journal articles. The emphasis in his early essays was on interpretation; in later essays speculative reconstruction and what he calls the hermeneutics of the present situation are addressed. The resources to which he appeals begin with the *Yijing*, which has been a continuing fascination for him; that very ancient book provides the themes in which Cheng sees China's distinctive philosophical identity and with which he engages the Western tradition of philosophy. He also takes seriously, both with hermeneutic intent and as resources for contemporary philosophy, the great writings of Daoists and Buddhists in China's history. In this regard he identifies clearly with the Song Neo-Confucians in their attempts to synthesize and criticize the vast range of texts of their past, not merely those identified as Confucian. But whereas the Song Neo-Confucians dealt with the Chinese cultural arena, Cheng incorporates into the synthesis and criticism the great texts of the Western tradition from Plato and Aristotle down to Whitehead and Heidegger.

Cheng provides an interesting contrast with the previous generation of Confucian scholars such as Mou Zongsan, who are sometimes called New Confucians because of the attention they paid to Western philosophers. That earlier generation pioneered in the interpretation of Western philosophy for the Chinese mind but generally with the overall intentionality of showing how the West could bolster threatened ideas within Confucianism and Daoism. Mou's "moral metaphysics," for instance, made good use of Kantian moral and epistemological idealism to defend the Mencian project. Cheng, by contrast, is far less concerned to bolster any Chinese project than to employ Chinese resources to address issues that Western philosophers also address and that define the contemporary situation.

For instance, after two hundred years in which most Western philosophers have abandoned philosophy of nature, leaving nature to the natural scientists and restricting philosophy to philosophy of science, it has become clear that we need a philosophy of nature that puts scientific technology in perspective and defines an ethical attitude toward the environment. Whitehead and Heidegger addressed this in their very different ways, offering conceptions of nature, creativity, relation, time, space, value, and human existence. Cheng picks up these very themes and argues that Chinese philosophy has resources for even subtler theories regarding these topics. His fascination with the *Yijing* comes in part from his concern to develop a contemporary philosophy of nature.

Ethics in recent Western philosophy, especially its analytic branches, has suffered from being abstractly removed from first-order problems, except when it deals nominalistically with case studies. It has also suffered from depending on a consensus arising from antecedently formed common sense. The common modern use of traditional

Confucian ethics is surprisingly similar, being formulaic and therefore abstract, and resting on received wisdom. Our situation has changed so much, however, with global economies and ecologically insensitive technologies, not to speak of new social relations, that received wisdom needs to be rethought; the metatheories that justified and embodied received wisdom need reconstruction also. Cheng's genius has been to see that a rethinking of ethics from either a Western or Confucian standpoint requires a speculative rethinking of the conception of the world itself. That speculative metaphysics cannot be a repetition of old Chinese or Western positions nor a mirroring of science but a critical reconstruction of all these into a new vision. In contrast to Mou's moral metaphysics it is helpful to think of Cheng's work as metaphysical morals: his intent, true to the Confucian (and Platonic) tradition, is essentially practical, but the practice needs to be informed by a new speculative worldview. Because of Cheng's efforts, whatever worldviews emerge to compete for our loyalties, they will include the themes of Chinese philosophy.

3.5. Wu Kuangming

Wu Kuangming differs from the above two positions in many important respects. Taiwanese born, Yale educated with specialties in Kant and Kierkegaard, Wu has spent most of his career in the philosophy department at the University of Wisconsin at Oshkosh. Deeply versed in Chinese and Western cultures, their arts as well as philosophies, and the Confucian texts as well as Buddhist and Daoist ones, Wu considers himself primarily to represent the Daoist vision. He also takes that to be the essential Chinese vision, in contrast to those who identify Chinese philosophy and culture primarily with Confucianism; in this respect he is a fellow spirit with Chang Chungyuan. Wu has slight patience with metaphysical speculation of Cheng's sort and even less patience with Tu's kind of Confucian scholar-official concern for public discourse (see section 5.1). He has in principle an affinity with Hall and Ames's construal of philosophy as philosophy of culture but does not see much in their generalizations and external application of classificatory categories.

Rather, Wu does what Ames and Hall say Chinese philosophy does generally, namely, work from the concrete to develop distinctions that can be expressed only in concrete terms such as stories, analogies, and telling metaphors. Because to assert something directly, Wu believes, is to distance yourself from it and thereby distort it, all serious expression is indirect and self-critically ironic. This is the position Wu developed as arising from Zhuangzi in his *Chuang Tzu: World Philosopher at Play* (1982). It was the position he illustrated copiously with line-by-line essays on Zhuangzi's text in *The Butterfly as Companion* (1990). And it is the position he explains by contrast and indirection in *On Chinese Body Thinking: A Cultural Hermeneutic* (1997) and *On the "Logic" of Togetherness—A Cultural Hermeneutic* (1998).

In both of the latter volumes Wu unfolds the cultural hermeneutics that follows from something like this world picture. Life contains only concrete processes, among which are we ourselves, and in these processes there is structure and grain, as in wood, but no abstract patterns replicable from one place to another. Unexpectedly, we can know other things, discriminate their structures, and comport ourselves so as to take these into account and behave appropriately. That is, there is a representative function in human life. How is this possible, given the concreteness?

Western culture has developed strategies of representation that involve asserting that reality is like the abstract structures of a proposition. To be sure, being *like* is not the same as being *the same as*, and many Western philosophies assert concreteness in the objects while remarking that the representations are only abstract. Nevertheless, the typical Western representative strategies first assert an abstract character to reality and then might possibly take it back. Some Western strategies do not take it back, for instance, most of those involved in scientific knowing.

Chinese representative strategies, Wu maintains, generally avoid the abstraction-negation dialectic by subordinating representation to comportment toward things, guided or oriented by representation. We come through knowledge to move in concert with things, thereby establishing concrete intermovements and wholes. In this Wu reinforces the linguistic argument of Chad Hansen (1983, 1992) that Chinese language primarily discriminates and orients rather than represents propositionally. In this concrete dance, representation is not self-reflective as such. But of course, the Chinese are as self-reflective as anyone else. So their reflection takes ironic forms of playing with the perspectives of the many things involved in the dance, allowing none the priority of being subject over the others as objects in representation. Hence, butterflies cannot be engaged concretely except by keeping open the question of who dreams whom (in Zhuangzi's famous story). More prosaically, Chinese culture and philosophy communicate more by telling stories that one understands to apply analogically to one's situation than by offering abstract descriptions. This is not to say that the Chinese cannot say how many people came to lunch or that Western philosophers cannot use telling metaphors and analogies for which there is no better direct speech. But it is to give priority, in the Chinese case, to representing the grain of things so that people concretely can dispose themselves appreciatively and deferentially toward them and, in the Western case, to getting the form of the thing in the mind, the form being at best still abstract. "Body thinking" is discriminating orientation and comportment, not getting the other thing in mind.

As Wu's philosophical project is coming to light in publications, it appears as a concrete working out of the Hegelian "labor of the notion" in respect of claims many have made about the immanence and concreteness of Chinese thought. Wu's argument, as often as not, is through analysis of Western philosophical positions. His very argument form is the abstract representation and criticism of philosophical positions. But unlike Ames and Hall, who seek to impose abstraction in order to distinguish and classify, or Cheng, who seeks to cultivate and express abstractions faithful to the Chinese as well as Western vision, Wu seeks to create a concrete apprehension of different grains in Chinese and Western thinking by a series of critical vignettes. In this he is like Tu who seeks to create a concrete conversation within which the Chinese vision can find expression and relevance beyond its world of origin. But whereas Tu strategizes the conversation and awaits the concrete deliberation, Wu's philosophy attempts to *be* the conversation. Wu's philosophy is not a little like Hegel's total system, a logic, though in a different sense of logic from Hegel's; rather, the way Kierkegaard is Hegel inverted. The potential limitation of Wu's strategy is that it is a conversation complete in itself into which it might be the case that no one else will join, a Zhuangzi tale *tour de force* that one can admire and affirm but not enter.

A criticism of Wu is that concreteness itself is an abstraction: we only engage things partially, in those selective respects in which our representations can interpret them. Things are always more than we ever engage even at our most real, and hence, our existential relations are always abstract in various senses. Life's philosophic questions are those about whether our partial engagements of things are engagements in the most important respects rather than trivial or irrelevant respects. Perhaps the best Chinese philosophy as well as the best Western philosophy is about that question rather than about concreteness. Wu's philosophy is still taking form and will doubtless address this question as it comes to consider some of the fundamental practical problems of our time.

The conclusions of this chapter are open-ended, but the chief one to draw is that a world conversation in philosophy has been started within which European and Chinese philosophical traditions are major participants. Looking to the future, however, the learned understanding and appreciation of all the great civilizations' traditions of philosophy will be required of all participants in the world conversation. We are privileged to live at the verge of that intercivilizational discourse. Seen in this light, Boston Confucianism is not an anomaly but merely a focal point.

4

Confucian Spirituality

4.1. Philosophy and Religion

Confucianism has been treated in the previous three chapters, especially the last, as a candidate world *philosophy*, but the question has not been raised whether philosophy in this sense embraces or is distinct from religion. The question is complicated. Contemporary Confucians' self-assessment is mixed. Tu Weiming comes down solidly on the side of saying that Confucianism is a religion, or at least has an important religious dimension. He emphasizes existential commitment to the way of the sage and understands personal transformation as a kind of immanent transcendence guided by principle. Because of the importance of religion for Tu's philosophy, the discussion of his work was not undertaken in chapter 3, where he deserves to be discussed in the array of normative contemporary thinkers, but is postponed until after the present chapter's discussion of the religious question. Rodney L. Taylor (1978, 1986, 1990) has done perhaps the most extensive analysis of Confucianism as a religion. The outline of his argument is that *tian* (heaven) functions as an absolute and that people are related to it so as to be capable of ultimate transformation (1990, introduction). He follows Frederick Streng (1985, 1–8) in defining religion in terms of ultimate transformation. On the other hand, the Chinese Academy of Social Sciences does not count Confucianism among the religions to be studied in its World Religions section. Perhaps this reflects the old communist disapproval of religion in general and its desire to give a more honored status to the traditional Chinese Confucian way of life, even when criticizing it. Whatever the ambient motive, the official Chinese establishment has not considered Confucianism to be religious.

The complications in the question come from the fact that categories such as philosophy and religion, arise from Western European culture. Except for recent Western influence, Chinese culture (like the cultures of India, Orthodoxy, Christianity, and the Islamic, not to mention the traditional cultures of Africa and elsewhere) did not sharply distinguish philosophy from religion. It had no words closely corresponding to the range of meanings of either "religion" or "philosophy" in the West, although of course they had ways of discussing all the elements the West embraces under these terms. All those cultures had "ways of life" that are extremely complex, pervasive, and manifested on many levels, including the basic levels of world-formation that Peter Berger (1967) calls "the sacred canopy." Within each culture there have been elite intellectuals who reflected deeply on those ways of life, and these thinkers are the ones that Western scholars have identified as "philosophers." Within each culture some of those intellectual elites have been critical of their way of life, recognizing that there are competing ways of life within each situation, and that no inherited way of life can remain unchanged as historical circumstances change and so encouraging changes. Thus there have been competing schools both within and among the great traditions as "ways of life," and this is like philosophy in the West.

Yet the intellectual elites are only a small fraction of the people living according to a "way of life," however much they might be the philosophical critics, leaders, and articulators. Rather, most people live within that "way" without much reflection on its express articulation and underlying principles, concentrating on concerns that accept or presuppose the "way's" framing. Or their kinds of reflection—while perhaps deep, insightful, and original—do not have the kind of public openness, universality, and precision in comparison with alternatives that are characteristic of philosophy, philosophical theology, and their analogues. Poets, painters, and politicians might know much about human nature and its ontological mirroring of the deep things of the cosmos and still not think directly about human nature as such as an endowment of heaven.

Moreover, not all aspects of a culture's "way of life" are directly involved with a religious dimension. Chinese ways of farming and diplomacy might be deeply shaped by Chinese religious practices and symbols, but they are really about growing food and politics: some great farmers and great statesmen might be acknowledged universally to be uninterested in religion or hostile to it. Yet this very distinction between farming and politics, on the one hand, and religion, on the other, within a great cultural "way of life" derives from the Western categories, which we should now explore.[1]

The sharp distinction between philosophy and religion is an artifact of the European Enlightenment and perhaps can be understood most economically through the development of philosophy of religion. David Hume's (1779) *Dialogues concerning Natural Religion* gave classic expression to an Enlightenment theme that drove a wedge between the practice of philosophy and the practice of religion. The Enlightenment asked how religious beliefs could be known to be true, and the question was put in ways that required religious beliefs to be grounded upon an absolutely certain starting point; it concluded with kindly but thoroughgoing skepticism.

One result was the conclusion that religion consists in practices based on beliefs that cannot be grounded in a properly philosophical or scientific way; this reinforced the older Enlightenment suspicion that religion is superstition rather than science. The Enlightenment project of "natural religion" had tried to free religion, indeed Christianity, from superstition, and Hume's critique ruined that effort.

The other result was the conclusion that philosophy consists essentially of skeptical epistemology that takes the cognitive stuffing out of religion (and much else besides). In most American philosophy departments at the end of the twentieth century, this foundationalist epistemology has created a skeptical mindset toward religion, even in universities and colleges that also support religion departments or even theological schools. Foundationalism itself is now under attack, but not by interests particularly friendly to religion. Postmodern critiques of foundationalism, such as those of Richard Rorty (1979), usually include attacks on objectivity of all sorts, including religious affirmations.

Hume, of course, was not the first Enlightenment thinker to move in this direction. Descartes famously is credited with setting modern European philosophy on the path of foundationalism. Hobbes had tried to understand religion scientifically. Locke, in his *The Reasonableness of Christianity*, had tried to separate out the superstitious elements from a rational core in ways that perforce diminish the importance and integrity of many religious practices, especially liturgical ones. After Hume, Kant could easily assume that philosophy about religion is epistemology, transcendental epistemology in his case. Though Kant retained a pietistic affirmation of religion, it was a religion devoid of the kind of cognitive content with which the Christian theological tradition had wrestled. Despite some attempts to broaden philosophy of religion from epistemology to include phenomenology, history of religions, or continental hermeneutics, the field as an academic discipline has gone where Hume directed it until this day.[2]

This European Enlightenment distinction between philosophy as skeptical epistemology and religion as practices based on ungroundable beliefs has not always characterized the West, though it has provided a hermeneutic perspective for reading Western culture in its terms. So, for instance, the modern reading of Socrates emphasizes his skeptical epistemological questioning whereas Plato, at least, saw Socrates as inaugurating a whole new "way of life," aiming to cultivate a rich civilization through critical inquiry. Surely the ancient philosophic schools had the forms of religion. Christianity from the beginning at least through Augustine saw itself as a rival philosophy to the pagan schools. Medieval thinkers such as Anselm, al-Ghazali, Thomas Aquinas, Maimonides, and Scotus cannot be classified as either philosophers or theologians to the exclusion of the other; the Thomistic distinction between knowledge based on revelation and that based on reason alone was rarely honored, even by Thomas. All of those thinkers were members of the intellectual elite working critically within the larger practices of their ways of life in their religious dimensions.

That the ideas of philosophy and religion are of Western origin and can vastly distort other cultural traditions when imposed with the assumption that they apply neatly, does not mean that they are false or useless. Rather it means that they need to be applied carefully so that biases can be controlled for. Of course, the use of those categories might raise questions of those other traditions that they do not easily or typically ask in their own terms. But this is not a bad thing. It rather is a new avenue of inquiry, if carried out circumspectly. Any comparative work whatsoever that compares cultural entities that have not previously engaged in dialogue is going to ask new questions of those entities. How to answer them depends on getting inside each enough to think like creative representatives of those cultural entities in the relevant respects.

We need to propose a working hypothesis that allows us to capture what is worthwhile in the concepts of religion and philosophy so as to be able to address the question of Confucian spirituality. How can we provisionally define religion in ways that are not ruined by cultural bias? Streng's (1985) approach through "ultimate transformation" is a good start that connects immediately with Tu's (1978) presentation of the religious dimension of Confucianism. But it does not pick up easily on the equally important aspects of religion's cultural and social embodiments. The same might be said of Whitehead's famous definition, "religion is what the individual does with his own solitariness."[3] Opposite to this are social science definitions of religion as in Durkheim (1915) and Berger (1967). John Milbank (1990) criticizes not only the social science definitions of religion but the validity of the social sciences themselves as secular enterprises, arguing that their own base is religious. Ninian Smart (1989) defines religion through the following dimensions: the practical and ritual, the experiential and emotional, the narrative and mythic, the doctrinal and philosophical, the ethical and legal, the social and institutional, and the material.

Religion can be defined here, provisionally, as the (1) ritual life; (2) mythic, cosmological, and philosophic conceptions; and (3) spiritual practices, both corporate and individual, by means of which people relate to what they take to be ultimate. Thus we need to acknowledge three interrelated religious phenomena: ritual, cognition, and spiritual practices, all shaped by religious symbols engaging what is taken to be ultimate (Neville 1996).

Ritual encompasses not only explicit liturgies but also the learnable, repetitive behaviors by means of which people epitomize something they take to be basic about relating to the world, for instance hunting, making crops fertile, celebrating birth, rehearsing dying, and so forth; the historical characters of religious traditions give their rituals particular shape. Religious ritual is but a small part of ritual in the broad Confucian senses, distinguished from the other parts by its relation to religious symbols of ultimacy.[4]

Myth, cosmology, and philosophy encompass assumptions and deliberations about what people take to be the basic categories and world-forming elements of their interpreted environment. Lived ways of life, when not reflecting directly on these foundational matters, assume that their myth, cosmology, or philosophy is iconic of reality, that is, that reality is somehow practically "like" what these narratives and schemes say.[5]

Spiritual practices encompass the range of behaviors, corporate and personal, aimed at communal or personal transformation so as better to relate to what is taken to be ultimate. Sometimes the transformations are matters of appropriation and enculturation, and sometimes they are matters of serious change, such as becoming a Confucian sage.[6]

There are so many definitions of ultimacy, contextualized in different traditions, that hardly any one sums up the others; roughly it means those limits of imagination and action beyond which a culture or person cannot go, though all the major world religions engage in some form of apophatic or negative theology and so do go beyond

any specifiable limits. Perhaps the most functional way to define ultimacy is as the cusp of negation when religious people try to say what
they really mean, knowing that anything they say is not yet or any
more what they mean. A more precise notion of ultimacy can be given
in terms of symbolic reference, and this will be explored shortly in this
chapter.[7]

Given this rough characterization of religion, Confucianism surely
qualifies, and it is hard to see why anyone would demure. It has two
and a half millennia of developments in ritual, myth, cosmology,
philosophy, and spiritual practices, and it has consistently interpreted
itself, though in inconsistent ways, as being the way to relate properly
to what is ultimate, usually symbolized as heaven, earth, and the dao.
Most of the chapters of this book will discuss various aspects and
instances of this.

The purpose of this chapter is not to explore Confucianism as a
religion in all its elements, but to focus on the third phenomenon,
spiritual practice. In developing a theory of spirituality, however, some
of the more general aspects of the definition offered here for religion
will be elaborated.

The argument here has begun with reflections on the nature of
spirituality in connection with some other elements of religion. The
next section presents a specific hypothesis about spirituality, which is
unfolded further in the following section, with all points illustrated by
Confucian examples. The argument then moves to consider some
particulars of Confucian spirituality as it might meet the needs of the
contemporary situation. The fourth section considers Confucianism in
a contemporary scientific culture, a problem widely understood to be
difficult for Christianity. The fifth considers the ability of Confucian
spirituality to meet the needs of different cultures in our global society
regarding matters of politics and ethics. The argument in this chapter
is further complicated by the consideration to come in section 10.5 of
multiple religious identities, that is, of being a Confucian plus something else.

4.2. Spirituality and Ultimate Reality: Defining Hypotheses

Spirituality has meant a great many things in the history of religions,
affected by different conceptions of the human, the ultimate or transcendent, and the world as susceptible to a spiritual dimension. The
prefaces to the volumes in Ewert Cousins's great series on World
Spirituality contain a characterizing statement that is likely to become

normative for the foreseeable future because of the monumental scale of the series and its legitimation of the disciplined notion of spirituality:

> The series focuses on that inner dimension of the person called by certain traditions "the spirit." This spiritual core is the deepest center of the person. It is here that the person is open to the transcendent dimension; it is here that the person experiences ultimate reality. The series explores the discovery of this core, the dynamics of its development, and its journey to the ultimate goal. It deals with prayer, spiritual direction, the various maps of the spiritual journey, and the methods of advancement in the spiritual ascent. (reprinted for instance, in Van Ness 1996, xii)

That statement calls up the metaphors of a *core* of the human person, a *transcendent dimension* or *ultimate reality* to which that core has access, *experience* as the mode of access, the *transformations* of the core by means of its experience of the transcendent, and the *journeys* according to which the transformations are understood for individual persons. All these have already been encountered in our discussion of Confucianism.

Spirituality is usually associated with religion in a broader sense, as defined previously, that includes founding persons, core texts and motifs, institutions for the ritual practice and transmission of traditions, conceptualities for understanding the human relation to the transcendent, and even organizations with membership in several senses of that term (see Neville 1978, 7–20, 104–16). Nevertheless, spirituality need not be closely associated with religions, as evidenced by the volume in the World Spirituality series entitled *Spirituality and the Secular Quest* (Van Ness 1996). Whereas it is unlikely that anyone could have much of a spiritual life without leaning heavily on one or several religious traditions, it is very possible these days to have a spiritual life with no positive allegiance to a religious community nor a commitment to the authority of a text or tradition. The major religious traditions themselves, it should be noted, differ widely in the importance they attach to membership and allegiance, with Islam being an extreme case insisting on self-conscious attachment and Confucianism paying much more attention to competence in the Confucian way than to membership or "denominational" commitment.

This section shall consider a more specific hypothesis about spirituality that makes precise general sense of Cousins's intuitions about the core human being, ultimate reality, experience, transformation, and journeys noted above. Any serious hypothesis characterizing spirituality needs to be enormously complex because spirituality itself engages so many areas of human life and cosmic reality. Indeed, the complexity in the hypothesis needs a special form. On the one hand, it needs interpretations of some of the main things to which spirituality is related, for instance, the self, ultimate reality, human experience, and such learning that transforms the self in deep ways. Each of these is a topic in its own right, but important for defining what spirituality relates to. On the other hand, the hypothesis needs to say just what spirituality is in relation to these things, over and above the collection of those several topics. The complex hypothesis about spirituality thus needs subhypotheses, on the one hand, relating to the various topics connected to spirituality and, on the other hand, defining what is essential to spirituality. The former can be called *conditional subhypotheses* because they interpret the topics that condition the topic of spirituality; the latter can be called *essential subhypotheses* because they pull together what spirituality is in relation to those other elements.

The complex overarching hypothesis here consists of one essential subhypothesis and several conditional subhypotheses that relate the essential one to various aspects of life and religion. Spirituality is not the essential subhypothesis alone but the harmony of that one with the rest, situating spirituality in a larger context. Moreover, the explication of the essential subhypothesis is by means of elaborating several of the conditional ones.

The distinction between essential and conditional subhypotheses is not philosophically innocent. It reflects a general thesis that to be a thing, any thing at all, is to be a harmony of essential and conditional features, the conditional ones constituting the thing as related to other things which condition it and the essential ones expressing the principles of its own-being. This conception of things as harmonies, especially as applied to changing things, is a contemporary reconstruction of the Neo-Confucian theme of harmony.[8] Following the lead of this notion, concepts should be defined by tracing out their harmony of conditional and essential features, and phenomena should be described that way too. In this sense, there are no "boundaries" to definitions, but harmonic structures; that is the way to get around essentialism. So the hypothesis about spirituality is a harmony of several subhypotheses, one essential and the others conditional.

The essential subhypothesis about spirituality is that it is *the deliberate effort to improve the human process of engaging ultimate reality truthfully by means of practices that shape the engagement with signs or religious symbols, that discern improved religious symbols for this purpose, that increase competence in the use of the symbols for engagement, and that foster the transformations of soul derivative from the engaging of ultimate reality with the symbols.*

This essential subhypothesis differs from the prefatory statement for the World Spirituality series quoted previously in several rhetorical ways in order to attain both greater tolerance for various spiritualities and greater precision in characterizing them. So, for instance, it substitutes *engagement* for *experience* in order to suggest the give and take of living with ultimate reality and the things that bear it, and to avoid the overly subjective connotations of *religious experience* that have been rightly criticized.[9] The subhypothesis does not suppose a natural "core" of the human person but suggests that some special integration might be the outcome of spiritual growth. It stresses the importance of religious symbols to shape the engagement and thus places the philosophy of spirituality within philosophical semiotics. It suggests that spiritual development or transformation can be a function of at least two things: improved or deeper symbols and changes in the person's capacity to employ the symbols in engaging the ultimate. These and other elements of the subhypothesis require brief comments that introduce some of the appropriate conditional subhypotheses.

To face the most controversial element first, it is necessary to justify reference to ultimate reality in a hypothesis about spirituality. The Kantian subjectivism of much contemporary philosophy of religion would prefer to treat spirituality wholly as an anthropological topic without ultimate references. The cautiousness of some contemporary Confucians about reference to transcendence, limiting it to "immanent transcendence," reinforces the anthropological circumscription of the topic.[10] But the attempt to characterize spirituality without reference to the ultimate is finally reductive and self-defeating; it would not be recognized by spiritual people. Therefore, we shall consider the following conditional subhypothesis about ultimate reality.

Ultimate reality in relation to spirituality consists in a finite-infinite contrast.[11] A finite-infinite contrast is anything a culture's or person's semiotic system takes to be a founding element of what is religiously important in the culture or person's world.

The finite side of the contrast is both what it is as merely finite and also what grounds or orients some crucial elements in the rest of the world, defining "worldness" as some part of the "sacred canopy," as Berger (1967) calls it. The finite side is some thing or process without which the world would not exist or be meaningful in some important religious respect. Cosmological existence, the ontological question, the coming into being of the world, is an obvious candidate and may well be universal among religions. The opening of Zhou Dunyi's *Explanation of the Diagram of the Great Ultimate* is a classic Confucian example:

> The Ultimate of Non-being and also the Great Ultimate (*T'ai-chi*)! The Great Ultimate through movement generates yang. When its activity reaches its limit, it becomes tranquil. Through tranquillity the Great Ultimate generates yin. When tranquillity reaches its limit, activity begins again. So movement and tranquillity alternate and become the root of each other, giving rise to the distinction of yin and yang, and the two modes are thus established. (in Chan 1963, 463)

Yin and yang form the five elements or agents which in turn form the ten thousand things at which point the world exists in its familiar temporal process. The Ultimate of Non-being and Great Ultimate in their process of generating diversity in unity constitute the finite side of a Confucian finite-infinite contrast.[12] Another Confucian example is the beginning of Zhang Zai's *Western Inscription*: "Heaven is my father and Earth is my mother, and even such a small creature as I finds an intimate place in their midst" (Chan 1963, 497, quoted in full in section 10.5). Here the conjunction of heaven and earth is the foundation of the intimacy of human belonging in the universe, a major Confucian religious theme. Yet another finite element in a Confucian finite-infinite contrast is the beginning of *The Doctrine of the Mean*: "What Heaven (*T'ien*, Nature) imparts to man is called human nature. To follow our nature is called the Way (*Tao*). Cultivating the Way is called education. The Way cannot be separated from us for a moment. What can be separated from us is not the Way" (in Chan 1963, 98). Here the finite element in the finite-infinite contrast is not so much the process of cosmic grounding, though it is that too, or a cosmic character that gives human beings an intimate place, though it is also that, but rather the founding of the human capacity to follow the dao, which is to be truly human and which derives from the ontological reality of heaven and is its gift.

In all these examples there is something that is finite at least in the sense that it can be described or symbolized. Moreover, without that finite thing or process, the world and human life would lack something extraordinarily important. Yet the finite thing or process cannot be taken by itself in any positivist fashion. For, its religious significance is its contrast with what would be if it were not there. So, without the process of the Great Ultimate generating yang and yin, there would be only the Ultimate of Non-being, that is, nothing determinate or finite at all, a completely empty infinite; Zhou is explicit about the connection of Non-being and the Great Ultimate (*wu-ji, tai-ji*) in his finite-infinite contrast, whether one interprets that connection to be reciprocity or the priority of Non-being to the Great Ultimate. In the case of Zhang Zai, it is the spousal embrace of heaven and earth in parenting that gives human life its cosmic intimacy. Without that, with no cosmic origins that could be symbolized in terms of sexual cooperation and mutual fit, the human place would not be intimate; consider the alienating metaphoric impact of the scientific notion that the cosmos is only matter in motion, or atoms in the void. The infinite side of the contrast for Zhang Zai would be an inhumane habitation, supposing that human beings arise some other way. In the case of *The Doctrine of the Mean*, the infinite side would be the failure of heaven to impart its basic character to human beings, with the result that human powers would not be able to accommodate life to what is most basic in reality; at best, they would be conventional fabrications.

In all these examples, and others from Confucianism and other traditions, the finite side is religiously or spiritually important only in connection with the infinite side, where the infinite is the condition that would obtain if the finite side were not a founding element of the world. There is thus a kind of apophatic element built in to the notion of a religious object as a finite-infinite contrast. The causal grounding of the cosmos as such is not religiously important except in light of what would be the case (if that language could be used) were that grounding not to be real. Similarly with the ontological harmony of elements in the cosmos as the ground of human cosmic intimacy, and with the human possession of the dao. *Of course*, the generation of yin and yang (or the Big Bang) is not what we mean as ultimate except in consideration of its contrast with the alternative; *of course*, the cosmic harmony of heaven and earth is just another fact and not ultimate except in consideration of its contrast with what its denial would mean for the cosmic harmony of human life; *of course*, heaven's imparting the dao to human beings is not more ultimate than the presence of elements from the periodic table in the human body except in consideration of what the alternative would mean to the human capacity to attain cosmic attunement. The finite sides are not ultimate except in contrast or conjunction with the infinite side in each case: the world would not exist, or would lack some religiously crucial feature, if the finite condition did not obtain. Some theistic religious theories give a kind of positive force to the infinite side, saying that the infinite creates the finite side; perhaps Zhou would agree.[13] But there is no need to say that all finite-infinite contrasts construe the relation between the finite and infinite elements this way.

Sociology of knowledge is involved in this subhypothesis about the ultimate insofar as it proposes that one of the main functions of religious symbols, myths, cosmologies, and so forth is to provide what Berger (1967) calls a "sacred canopy" defining the limits and meaning of the world. The symbols are foundational for what counts as real and important in the world and thus are not to be taken only at face value but also in their founding roles. Without the legitimating viability of the symbols in the sacred canopy, the culture whose canopy it is supposed to be is confused and disoriented about what is real and important. That a culture's symbols of the ultimate are viable, and in practice serve to legitimate its worldview, does not mean that they are true and refer correctly to what really is ultimate. But if they are not viable and lead to disorientation, this shows that they are false in at least some respects; and if they are viable, this shows that in at least some respects they keep the culture successfully oriented to what is genuinely real.

This subhypothesis about ultimate reality as finite-infinite contrasts locates spirituality's reference to the ultimate or transcendent squarely within semiotics. Thus, the connection averred in previous chapters of Confucianism with pragmatism, especially pragmatic semiotics, has an important illustration here.

A crucial moral for the contemporary Confucian discussion should be drawn from the argument so far, namely, that Confucian reference to ultimate reality is far more substantial and important than might be supposed from limitations of the discussion to the immanent transcendent or to anthropocosmic unity, the common ultimate references of Tu Weiming (1979), surely the most forward proponent of Confucian religiousness and spirituality. Rather, Confucians need to pay direct attention to such notions as the dao, the Great Ultimate, heaven and earth, principle and material force, and other metaphysical or ontological conceptions that have been so richly articulated in the tradition, and which Tu also thematizes in various places. The attention these notions require is nothing less than a contemporary reconstruction. Contemporary Confucianism needs to be directly metaphysical with a metaphysics faithful to its roots, on the one hand, and plausible for the modern age, on the other. If the direct ontological significance of these notions is not explored as the essential foundation of spirituality, then it will be impossible to give Confucian spirituality a seriousness required for any full-blown spiritual tradition.

And, of course, those transcendent elements are pervasive in the Confucian tradition. Only when transcendence is taken to mean only something that is separate and real apart from the world, as some Christians believe about God, could it be said that Confucianism does not have transcendence in the sense of ultimate realities as finite-infinite contrasts. David Hall and Roger Ames, as noted in section 3.3, have argued with great vigor, especially in *Thinking from the Han* (1998), that Chinese thought in its ancient forms does not have anything like the Western notion of transcendence. But they define transcendence in a narrow or "strict" way to mean an independent being or principle separate from and asymmetrically related to the world such that the transcendent conditions the immanent but the immanent does not condition the transcendent (198–93). They then argue that people who do not use transcendence this way merely sneak that way in under the disguise of an "informal" use of transcendence. There is a bitter antitheism polemic in their argument, which is strange for scholars of a culture whose ancient Shang Di is as good a sky god as you get anywhere.

For many monotheists, God is not to be construed as separate and real apart from the world; consider Aquinas's conception of God as Act of Esse, or Tillich's as Ground of Being. The Western monotheistic traditions are highly diverse in their various interpretations of the relation of God to the world. Several, for instance the Neo-Platonic and the creation *ex nihilo* mysticism traditions, argue that the sense of God sundered from definition by relation to the world turns out to be nothing, Nothing, Non-being, *Wuji*. Chapter 8 will discuss the comparative notions of transcendence in greater detail. Sufficient for the present chapter is the fact that any world-founding element has an asymmetrical relation to the rest of what it founds, and thus is transcendent in Hall and Ames's sense. Any finite-infinite contrast thus marks something transcendent. The human nature heaven imparts to us, according to *The Doctrine of the Mean*, marks heaven as transcendent; the familial belongingness of Zhang Zai marks heaven and earth as his transcendent parents.

That these ontological considerations are important for contemporary Confucian spirituality means that their contemporary viability needs to be assessed, just as the Christian conception of God needs contemporary viability. Sections 4.4 and 4.5 will return to this topic.

4.3. Self, Truth, and Transformation

The conception of the self or soul in the essential subhypothesis discussed previously about spirituality is vaguer than the Western metaphor of "core." All the conception supposes is that a self can engage finite-infinite contrasts by means of symbol systems and be transformed in the process. Another conditional subhypothesis, this one about the self, can make this clear:

A self or soul consists of a person's engagements with realities, ultimate and otherwise, and its structures have to do with how the person is oriented with reference to the realities and integrates the different structures of orientation.

Thus the self is always defined in reference to its orientations to things so as to engage them, and how it puts its orientations together. Minimal engagement with ultimate realities as finite-infinite contrasts is simply to exist as shaped by the contrasts—for instance, as a materially existing thing, intimately placed in the cosmos, capable of acting in cosmic harmony. Persons unaware of this engagement are likely to act in ways contrary to their founding conditions, and hence to be in some alienation from themselves and their world. To be spiritual is to engage interpretively with the finite-infinite contrasts and to attempt to be oriented properly to them. This hypothesis is vague enough to allow for Aristotelian conceptions of substantial cores for human beings. But it is also vague enough to allow for Buddhist rejections of the self—the no-self doctrine—and to sustain only the claim that persons can be properly oriented to what is real (for instance, suchness as empty). Of course it also allows for the Confucian conception of the self as described in *The Doctrines of the Mean* and elsewhere, which stresses the structural integration of principle or dao as resident in the perspective of one's body with the persons, institutions, and natural surroundings that constitute the ten thousand things to which the mean relates.[14]

That spiritual engagement is interpretive and aims to be true requires an epistemological conditional subhypothesis about truth: *The truth of our engagements with ultimate realities consists in the carryover of the value in those realities (finite-infinite contrasts) into the interpreters' lives, in the respects in which the engagements interpret the realities, and as qualified by the biological, cultural, semiotic, and intentional characters of the interpreters.*[15]

Two interesting deviations from customary epistemologies should be noted in this hypothesis, namely, its orientation to causation and to value.

To claim that truth is a causal matter—a relation of accurate transmission from object to subject—is to subvert much of the modern European mind-body distinction (see section 9.1). It is also to buy into the claim that Confucianism is a naturalism in philosophy, and it does so by linking Confucianism to American pragmatism from which the semiotics employed here derives. Enormous complexities lie in the way of calibrating the causal mechanism to carry over something real and external into the interpreter. The crucial conceptual tool is a semiotic theory that analyzes (1) how signs refer to objects outside the semiotic system (not just to other signs within that system), (2) how meanings evolve culturally and also devolve, and (3) how communities and persons interpret realities by means of signs which are taken to stand for the realities in certain respects (Neville 1996, chapters 2 to 4). The defense of the claim that a semiotic system and interpretive mental behavior are natural parts of human life is somewhat difficult in a Kantian environment, which supposes that only science speaks authoritatively about nature and that philosophy is limited to philosophy of science. Nevertheless, it can be shown that the Kantian project is as limited as the European Enlightenment project which is now subject to so much criticism. Moreover, there are contemporary alternative theories of nature, for instance, those deriving from process philosophy or pragmatism, that demonstrate how knowing is a part of natural life and not a transcendental (supernaturalistic) commentary.[16] Confucianism from its ancient sources onward should flourish in such a naturalistic epistemological environment.

The other peculiar part of the hypothesis about truth is that it is the carryover of *value*. Aristotle, who also had a causal theory of truth (as touch), believed that the carryover was of *form*: for Aristotle, the form of the object, minus its material substrate, is to be carried over from the object into the substance of the mind to be (part of) the mind's form. We now see this to be implausible for at least two reasons. The form of an inert material object such as the fortress-city at Mycenae simply does not fit into a meat-brain interpreter such as Agamemnon. To get the "same thing" into Agamemnon's mind it is necessary to "change" the material form as might be analyzed by a positivist physicist into (1) the visual-auditory-olfactory-touch-kinesthetic signs of the human body, (2) the respects of interpretation that reflect what Mycenaean culture thinks is important, (3) the signs of its specific semiotic systems that allow for interactive interpretation, and (4) the interests directing interpretation that come from its society and Agamemnon's personal intentions.[17] It is far better to get what is *important* in the object, its value, into the interpreters so that they can intentionally comport themselves toward it well, especially as such comportment might require a different form. To be sure, there is no *mirroring*, for that is a *formal* metaphor. Interpreting something addresses what it is only in the respect in which the sign interprets the object. There is much more to the object than the interpretation picks up. But the interpretation is better or worse insofar as it picks up on what is valuable in the object and makes that important or significant in the interpreter who intends to interpret the object in a certain respect. The fact-value distinction of the early European Renaissance and Enlightenment project is a false lead and needs to be repudiated in terms of a naturalistic theory of the carryover of value that can render not only scientific hypotheses about what the forms of things are but also ethical, political, and aesthetic hypotheses, all as much subject to correction as the scientific hypotheses.[18]

That truth is the carryover of value means that the soul or self needs to be ready to receive and embody the value as the object is interpreted in the proper respect. Neurophysiological development of the ordinary sort determines that we can interpret ordinary physical objects. Ordinary maturation in physical and social terms determines that we can interpret complex phenomena, such as the perceptions required for driving a car and whether the mood at a gathering is happy or hostile. Specialized training cultivates the sensibilities of musicians to hear more in music than most of us can, of scientists to have more discriminating taste with respect to experiments than is common, of parents to discern the special moods of their children, and of religious people to engage ultimate realities with sophistication most of us lack. As the essential subhypothesis says, spiritual progress can be made in at least two ways. First, one can learn better, more profound symbols for engaging ultimate realities. Second, one can become better at the employment of those symbols so as to affect engagement more thoroughly and directly (direct but not immediate, because the signs always mediate).

Philosophy and theology are the critical disciplines charged with the improvement of symbols. In addition, however, are the spiritual practices that transform the soul to be more adept at engaging the ultimate realities with the symbols. The East Asian traditions have emphasized the importance of yoga as the discipline of working through and reading life under the interpretive guidance of texts and gurus with founding spiritual symbols. The more profound spiritual symbols require the development of just as much unordinary capacity as the more complex musical symbols.

This leads to yet another conditional subhypothesis, this time concerning the psychology of transformation: *The soul is both shaped and developed by acquiring the capacities to employ symbols so as to engage the world in ever more accurate and true appropriations of the values of things.*

Human personal and social identities are formed by the individuation of relations toward things in symbolically rich interactions, a prominent Confucian theme. Spirituality, which deals with the transformations of soul occasioned by engagement with the ultimate, thus supposes from the outset that selves are malleable and that spiritual life will change the self. The purpose in the long run is to transform the self so it becomes able to embody and bring into its constitution and behavior the values of the religious objects. This means conforming one's life to the bearing of the finite-infinite contrasts upon it, becoming holy as Christianity would put it, or "manifesting the clear character" as Confucianism would.

Embodying the value of ultimate realities has immense practical consequences. Confucianism is clear that this involves continued pursuit of personal transformation so as to become more and more sage-like: sages are the ones attuned most thoroughly to the dao, the existential intimacy, and the contingency of ontological flourishing arising from Non-being and the Great Ultimate. But more than what some Christians might suppose is a merely individualistic rendition of transformation, Confucians would emphasize the communal aspect. If the self consists in the relations it individuates with the persons, institutions, and natural elements around it, then personal transformation requires transforming one's neighborhood, a point as familiar to John Wesley as to Wang Yangming. Tu Weiming brilliantly expresses this point by saying that one relates to transcendent things only through first participating in the fiduciary community (Tu 1976b).[19]

This section and the preceding one have expressed a complex hypothesis about spirituality, consisting of an essential subhypothesis that says that spirituality is the engagement of ultimate reality by means of signs, and several conditional subhypotheses that interpret ultimate reality, the self, transformation, truth, and interpretation. The implication of this argument is the displacement of purely anthropological and immanent approaches to spirituality in favor of one essentially referring to ultimacy and conditionally related to several other disciplines. At this point, the crucial theses to remember are that spiritual discernment aims to be true and that spiritual development aims to embody with increasing fullness and exactitude what is real and relevant to human life. Spirituality is fundamentally practical: its goal is the deepening of one's engagement with ultimate reality and it pursues that goal by means of specific practices that include prayer and meditation but also action in the world.

4.4. Confucian Spirituality in a Scientific Society

Like any traditional religion at the end of the twentieth century, Confucianism faces three major problems for which its ancient roots, core texts, and motifs do not provide immediate satisfaction. These are, first, coming to terms with the cosmos as understood by modern science; second, envisioning a global social ethic that can interpret distributive justice now that we have a global economic and the political means to do something about oppression and inequalities; and third, articulating the moral structure of human beings' relations with the natural environment now that science has shown us something of the complexity of the vast web of interconnectedness and the hitherto hidden consequences of human modifications of our niche. Contemporary Confucianism is very well positioned to make helpful responses to these problems, although those answers will require creative transformations of the tradition.

The challenge here is not to religion in general but to spirituality, and with regard to this topic contemporary Confucianism has variations on these special issues. Three Confucian problematics regarding spirituality will be discussed; only the first will be discussed in detail, in this section, and the second and third more briefly in the section to follow.

As argued in section 4.2, contemporary Confucian spirituality requires a conception of Confucian ultimate realities adequate to the world of modern science yet expressing the dominant motifs of the Confucian tradition that can be used to guide spiritual engagement. The ancient picture of heaven above and earth below cannot by itself provide resonance to strike the heart of contemporary Confucians, and therefore it cannot function at face value to guide our engagements. That picture must be reconstructed and its ancient motifs reinterpreted as symbols that say something other than what they seem to say if interpreted as scientific claims. It would be disastrous for contemporary Confucian spirituality to retreat to "mere humanism" in order to avoid the challenge of modern science, for there is nothing ultimate about human nature, according to the Confucian conception, unless it is indeed connected to the ultimate dao, given an intimate place in the cosmos, and construed as the self-conscious perceiving outcome of the ontogenesis process as Zhou described it, a moral he draws immediately after the material quoted above.

> It is man alone who receives (the five Agents) in their highest excellence, and therefore he is most intelligent. His physical form

appears, and his spirit develops consciousness. The five moral principles of his nature (humanity or *jen*, righteousness, propriety, wisdom, and faithfulness) are aroused by, and react to, the external world and engage in activity; good and evil are distinguished; and human affairs take place. The sage settles these affairs by the principles of the Mean, correctness, humanity, and righteousness . . . , regarding tranquillity as fundamental. . . . Thus he establishes himself as the ultimate standard for man. Hence the character of the sage is "identical with that of Heaven and Earth; . . ." The superior man cultivates these moral qualities and enjoys good fortune, whereas the inferior man violates them and suffers evil fortune. (in Chan, 463–64)

This is to say that Confucian spirituality, in contrast to a blander Confucian humanism of moral striving, needs to relate human life to the ultimate, and therefore needs symbols of the ultimate that resonate with the vastness and impersonality of what we now understand the world to be.

Like the great monotheistic spiritual traditions and several of those of India, Confucianism has thematized ultimacy in terms of the foundation of the physical-spiritual cosmos, as in the quote from Zhou above. How these ontogenetic Confucian themes can be reconstructed to accord with modern physical theory, for instance the Big Bang cosmology, is not so much different from the similar reconstructions required of monotheistic creation theories or Brahman-Isvara world theories.[20] For all such ontogenetic concerns, a contemporary theory and resultant set of symbols need to be developed that meet two conditions. On the one hand, they need to point to the grounding Act or Process without making that one more thing to be grounded, which would produce a bad infinite regress. On the other hand, they need to represent the world as determinate but in a sufficiently vague sense that can accommodate whatever science discovers empirically that the world is.[21] Such an ontology and symbology can be employed to give contemporary meaning to the core texts and motifs of each of the world's great spiritual traditions, or at least those with ancient ontogenesis themes.[22]

The special focus of Confucian ontogenesis, however, is less the grounding of physical existence than the grounding of the real value that existence bears and of the very definition of the human as the value-seeker. This positive axiological commitment is expressed in the general Chinese sensibility that the world and human life are good, in the sense that human beings are intimately, rightly, fitly, placed in the cosmos relative to the ultimate (Zhang Zai, and the notion that the human forms a trinity with heaven and earth), in the motif that the human is given the dao as part of its essential nature (*The Doctrine of the Mean*) and, as the Neo-Confucians put it, that the one principle is manifested in every thing and especially in the human character. Both the Cheng-Zhu and the Lu-Wang schools agree that principle in the heart anticipates and is responsive to principle in things, and requires a cultivated expression in personal and social life so as to constitute sage virtue. Like all moral traditions, Confucianism has recognized from the beginning that, in the human case, existence and optimal value do not go together automatically but require deliberate discernment of the ideal relative to the actual and possible, and then controlled and disciplined behavior to accomplish that ideal. The Neo-Confucian conception of principle, say, in the Cheng brothers, as that which would harmonize anything that needs harmonization and which is a ready cognitive impulse in human nature, is as sophisticated a theory of moral realism as has been developed in any tradition.

Modern science, however, poses an extraordinary obstacle to the Confucian claim that ultimate reality is good, that it can be known as good expressed throughout nature, and that human moral striving is possible as a realistic way of relating to ultimate reality, that is, that moral behavior can have a spiritual dimension. The obstacle is not so much in the science itself as in the conception of knowledge associated with science in modern European philosophy. Although the European Christian tradition had long maintained that the creation is good and that moral behavior is part of holiness, the fact-value split adopted by much early modern European philosophy undermined that. Facts are the province of science, and alone are objects of cognition; values cannot be known but are somehow functions of human subjectivity, projection, or contract. The story of the development of the fact-value split is extremely complex, beginning with Descartes and Hobbes. By the beginning of the twentieth century, however, it was manifested in science as conceived by positivism and in value theory as a function of the Nietzschean will to power. Even most critics of scientific positivism who insist that all theories and observations are value-laden suppose that the values are functions of interest and power rather than cognition of the worth of things. The dimension of Confucian spirituality that relates to the ultimate as grounding value and human value discernment is simply impossible for contemporary persons whose sensibilities are deeply formed by the fact-value dichotomy suppositions of the theory of knowledge usually associated with modern science.

Therefore, contemporary Confucianism needs to develop a comprehensive conception of knowledge expressive of its core motifs of value and valuation, a kind of axiology of thinking. On the one hand, this axiology needs to be compatible with science and in fact to provide accounts of fallibility in both science and morals and of the justification of the interests that guide science, as well as those that guide aesthetic, moral, and political life. In this respect, fact and theory-oriented science needs to be represented as an abstraction from a richer, value-laden concrete reality, which also can be known in appreciative and evaluative ways. On the other hand, the axiology of thinking needs to reconstruct the valuative elements of the Confucian tradition's symbols, from Mencius' Four Beginnings to Mou Zongsan's moral metaphysics. Confucian spiritual engagement as grounding value is impossible without a reconstruction of the Confucian symbols in terms that address and circumvent the value-subjectivizing ideology of modern science.

A successful axiology would have to address four families of thinking: imagination, interpretation, theory, and practical reason.[23] *Imagination* has many levels, from the elementary forms of cognitive synthesis by which we transform physical stimuli into an experiential field through the religious images of worldliness to the spiritual images of connection with the ultimate. The elements in Berger's sacred canopy, in fact, can be analyzed as falling on diverse levels, some as elementary as space-time perception, others reflecting cultural constructions of focus-field distinctions, and other systems of narrative and mythic structure. The central axiological claims about imagination are that it consists in valuation and that *form is a function of valuation* rather than the other way around (as in Aristotelianism). Imagination by itself is not true or false, only productive of the forms by which we engage reality.

An axiological theory of interpretation needs, on the one hand, to show how *interpretation* is a part of natural process, representing intentionality, judgment, discernment, and the like as special functions within nature, a project congenial to Confucianism.[24] On the other hand, it needs to show how real values in nature—natural things as valuable and evaluable by human beings—are known in interpretation. The axiological formula for the latter condition is that interpretive truth is the carryover of value from the object interpreted into the interpreter in the respects in which the object is interpreted, with the form of the value qualified by the biology, culture, semiotics, and purposes of the interpreter. Interpretations are cognitive engagements with specific objects, connected by the semiotic systems providing the interpretive signs.

Theories, the third family of kinds of thinking, are self-conscious cognitive constructions of how interpretations hang together and are vulnerable to criticism, one of another.[25] The axiological problem for theorizing is to prevent the values resident in the forms of theories—whether will-to-power interests, value-biases of form as such, or private evaluations—from prejudicing what is valuable or important in the phenomena encompassed within the theory. Therefore, an axiological theory of theories needs to show how good theories are vulnerable to correction by engagements with the phenomena. Imagination makes engagement possible, interpretation engages reality with intentionality, and theorizing allows us some disciplined way of understanding and criticizing the background within which our specific interpretations are situated.

How we imagine, interpret, and theoretically situate ourselves in reality are all ways of thinking that affect what we do. But the *pursuit of responsibility,* as a Confucian might put it, or *practical reason,* is a family of thought processes issuing in actions that define moral identity.[26] An axiological approach to responsibility needs to be able to show how the real values of things make a difference to what should be done and thus define obligation: Confucianism is committed to a strong objectivism in ethics. A contemporary axiology needs to show how general obligation of the sort that "somebody ought to do something about that" can fall to individuals as their own responsibility: Confucianism is committed to identifying particular loci of responsibility depending on both need and personal position. A contemporary axiology needs to show how nearly all actions are not merely individual but conjoint and social, reflecting cultural valuations and embodied in social rituals that frame conjoint behavior: Confucianism's most unique contribution to contemporary world philosophy is its deployment of ritual to interpret conjoint action and practical reason. A contemporary axiology needs finally to account for how different cultures define obligation and human nature differently and yet should accept obligations to normatively good intercultural social interaction (something better than the "clash of civilizations"): Confucianism has long understood that social forms are conventional but normative at the same time.

Imagination, interpretation, theorizing, and the pursuit of responsibility are the four families of kinds of thought that need an axiological interpretation if the Confucian emphasis on the ultimacy of goodness and its demands is to be a viable system of symbols for spirituality. Developing a reconstructed set of Confucian symbols of the ultimate that embody Confucianism's concern for the grounding of value in the world, and true valuation and practice in the human being, is the most essential cognitive task for contemporary Confucian spirituality, without which such spirituality is but wishful thinking. Only this will allow Confucian spirituality to let the ultimate be carried over into persons with the sensibility of modern science in the contemporary world, which is a contemporary requirement for "manifesting the clear character."

Confucian spirituality is not only the direct engagement of what is ultimate but also the playing out of this engagement with the rest of life, especially in our relations with other people and with nature as our home in the cosmos. Whereas the engagement of the ultimate is the essence of spirituality, connecting this with people and nature are its conditions. Together the essence and the conditions constitute the harmony of things in which spirituality consists. From this follow the second and third points about contemporary Confucian spirituality, briefly considered.

4.5. Confucian Spirituality in a Global Moral Democracy and Ecology

We live in a moral situation very different from that obtaining during most of the period of Confucian thinking. There are two important changes. The first is that because of the development of the social sciences we can now envision global social structures and global social engineering. This gives a point to questions of structural oppression and unjust economic inequalities. Before the twentieth century Confucianism had thought only rarely about structural issues of justice on a global scale, though of course it has focused on how China can keep its soul in the modern world. To some extent, the globalization of structural issues of justice runs in tension with Confucianism's focus on attending first to what is close to home based on the person-to-person genesis of moral character in filiality, a major theme of Tu's *Centrality and Commonality*, and Confucianism's polemic against Mozi in which it defended "love with distinctions" (in Chan 1963, chapter 9).

The second change in the moral situation is the increasingly widespread appreciation of the double value of democratic equality with meritocratic rewards, on the one hand and respect for personal and cultural otherness—pluralism—on the other. Neither democracy nor pluralism is native to the Confucian moral tradition. Both developed from the European Enlightenment. Yet in their Enlightenment forms, democratic equality and meritocracy can be given empty procedural meanings, and otherness and pluralism can be so privatized as to be trivial and alienating. The Confucian emphasis on the need to cultivate concrete content to individuating relationships is a fine counterweight to Enlightenment abstraction. Moreover, the Confucian insistence on attending to the institutions of human interaction, from family to state, as more determinative of effects on human beings than isolated face-to-face interactions, is a fine counterweight to the rather thin Enlightenment view of institutions as reduced to public procedures and private rituals (Neville 1987a).

Without claiming that Confucianism has only one contribution to make to the changed moral situation, the first two chapters above argued that its most important contribution would be a reconstruction of its theory of ritual, especially as anciently framed by Xunzi. For Xunzi, rituals are the invented and learned general social habits that constitute the frameworks within which specific civilized human interactions can take place. In a ritual, all the players are brought into a conjoint action. Now with respect to global structural injustices, the problem lies not so much with specific policies or actions but with the social habits, often affirmed by all parties, that constitute an unjust ritual dance. Social classes, for instance, are people grouped by different roles in structured habitual interactions. A Confucian ritual analysis of global structural problems of injustice would locate the problems in the generalities of the habits, rather than specific acts and policies, and would be able to show why even those who suffer seem often to accept the roles they play. The Confucian moral solution would be to criticize the current global rituals and invent improved ones, and then to administer the changes in specific acts and policies that would establish the new rituals. The Secretary General of the United Nations should be a Confucian Ritual Master.

A similar point can be made about giving humanizing concreteness to democratic equality and meritocracy and to cultural and personal pluralism. Although these particular values have not been prominent in the Confucian tradition, what is a Confucian ritual except a complicated social dance form in which all can participate (democracy) and yet can play roles that recognize their vast differences from one another (pluralism)? Contemporary Confucians should develop rituals that allow all persons to participate equally with regard to political power and be rewarded with placement and wealth according to their merit and that allow persons to interact respectfully and concretely with people very different from themselves. The key is rituals that require affirming ritual participation without necessarily agreeing to affirm the character and values of those importantly different from oneself (except to respect them in the ritually defined social construction).

Contemporary Confucian spirituality requires a practical orientation to moral action, which in turn requires moral programs that address the changed moral situation of issues of global justice and the combination of democracy and pluralism. Without those new Confucian programs, Confucian morals will be parochial and disconnected from spiritual life. The Confucian spiritual life will be vital when Confucianism has a program that addresses the most important questions of contemporary morality. This is "renovating the people."

The last issue for contemporary Confucian spirituality to be discussed here is the redefinition of our orientation to the universe in light of the new knowledge deriving from ecology. Partly this is a moral matter, and Confucians should let ecological awareness shape the rituals developed for habitual social interaction. What should be stressed, however, is less the moral dimension than that of orienta- . tion. Here the Confucian tradition is far more advanced than most others in grasping the contemporary problem. Xunzi said in his treatise on heaven that we are oriented one way to the regular processes we cannot affect, such as the rotation of the heavens; that orientation involves wonder and appreciation, perhaps ritual celebration.[27] We are oriented another way to the rotation of the seasons to which we need to respond adroitly to avoid starvation and disaster; this orientation requires the kind of social habits passed down generation to generation in peasant culture, and now more technologically advanced forms of this. We are oriented in yet a third way, said Xunzi, toward irregular events for which preparation should be made, for instance floods and droughts and the appearance of the barbarians over the hill; this orientation requires political organization to provide for relief, storage, and military readiness. Taking Xunzi's analysis as a clue, we can note that we have orientations toward our families that differ from those toward the workplace, toward our universities that differ from those toward our professional public, toward our neighborhood that differ from those toward our country, toward our garden that differ from those toward the wilderness, and so on. Ecological knowledge of nature has forced upon us issues of orientation toward many facets of our habitation that previously we ignored more or less. An orientation is not an action, but the general habit or behavioral and interpretive context within which an action toward the object of orientation is shaped, much the way a ritual is a context for social interaction.

One of the geniuses of Confucianism has been to recognize that our lives require orientations to many different things and that what is required does not easily fit together. To balance out our orientations is to have poise, to keep one's balance in the constant shift of attention required for responsiveness. A person's poise is structured, and the structure of one's poise determines much of one's personal identity. That identity also includes what goes on specifically with regard to each of the things to which the person is oriented, but the person's character out of which the actions spring lies in the structure of poise with regard to orientations. The Confucian way of specifying the vague notion of self is neither to claim it has a core nor that it is wholly to be negated in terms of relations but that it is a structure of poised balancing of orientations to the ten thousand things. The poise issues from the ready responsiveness of principle within each person and from the attunement, such as it is, of our various orientations to the principle or worth in the things to which we are oriented (see section 9.5). Righteousness is getting our orientations right. Humanity is the poise to keep them in balance.

Ecology has shown a new domain of things with respect to which we should be oriented and whose integration into family, economic, and political life-orientations will require new forms of poise. Confucian spirituality is well-placed to develop such new forms, and new humane orientations, that situate us more accurately in respect of what we now know to be of very great value in the cosmos. This is "abiding in the highest good."

5

Tu Weiming's Confucianism

5.1. Conversation and Existential Choice: Way of the Sage

No contemporary Confucian, or New Confucian, has been clearer than Tu Weiming in claiming that Confucianism is a religion or, at least, has a serious religious dimension.[1] The trajectory of Tu's thought has moved from interpreting the Chinese classics, especially in respect of *ren*, to manifesting the contributions of the Confucian intellectual in the present world conversation, which contributions have to do with elaborating the implications of *ren* (humaneness) for the contemporary situation. Along the way he has focused on the nature of the self and its existential process of taking on the way of the sage. From the beginning this existentialist orientation has always been with regard to the way of the sage in the modern world, not merely the world of Confucius, Zhou Dunyi, or Wang Yangming. Sensing the anomaly to Western thinking of the Confucian emphasis on ritual, Tu has argued that ritual propriety is the set of external forms required for *ren* to be expressed in human relations. Without ritual propriety or decorum, human relationships could not be established that might be quickened by *ren*. Tu has always been clear that the way of the sage is not merely a matter of personal self-cultivation but also of the cultivation of one's relationships.

In his later thought he has turned more to the issues of cultivating a community within which life can flourish under the conditions of modernity within a global society, defined by economic and other interactions, but with a conflict of competing and fractured cultures. Specifically, he has examined the European Enlightenment project and its challenges to Confucianism. Part of this concern is expressed with respect to the modernization of China—with Marxism, liberal

democracy, and modern science seen as expressions of the Enlightenment. Another part of the concern has to do with the effects of Enlightenment thinking on family structures and personal relationships so
crucial to the Confucian conceptions of self and society. Yet another
part has to do with the critiques of the Enlightenment project itself.
Some of those critiques are external, as from postmodernists, on the
one hand, and from nativist reactionaries, on the other. Others are
internal critiques such as the self-destruction of communist governments, the apparent difficulty of liberal democracies to sustain the
tolerance and pluralism they require for mutual cooperation, and the
self-betrayal of scientific technologies by ecological crises of their own
making. In all of this Tu argues for the relevance and importance of
Confucian values, appropriately adapted to the conditions of our time.[2]
That one would want to shape a community's discourse is itself a
Confucian project: Not by the arts or by laws or by abstract speculation should we try to govern ourselves but by the creation of a community of discourse in which all are respected, all cultures and
perspectives, and the Confucian virtues of what Tu calls the fiduciary
community can be practiced. Tu is the Confucian ritual master of
important public conversation. His leadership of Boston Confucianism is a central part of this work. Whereas the other chapters of this
book are "about" their topics, this chapter has the form of a ritual
offering in dialogue.

There is something bland, alas, about the rhetoric of "conversation" and "discourse." The former word suffers from the effects of
Richard Rorty's (1979) claim that conversation has no real referent,
and hence no real truth or falsity. The latter suffers from the effete
academicism of "postmodern discourse" (Neville 1992, introduction).
Indeed, despite the arguments of chapter 4, for many of our contem-
poraries Confucianism has the public image of bland religiosity, of the
bureaucratization of existential concerns.

Tu Weiming gives the lie to this blandness. His early writings are
directly existential and should be viewed as underlying all his subsequent thought. Of Herbert Fingarette's two themes, humanity (*ren*)
and ritual propriety (*li*), the former is congenial in a vague way to
Western humanism and the latter explains why Confucianism seems
so strange to the Western sensibility. While deeply respecting
Fingarette's work, Tu comes to the topic of Confucian emphasis differently. He takes humanity to be far the more important Confucian theme
than ritual, and thus has direct entry into the Western sensibility. Tu's
interpretation of humanity is that it rests on the existential choice to

enter onto the path of self-transformation to sagehood. For these reasons, Tu should be called an *existential Confucian*.

The point can be introduced by citing Tu's corrective of a claim by Etienne Balazs that "all Chinese philosophy [is] social philosophy." Tu (1979) writes:

> Strictly speaking, the point of departure in Confucianism is self-cultivation (*hsiu-shen*) rather than social responsibility. It is true that Confucian self-cultivation necessarily leads to social responsibility, and furthermore, the process of self-cultivation in the Confucian sense ought to be carried out in a social context. Still it can be maintained that the perfecting self rather than the corresponding society is really the focus of attention. (71)

With reference to the contours of Confucianism as a religion, he says:

> For example, if Confucianism is described as a religion and by religion is meant a kind of spiritualism purportedly detached from the secular world, the whole dimension of sociality in Confucianism will be left out. If Confucianism is described as a social philosophy, its central concern of relating the self to the most generalized level of universality, of *t'ien* (heaven), will be ignored. If the spiritual aspect of Confucian self-cultivation is emphasized exclusively, its intention of complete self-fulfillment, which must also embrace the whole area of corporality, will be misunderstood. On the other hand, if the Confucian insistence on man as a sociopolitical being is overstated, its ideal of self-transcendence in the form of being one with Heaven and Earth will become incomprehensible. (86)

Tu puts the point about self-cultivation in the following words:

> Yet despite the tension and conflict within the Neo-Confucian tradition, it seems that there is an agreement among virtually all of the Neo-Confucianists: man is a moral being who through self-effort extends his human sensitivity to all the beings of the universe so as to realize himself in the midst of the world and as an integral part of it, in the sense that his self-perfection necessarily embodies the perfection of the universe as a whole. (79)

Now these remarks about self-cultivation can be given a bland or a piquant interpretation, and here is where the charge of Confucian blandness must be faced.

The bland interpretation is that human beings are defined by an ideal of sagehood and that they can advance by trying a little harder at each stage of life. Self-cultivation is strictly a human matter, on this view, with nothing like a theistic notion of divine intervention or grace. The impediments to self-cultivation are miseducation, selfishness, and moral torpor. The underlying supposition is that the inborn nature of people is perfectible, and conditional upon personal perfectibility is the perfectibility of the society. All of these points can be found in Tu's writings, both in his interpretation of the Confucian tradition and in his positive assertions.

The piquant interpretation accepts these points but makes them all problematic. At the heart of the problem is the fact that effort at self-cultivation depends on an

> existential decision in the Kierkegaardian sense: it is a funda-
> mental choice that requires an ultimate commitment; it is a quali-
> tative change that affects the entire dimension of one's being;
> and it is an unceasing process that demands constant reaffirma-
> tion. (Tu 1979, 89)

Although Tu is careful to qualify the association with Kierkegaard's approach, his emphasis on decision is straightforwardly existential. Decision, in fact, is something like conversion, a turning of the soul from outward preoccupations to an inward human nature which, if engaged sincerely, can power the process of self-cultivation. Tu develops this point in his discussions of Wang Yangming.

The mind always has an intentional direction, arising from heavenly principle in its heart, and oriented to objects of various sorts. Tu says, "ontologically the mind is the affective manifestation of the Heavenly Principle, and the Heavenly Principle is the original substance of the mind" (1979, 154). This reflects the classic *ti-yong*, or substance-function construction. Tu follows Wang in interpreting mind to be an integral part of a psychophysical organism. Now the existential problem is that

> when the mind encounters a thing, it faces the danger of being
> fixated in its intended object. If such a fixation is prolonged, the
> mind is gradually "materialized" (*wu-hua*) by the inertia of the
> thing. When this occurs, the Heavenly Principle becomes func-

tionally neutralized. Consequently the dynamism and creativity essential to self-realization will not be generated, and the original substance of the mind is "buried." (1979, 154)

Fixation on intended objects is what the Confucian tradition has interpreted as "selfish desires." Desire is not bad itself and indeed is the affective and responsive element of heavenly principle expressed through embodied mind. But desire is selfish when the fixation distorts or neglects its root in principle and the true nature of its object.

Selfish desires are not only individually destructive but constitute a personal character that becomes hardened into habit. "The ontological identification of the mind and the heavenly principle notwithstanding, in the conduct of daily affairs, the mind may existentially be controlled by human desires. As a result, its normal functions are obstructed and distorted" (154). Therefore,

> In a paradoxical sense human desires are not at all human; for as selfish expressions of the mind, they have already obstructed and distorted its true intentions, which means that the mind is existentially alienated from its original substance. (154)

The central problem for self-cultivation, therefore, is that the ordinary state of affairs is that we are existentially alienated from our original substance. In the state of existential alienation, merely trying harder to be a sage is not enough, contrary to the bland approach. Rather, the alienation itself needs to be reversed.

Tu follows Wang Yangming in giving a dual prescription for reversing alienation. One medicine is the discipline of vigorous extirpation of selfish desires, those that are merely human and not manifestations of heavenly principle. The other is the direct turning of the intention inward to the heavenly principle itself. Tu follows Wang and much of the rest of the ancient and Neo-Confucian tradition in advocating rigorous self-criticism and the cultivation of self-control, as the ways to take the first medicine. His special contribution, however, is to accentuate a theme of Wang's, namely, the recovery of heavenly principle in the heart, the second medicine. By turning inward to principle and attaining sincerity, in which heavenly principle is neither obscured nor paralyzed, suddenly the mind can turn back outward to objects sincerely and without fixation, interpreting and responding to them with something like spontaneous rightness. This is Wang's notion of *liang-zhi* (innate Knowledge affectively expressive in action). With a proper orientation to heavenly principle in the heart, the mind, indeed, the whole person, can find and conform to heavenly principle in all its objects and in the structures of its own responses. The ontological point is that everything that exists arises from heavenly principle, and the existential point is that when this clearly or sincerely informs the mind, the mind acts to make us "one body with the world." But the ordinary existential situation is that we are alienated from the heavenly principle that constitutes our very hearts.

5.2. The Question of Conversion

The existential question then is how one goes about turning inward to heavenly principle. There is no question for Confucianism that heavenly principle lies in the heart of the mind, as Mencius' "Four Beginnings" are ineradicable however much they are frustrated. But how is heavenly principle accessed from a state of alienation? Tu's answer is that we must make a deliberate act of commitment to the way of the sage (1979, 66–68). Self-cultivation is not just more effort at perfection but the conscious existential act of committing oneself to the process, of taking on the identity of the one who will struggle toward perfection.

> If man is not merely a conglomeration of externalizable physiological, psychological, and sociological states, a conscious choice is required to establish his spiritual identity. . . . The decision to learn, which in the classical sense means to be engaged in self-enlightenment, thus symbolizes a qualitative change in the orientation of one's life. . . . Learning so conceived is a conscious attempt to change oneself from being in a state of mere psychophysiological growth to that of ethicoreligious existence. (1979, 89)

Once that act of commitment is made, and so long as it is constantly reaffirmed, heavenly principle in the heart, to the extent it is discerned, is given power to push through selfish desires and to deconstruct institutionalized habits and engage the world with clarity. Tu emphasizes the gradual character of self-cultivation, with slowly growing discernment of heavenly principle and its transformative powers in the self. But at whatever stage of development the person might be, the existential act of commitment to self-cultivation guided by principle is the key.

In the East Asian tradition, this theme in Wang Yangming owes much to Buddhism and the Bodhisattva's vows. Tu likens it to the act of faith in existential Christianity. He links his conception of

Confucian religiosity to "the mystical elements of Plato, the writings of St. Augustine, the Stoics, the medieval saints, Pascal, Kierkegaard, and the works of modern philosophers such as Martin Buber, Gabriel Marcel, and Martin Heidegger" (1979, 83). The qualification Tu insists upon to the analogy with that Western tradition, especially Christianity, is the denial that Confucianism requires an either-or decision; rather, Confucianism insists on "both-and":

> Paradoxically, neither the fundamental choice nor the qualitative change appears as merely a discrete moment in one's life history. Since Confucianism is not a revealed religion, the "establishment of the will" is not so much a mystic experience of the transcendent Absolute as it is an enlightening experience of the immanent Self. Therefore the never-ending process it entails does not take the form of a dialogical relationship with the "wholly other;" rather, it takes the form of a dialectical development of the Self. . . . Thus the establishment of the will is both a single act and a continuous process. As a single act, it so shakes the foundation of one's temporal existence as to enable one to arrive at a deeper dimension of self-awareness. As a continuous process it reaffirms the bedrock of one's being in an unending effort of self-realization. (1979, 90)

Tu's characterization of Christianity in this early writing is limited to Karl Barth's version of Kierkegaard, emphasizing God as the Wholly Other and downplaying the importance for salvation of the continuous pursuit of holiness. Paul Tillich contrasted the approach to God as an other with the approach to God as the internal ground of being, "closer to us than we are to ourselves," to use Augustine's phrase (Tillich 1959, chapter 2). Christians also have emphasized the abiding image of God in human beings, an image that might be distorted and rendered impotent by sin, but abiding nevertheless and the source of the human capacity to turn back to God (see section 8.4), a rather close analogy to the heavenly principle by which heaven gifts human nature. Tu positively appropriates the point from the opening of *The Doctrine of the Mean:* "What Heaven imparts to man is called human nature. To follow our nature is called the Way" (in Chan 1963, 98). Human nature in that sense is the heavenly principle discussed by Wang, and it lies very close to the Christian conceptions of God as the interior ground of one's being and the image of God in human beings. So far as these matters go, Tu's position is compatible with Christianity, and in fact the two traditions are complementary here.

The question that still must be posed to Tu, however, concerns the seriousness of the alienation from heavenly principle or divinity in one's heart and the correlative question of the role of heavenly principle or divinity as a necessary means of grace for the recovery from alienation. It is common for scholars to say that Confucianism has no reference to grace, only to human self-development. The Christian position was most neatly expressed by Augustine who agreed that, so long as one is rightly turned to God, one's intentional orientation to the things of the world is not sinful but appreciative, helpful, and loving. Augustine, however, had a stern view, stern beyond piquancy, of sin as the state of being turned away from God.[3] In *The Confessions*, book 2, Augustine epitomized his view of sin with the story of his joining a group of teen-aged friends in stealing pears from a neighbor's tree. Although various commentators have dismissed this story as exaggerating a trivial sin or merely expressing a Freudian guilt pathology, in fact, it is a deep analysis of sin. If the boys had stolen the pears because they were hungry, the legally wrongful act might have been justified on utilitarian grounds, but they threw the pears away without eating them. If the neighbor's pears had been especially good, the wrongful act might have been understood, if not justified, on aesthetic grounds; but Augustine's father's trees had better pears. If Augustine had joined out of peer pressure or to be one of the boys, the theft could be understood in terms of elementary male bonding or the terrors of an adolescent's psychology, but the episode ruined the friendship among the boys because they knew they were ruining one another. Augustine said he would not have committed the theft alone but did it precisely because it was gratuitous theft committed for its own sake in the company of others, a group sinning for the sake of sinning itself and for no other reason. The result was that Augustine and his friends had chosen what was alien from God for no reason except that it was alien from God. Having done that, they could not simply turn back to God but had defined themselves as taking pleasure in that alienation.

Augustine's account in book 8 of his conversion back to God acknowledges God's presence in his heart which continued to long for God, in the sustaining love of his mother and other Christians, in the philosophy and theology he encountered as an adult, and in his knowledge of the Bible. As the pressures converged toward his conversion, he even wanted to convert, but could not bring himself to do it because of the power of alienation, not focused now on pears but on his concubine whom he loved with a love he thought wrong. And he could not convert, crying to God, "How long, how long? Tomorrow and tomorrow? Why not now? Why not this very hour make an end to my uncleanness?" (Augustine 1955, 175) Then circumstances led him to look at the biblical verse that simply told him to give up the lusts of the flesh and "put on the Lord Jesus Christ." "Putting on Jesus Christ," like putting on clothes, means taking up Jesus' way. Perceiving this as an invitation, Augustine then committed himself to the Christian way which was in fact his conversion. From then on, despite frailties and reversals, he was turned to God and went on to a powerful Christian career. His conversion was not a single act of God, nor a single act of himself, but a complex interweaving of prevenient grace and human response.

The question to be posed here is whether anything in Tu's Confucian vision is as stern and definitive of human nature as a self that determines itself to be turned away from heavenly principle and thus incapable by itself of the kind of self-cultivation that requires and fosters sincerity. Do infatuation and obsession with an object get as seriously alienating as this? Augustine's analysis of the human condition is not merely that we are selfish and alienated and need to choose to turn to God, or to heavenly principle. It is rather that we choose to be alienated and make ourselves that, but that we need to give up that choice and choose another thing, God. Christians of Augustine's sort assert a human responsibility for sin that goes beyond finding ourselves in a predicament but in addition is the deliberate choice of that predicament.

Confucians might dismiss that choice of alienation as guilty overkill and say only that alienated people need to be educated back to the Dao. Does Tu's insistence on the existential commitment to undertake the way of the sage recognize that, at least for some people, this commitment requires the choice to abandon a contrary commitment? If so, the Confucian medicine of extirpating selfish desires requires not only self-criticism and effort but also the problematic that Christians address with notions of repentence and confession.

The treatment here of the theme of conversion in Tu has focused on his discussion in *Humanity and Self-Cultivation* (1979) to the neglect of his analysis of the social dimensions of self-cultivation in *Centrality and Commonality* (1976b), where he develops the idea of the fiduciary community and in *Confucian Thought: Selfhood as Creative Transformation* (1985). In those books he emphasizes the creative capacity of *ren* (humanity, goodness, or love) to fuel the process of self-cultivation. His discussions of filial piety are particularly appealing for their demonstration of the learning of humanity. Nevertheless, the question of the choice of alienation versus the choice of the way of the sage can be raised within the problematic of humanity and its problematic engagement as well as the context discussed above. Before turning to the question of humanity or love, however, the question of ritual needs to be introduced.

5.3. The Question of Ritual

Tu begins *Humanity and Self-Cultivation* with two essays about ritual propriety (*li*) in relation to humanity (*ren*). The basic idea is that humanity is the inner essence of human nature, the heavenly principle, that needs to express itself externally in social relations. Tu is far too subtle to make a simple distinction between inner human nature and outer action, but the process of self-cultivation involves a dialectic of determining one's relations with others and with the structures of society. He interprets ritual propriety as the structure for expressing humanity in action:

> *Li* can be conceived as an externalization of *jen* in a specific social context. No matter how abstract it appears, *jen* almost by definition requires concrete manifestation. . . . [S]ocial impact is inherent in the principle of inwardness because the main point is not to achieve perfect equilibrium in order to eliminate all worldly entanglements but to be of great "use," although this is quite different from both positivistic utiltarianism and Dewey-type instrumentalism. Nevertheless, it is in this concern for workability and practicability that the true "meaning" of *li* should be found. (1979, 10–11)

Tu rejects the view that *li* refers to structured ceremonies per se but says that it "points to a concrete way whereby one enters into communion with others" (24). That way is a process that moves through cultivating personal life, regulating familial relations, ordering the affairs of the state, and bringing peace to the world, all of which reflects the order of learning in the *Da Xue* (Tu 1979, 27–28). Tu is very clear, however, that the process begins from the inward cultivation of the self and is for the sake of that:

> sociality as a spiritual value is justified neither on grounds of transcendent reference nor on grounds of collective goal. It is in the perfectibility of man as an ethicoreligious being that the justification for sociality really lies. Indeed, a Confucian tries to be social for the sake of self-realization. His personal authenticity is inseparable from his sociality. If he fails to relate himself to

others in a meaningful way, he does violence not only to his social relations but also to his authentic self. Unless he cultivates himself in the context of human-relatedness, no matter how high a spiritual level he is able to attain, from the Confucian point of view, his claim to self-realization is inauthentic. (1979, 26)

For Tu, human beings cannot realize or cultivate themselves without sociality, which requires ritual propriety. But the value of ritual is precisely that it makes self-cultivation possible.

Tu's contribution here is an authentic development of the Mencian strain of Confucianism. Coupled with the emphasis on existential commitment to the process of self-cultivation, a commitment to the way of the sage, Tu's approach to ritual propriety directly addresses the late-modern problem of authentic life in a society that is deeply fragmented and therefore in need of rituals that make personal development possible.

But there is an equally profound strain of Confucian thinking about ritual, as has been argued above, that proceeds from Xunzi which can serve as a balance to Tu's approach. *Li* is as primordial as *ren* in its own way, and in its own way prior to *ren*. To recall the argument in section 2.2, Xunzi pointed out in his essay on *tian* (heaven or nature) that the natural endowment provided human beings by heaven and earth is not yet human. On the one hand, people are given capacities for sensation and response through the ear, eye, nose, mouth, and body (touch), and on the other hand, people are given feelings such as desire, aversion, delight, anger, grief, and joy. There is also an inborn general mental capacity to control behavior, and a kind of discernment that is able to tell when something is fulfilling or frustrating its dao, which Xunzi calls the "governor." But there is nothing in the human natural endowment that sets the feelings to their appropriate objects, so we love what we should fear, avoid what we should desire, and in general become fixated on objects inappropriately, as Tu would say.

The reason for this is that the human endowments are underdetermined. Our bodies have a great flexibility of movement, but we have to learn some specific way of moving in order to live, some specific gait for walking, particular habits of eye contact for social relations, some specific language for speaking. All of these are conventional, or matters of learned ritual. Our sense organs can discern many things but cannot sort them with good taste until taste is learned. Our feelings can provide emotive power in all directions, regarding just about anything, but need learned discrimination to find appropriate objects and appropriate responses. All of this comes from the conventions of civilization. In fact, to be human is to engage in significant activity as such, activity shaped by signs, which are conventional. Xunzi never suggested that "conventional" means "non-normative"; on the contrary, conventions are good as they shape behavior to be civilized and normatively human. But they are conventional nonetheless.

The point of all this is that people need to be formed ritually before matters of *ren*, or humanity, are possible or can become problematic. People are defined as much by the conventions that make them human as by the human-heartedness that expresses their inner principle. In fact, the very notion of thought, feeling, and behavior expressive of heavenly principle or humanity needs to be articulated through the ritual conventions that give it human shape. Ritual is needed not just to express sociality toward others but to make a person human in the first place. Whereas Tu interprets *The Doctrine of the Mean*, the *Zhong Yung*, to give priority to *zhong*, the inner heart, it can also be interpreted to assert an exact reciprocity such that a person is constituted, actually and ideally in respective senses, by the continuum between inner principle whence humanity springs and the ten thousand things *to which we are related through signs that shape even our physical movements.*

In a sense, the issue is merely a matter of emphasis. Tu would not reject any of the phenomena, principles, or functions that come from Xunzi's line down to the pragmatism defended here. But the difference in emphasis leads to fairly important differences in representations of Confucianism's contributions to the world of late-modern culture, two of which shall be mentioned, a metaphysical one and an ethical one, stressing the contributions of Xunzi's pragmatism.

The metaphysical contribution is that the emphasis on ritual as constitutive of the human in its very essence connects immediately with the pragmatic analysis of signs initiated by Peirce, as argued in section 1.3. According to Peirce, not only is all activity shaped by signs, but human beings themselves are to be understood as signs (Neville 1992, chapter 1). A contemporary Confucian theory of ritual thus has at its disposal the extremely rich pragmatic theory of semiotics and, through that, connections with the entire Western tradition of philosophy as well as with the analyses of sign-shaped behavior by the contemporary social sciences. Contemporary Confucian ritual theory can cite Mencius and Xunzi for inspiration and to display the authenticity of its lineage, but it is to be formulated for philosophic purposes in terms of the best semiotic science of our time.

On the other side, it must be admitted that Western semiotics and the social sciences are sometimes lame and stumbling over normative matters, deeply confused by positivist claims to value neutrality. If we affiliate them with a contemporary Confucian theory of ritual, however, they have at their disposal a profound Confucian tradition of more than two milennia that reflects on the differences between civilized and barbaric rituals, between better norms for personal and social life and worse ones, between better conventions and worse ones. Odd as it might seem, Confucianism might well become the salvation of the social sciences.

This is a metaphysical contribution of Confucianism because it has to do with ritual as a constitutive element of human nature defined in connection with all the rest of nature. The ethical contribution, by contrast, has to do with the focusing of ethical attention.

If ritual conventions are constitutive of individuals because they allow individuals to act with shared meanings, and thus to be individual by being social, this suggests, as argued in sections 1.4 and 1.5, that ethical attention ought to be focused on the ritual structures of gesture, language, interpersonal behavior, and social institutions. Western ethical theory has tended to focus on individual acts and the principles or goals of such actions, that is, on deontology and teleology; Western political and social theory has focused on actual historical institutions and social structures. Ritual conventions lie between these two and embrace much of what is normative in both. Often what is important about individual actions is not their particularity but their conventionally structured possibilities. Kant was groping for something like this in his notion of a maxim for action. What is important about social institutions is not always their historical particularity but the general ways they make action and production possible through conventional social habits. We should not neglect either the ethical analysis of particular actions and policies or the criticism of actual institutions. But we also should turn our attention in systematic ways to the analysis and improvement of the sign systems, the rituals, that make social intercourse possible. Miss Manners might be a more important political theorist than we have suspected.

Ethical analysis in our time is especially complicated by the fact that we live in a plurality of cultures, each with its ritual systems and norms. Every culture says what is normative, and yet every one is conventional and in these late-modern days knows it is conventional. The Confucian tradition has long known that ritual is both conventional and normative, and different conventions can be equally normative in noncompetitive ways. The more we can understand our ethical and political problems through the theory of ritual, the more resources we have for adjudicating the clash of civilizations in normative, civilized ways. Whereas Tu's existential Confucianism has many Western analogues in its treatment of choice and commitment, especially within Christianity, there is little Western analogue to the ritual theory of normative cultures.

Tu Weiming's Boston Confucianism of humanization, self-cultivation, and existential commitment to the way of the sage has not only shown the viability of the Confucian tradition for the late-modern world and led many of his peers in the articulation of that point. It has also provided a profound answer to the moral and political relativism that seems to plague late-modernity. Western existentialism has been part of the glorification of will that makes power the source of the definition of the right. Even those who are aggrieved by the conditions of our time so often think that the solution is for them to have power rather than their oppressors. Tu has shown that individuating choice and commitment are to be understood as the appropriation of the normative principles of human nature. Although the norms for human nature are contextual and situational on his view, they are not at all relative. That is an extraordinary contribution to ethical theory. To couple Tu's Boston Confucianism so described with a Boston Confucian theory of ritual convention as constitutive of humanity in both personal and social dimensions provides an even more effective approach to norms in an age of pluralism, social disintegration, and conflict.

5.4. The Question of Love (Ren)

Tu Weiming's central concern from the beginning of his career has been the Confucian problematic of *ren*, with the range of meanings from humaneness to love. There must be something important to the idea of love because it is central to so many of the world's major religious traditions, albeit with different stresses and nuances. The concept of love has an extremely broad extension in both Christianity and Confucianism, beginning as a human virtue, the chief virtue, the virtue that defines authentic or holy humanity. Love lends itself finally to the root metaphoric work for ontology, in the Christian notion that the divine act of creation of the world is pure love, that love is creativity, and in the Confucian notion, spelled out in Zhu Xi's *Treatise on Jen*, that love is the empowering principle of coming to be, developing, flourishing, and having consequences (in Chan 1963, 594). Tu puts the point well in his interpretive summary of *The Doctrine of the Mean*: "it can be understood and appreciated as the unfolding of an ethicoreligious vision on the inseparability of the Human Way and the Way of Heaven" (1976b, 3). The argument here will not deal with the ontological uses of the notion of love but will examine the personal or existential.

Little needs to be said to substantiate the claim that love is an important virtue in both Confucianism and Christianity. The Confucian concept of *ren* dates to Confucius himself, as in his discussions in Book 4 of *The Analects*. Its range of meanings include, besides love, benevolence, perfect virtue, goodness, human-heartedness, and altruism. Wing-tsit Chan points out that "Neo-Confucianists interpreted it as impartiality, the character of production and reproduction, consciousness, seeds that generate, the will to grow, one who forms one body with Heaven and Earth, or 'the character of love and the principle of mind.' "[4] These latter meanings illustrate the more ontological senses of the term. Translating *ren* in *The Analects,* D. C. Lau (Confucius 1979) uses benevolence, whereas Wing-tsit Chan uses humanity; Tu follows Chan in his discussion of the text of the *Zhong-Yung*.

Love is central to the Christianity of the New Testament. It is the chief characteristic Jesus ascribed to God, and the virtue he advocated for people in their relations with one another. He also asked the disciples to love him and to love God.[5] Saint Paul's hymn to love in *1 Corinthians* 13 is a classic that transcends the Christian tradition, and it ends by saying that love is the greatest of virtues, greater than faith or hope, both of which were more the focus of his own writings than love. Jesus was clear that love is the greatest virtue when he gave the great commandment summarizing all the law: "You shall love the lord your God with all your heart, and with all your soul, and with all your mind, and with all your strength. . . . You shall love your neighbor as yourself." (*Mark* 12:30–31; see also *Matthew* 22:34–40, and *Luke* 10:25–28).

That love, or *ren*, is the cardinal virtue in Confucianism is stated in the *Zhong-Yung* (chapter 20), where it says that *ren* is the distinguishing character of the human; *ren* is *ren* (Chan 1963, 104; Tu 1976a, 50). Mencius repeats the saying in 7B:16, and in his famous discussion of the Four Beginnings at 2A:6, humanity is the first virtue begun from commiseration or fellow-feeling. Both Confucianism and Christianity go so far as to say that *ren* or love is what makes people human, a normative definition of human nature; thus Christianity can say that love constitutes humaneness.[6]

The Chinese character for *ren* shows two people together, and as a virtue it is the ideal of "human-relatedness," a phrase with which Tu often translates *ren*. He points out that the Confucian tradition never defined human beings as social beings or symbol users, as is common in the West, but as *ren*, as capable of expressing humanity. This has two related parts. On the one hand is the inner cultivation of an in-born tendency to be humane, especially as this is explicated in the Mencian tradition. On the other hand, *ren* means establishing real loving relations with other people, a matter of acting in society. The forms by which humanity is established with others are those of ritual propri-ety, which Tu interprets as the externalization and codification of inner *ren*. It was argued before that ritual propriety in the form of conven-tions of symbolic behavior is necessary for any human relations at all, and that ritual thus is a precondition for the expression of anything social in one's inner nature. But this is only to make Tu's point about the need for love to find expression in external human relations all the stronger. A human being is someone who is capable of, and has im-pulses toward, good human relations, and a good human being is one who exercises and perfects that capability through practice. This means not only following the right ritual forms with one's companions but also individuating and perfecting particular relations with specific family, friends, and fellow citizens.

Confucians and Christians agree that the capacity for love is inborn and definitive of what it means to be human. *The Doctrine of the Mean* opens with the claim that the Way, which later is identified with *ren*, is imparted by heaven, and as we have seen, the Neo-Confucians developed this into the subtle position that heavenly principle is embodied in every person as the essence of human nature. Christians say that persons are created in the image of God, and although this has meant a great many things, one of the most important is that persons are formed in the image of God's creative love, or at least have that capacity in a limited way. The differentiated comparison between Confucianism and Christianity gets interesting at the points of asking how the inborn capacity gets aroused and cultivated, and what might go wrong so as to make that cultivation problematic.

It is noteworthy that neither Confucianism nor Christianity treats sexual attraction as the initiating point of love, which was Plato's way. In the *Phaedrus* and even more directly in the *Symposium*, Plato said that sexual love, which everyone has in some form however crude, can be cultivated to higher and higher levels of erotic love until good things are appreciated for their own sakes, not for any special gratification of the lover. Enriching the metaphors of erotic love, Plato elaborated the dimensions of love that involve friendship and altru-ism so that the highest kind of love is the cultivation of the next generation with institutions that fulfill them in such ways as they themselves can become lovers after their various types.[7] Neither Confucianism nor Christianity begins this way.

Both begin with parental love. In the Confucian case this is closely connected with the relations usually explained as filial piety. Parents naturally, biologically as it were, love their infants. Parental love is also, and more importantly, a process of growth in love. As children grow, parents learn the subtle art of providing care while slowly relinquishing control so that the children learn responsibility; perhaps it is mainly in parenting that the profoundest lessons of boundary-setting and individuation are learned. Children, of course, get into trouble and disappoint us. They get sick and sometimes die. In all this parental love is tested and grown. By the time children reach adolescence, parents in every culture of the world would grit their teeth and agree with Saint Paul that love "bears all things, believes all things, hopes all things, endures all things" (*1 Corinthians* 13:7). Because parental love wants children to be fulfilled and as perfect as possible, it wants the children to become parents themselves in order to learn how to love fully as parents do. In East Asian Confucian cultures children have the filial duty to provide their parents with grandchildren. This has often been given an economic interpretation, and there might be something to that. But the true religious motivation is that the long course of parenting is how one learns love in its fulness, and this is what good parents want for their children. Tu Weiming says that filial piety is not so much taking care of your parents when they get old but rather becoming so virtuous yourself as to set them free from further work in bringing you up to be a good person.

Becoming a good person, says Tu, means learning how to love, which is the way of humanity and the dao of heaven: the paradigmatic curriculum for learning how to love is being a parent. Little children are turned on to love by receiving love and slowly learning those things necessary for adult responsible life. The greatest responsibility is raising children of their own. Of course, not all adults have, or should have, children, but there are many surrogate contexts of long-term caring that express the same learning of love.

Tu argues that parental love is not only a domestic virtue but is at the heart of politics. The greatest power the emperor has is his capacity to inspire others to imitate his virtue, and the central virtue in which *ren* is most conspicuous is parental love, extended to love of one's family and beyond. Whereas egalitarian Westerners might take nepotism to be a vice, in classical Confucian thinking the people should see how the emperor loves the members of his family, disciplining them like a parent but also setting them up with rewards and a living. Of course, the emperor ought not put a corrupt or incompetent relative into a ministry, because the empire would suffer, but short of that, his care of his family is exemplary and when displayed in practice and policy should encourage others to do that. As Tu (1976b, 87) says,

> [T]he ruler cannot exercise his power directly on the people; his political influence can only be extended gradually through the mediation of appointed offices. If he fails to identify himself with the welfare of those who are responsible for the execution of his policies, his leadership will be greatly weakened. What he must do, then, is to see to it that his esteem for the worthy, his care for his proximity of blood, and his respect for the great ministers do not hamper his consideration for all officialdom—including the host of subordinate bureaucrats as well. Indeed, this process of inclusion must also involve artisans, farmers, and even strangers from far countries. The ruler's moral persuasion can be truly effective only if it is conducted in the spirit of impartiality. Once the ruler's concern is limited to special interest groups, his efficacy as a leader for the whole country becomes problematical.

The fiduciary community, as Tu calls it, is based not on trust in contracts but in the mutually reinforcing resonances of parental love reciprocated by filial piety, in family after family from the emperor to the rudest peasant (Tu 1976b, chapter 3). Confucians emphasize "love with distinctions," paying closest attention and care to one's immediate relatives, then distant relations, then unrelated neighbors, and finally to strangers in distant parts (*Mencius* 3A:5, in Chan 1963, 71). This does not lead to a justice of equality, as the Moists pointed out, but it does lead to regarding even the most distant person as subject to a degree of the regard you would have for your beloved children.

Of course, there are many human relations besides that of a parent loving a child, including relations between wife and husband, among siblings, cousins, friends, villagers, officials, distant citizens, and with the barbarians. These all have complicated proper forms, and the proper way to love your friend is not likely to be the way you properly love your children. Nevertheless, the model of parental love is like a flywheel that keeps all these other relations in balance. You should love your siblings as children beloved of your parents. You should treat your neighbors with the respect that honors their own parents' love of them. You should treat all citizens as distant children of the emperor, and the barbarians as people who would greatly benefit from having a father like your emperor. To be fully human is to have realized the fullness of parental love, reciprocating it in filial piety toward your parents, and living out its implications in all your human relationships, according to Tu's Confucianism.

Beginning with Jesus, Christians too have taken the father's, or the parents', love as the paradigm of the love God is understood to have and also that is ideal for the human practice of love. But unlike the Confucians—indeed, in very stark contrast with them—Christians do not assume that everyone has good parents from whom to learn love or that they themselves can be good parents so as to perfect that love. Christianity is a religion for widows and orphans, for broken families (see section 10.2). If a person is so fortunate as to have loving parents, and to live in such settled and prosperous times as to be able to bring one's own children up in love and security, that is a great blessing, but a rare one. So Jesus developed a strange dialectic in describing ideal parents (actually, like the Confucians, just "fathers"). He used this human ideal as a description of God who cares for the birds of the air and all his earthly children even more, giving them bread and fish rather than stones and snakes (*Luke* 12:22–34). He described ideal fathers such as the father of the prodigal son as images of God (*Luke* 15:11–32). We should look to God as our ideal father, on the one hand, because God is our creator, the Father of All, and, on the other hand, because God's character is loving in a symbolic parental way. Then we should use the image of God as loving parent to guide our own human love, caring for others. Our own parenting should be in imitation of God's love.

Jesus took the kinship relations and universalized them: all human beings are brothers and sisters, and God is the Father of all. Like the Confucians, Jesus and the early Christians construed all human relations, whatever their formal roles, as being tinged with family affection, all people being recognized as children of God and all obliged to some version of filial piety or gratitude. Unlike the Moists, the Christian conception of the universal human family was based on love like that of siblings all loved by the Heavenly Father, not a matter of mere impersonal justice.

For Christians, a human being's inmost defining nature, which is to be an image of God, is brought to full expression only in a community in which people love one another in appropriate ways as children of God and love God with all their heart, mind, soul, and strength, as their true father. Tu has argued that for Confucianism one's inmost nature as a *ren* person can be expressed, developed, and fulfilled only in the cultivation of rich human relations within a community. Christianity says the same thing about the image of God: it is not a private virtue or faculty such as reason or will, but all the human faculties aimed at social living characterized as loving the family of God.

5.5. The Question of Evil

But now we must face up to the problem of real evil. If the capacity for love is built into the heart of human nature and is as easy as being seduced by an infant, if in fact God is like a father and all people are sisters and brothers, why is the world such a mess? The phrase "learning to love," is profoundly ambiguous. On the one hand, it has a merely developmental dimension, as one is supposed to learn love in the family or the religious community. But on the other hand, that learning in reality often is blocked so that something as dislocating as an existential decision is required to gain access to the innate or nascent love in the soul. Even in good families, Tu would say, it is necessary for a would-be sage to make a serious decision to follow the path of unfolding love or humaneness. Evil is not merely immaturity.

The standard Confucian position is that inborn love or *ren* is corrupted or thwarted by selfishness, and there are two main traditions accounting for selfishness. One following from Mencius says that society corrupts the natural tendencies to humane development. The other following from Xunzi says that society fails to teach the complicated ways or rituals by which love can be expressed beyond the elementary level, and people are thrown back on competition, breeding selfishness. Xunzi is supposed to have said that human nature is evil, not *ren*, contrary to Mencius' belief that *ren* is always in the heart ready to rise again like new shoots in a logged-over forest. But Xunzi's point is that *ren* finds no natural expression unless it has symbolic forms in which to express itself. He was not a nature romantic but insisted that everything human has to be shaped by learned conventions or forms, that is, symbolic meaning. He never denied that the human heart would fail to respond in *ren* if the proper forms were present and ingrained. Most Confucians from both strains say that some people are natively large-minded and loving persons and that others are natively small-minded and have to work much harder to overcome selfishness. But everyone can learn to be humane, loving, and fulfilled in *ren*. All they need is effort, and they might first need to gain the possibility of applying effort.

Tu, as we have seen, gives a far more forceful and interesting interpretation of selfishness and its remedy than the standard one. The central problem for Tu's self-cultivation is that in the ordinary state of affairs we are existentially alienated from our original substance. In the state of existential alienation, merely trying harder to be a sage is not enough. Rather, the alienation itself needs to be reversed. This is indeed like Saint Paul's famous claim (*Romans* 5–7) that the sinful person degenerates into slavery to sin in his members, which comes from turning away from God; salvation consists in turning back to God. How? Tu's answer as we have seen is that we must make a deliberate act of commitment to the way of the sage, an act of faith. Self-cultivation is not just more effort at perfection but the conscious existential act of committing oneself to the process of taking on the identity of the one who will struggle toward perfection.

Both Confucianism and Christianity face the dilemma of alienation: although heavenly principle (in the former case) and the image of God (in the latter) lie in the heart, and from them mature humaneness and love might grow, the ordinary existential situation is that people are alienated from them and cannot access them. Both traditions also respond with the same strategy: developed humaneness or love needs to be encountered in a concrete human being who provides a model. In the Confucian case, that is a parent, an ancestor or sage-emperor, more likely a teacher; in the Christian case, Jesus or a saint bearing Jesus' love. This Confucian-Christian agreement in strategy will be developed more in sections 10.2 to 10.4. But despite the similarity of strategies, the metaphoric systems of Christianity and Confucianism in this regard seem far apart.

The Christian symbols are that God's parental love intervenes to create the child over again, into a New Being, as Paul put it and as will be elaborated more fully in section 10.2. This is done by overwhelming the diminished self with love, as a parent takes back a wicked, broken prodigal child. If God, who knows the sinner's deepest sin, can still love the sinner, then the sinner who accepts this love can have the courage or power to turn back to God. There are many Christian accounts of how God's love is manifested in an overwhelming way, and they are not mutually compatible. But they have in common that this is accomplished or initiated by Jesus. The most minimalist account is that Jesus himself had an extraordinary capacity to love that derived from his own worshipful and prayerful relation with God, and that this attracted people to him. He taught a way of life consisting in fellowship, in carrying on a ministry of care for those who need it, and in teaching both that we are in God's kingdom rather than a kingdom defined in merely worldly terms and that God is merciful, forgiving sins. By dedicating themselves to Jesus' way, the disciples discover step by step that God loves them and that they are accepted. This gives greater and greater power until finally they can accept themselves as accepted, to use Tillich's phrase, and with this self-acceptance have the power to turn back to God directly (Tillich 1948, "You Are Accepted"). Perceiving God's love of them, as manifested through following Jesus' way, people respond in thanksgiving to God. This thanksgiving is locking onto God who is then embraced in an act of faith, which empowers the process of growth in love.

By contrast with the deep anthropomorphic symbols of Christianity in which God is personified as a lover, Confucianism, including Tu's representation, stays with a cool appeal to embodied principle. Christian personification of God is difficult to sustain in the world of late-modern science and intercultural skepticism. Confucianism has an advantage in this regard. But the question for Tu is whether the cool model of a humane person is sufficient to break through the common alienation from the self and fuel an existential commitment. This is a genuine question to which there is no ready answer. Perhaps Tu would say no more than Augustine about the leap of faith.

This chapter has been a study of a preeminent Confucian thinker of our time, the leading thinker of the Boston Confucians. It has pointed out the relevance of his thought for the Western problematic of existential alienation in the modern world and shown how Confucianism has a vast range of resources to bring to that issue. But at the same time, by indirection this chapter has indicated two points on which Boston Confucianism needs to look to Western resources. The first is the fruitfulness of connecting Confucian ritual theory with American pragmatism, a point made earlier but here integrated with Tu's theory of humaneness. The second is the more religious issue of conversion, or the overcoming of alienation so as to tap into the ontological foundations of love or humaneness. If one is seriously alienated, it is not clear that the commitment to overcome alienation is possible without some extra intervention.

Such interventions Christians call grace, and Tu declines to adopt a Christian notion of grace. To be sure, there are many such Christian conceptions, and they are not mutually consistent. But it would seem that this ancient Christian problematic is one that Tu's contemporary Confucianism needs to investigate. Or has his early existential thinking overstated the seriousness of alienation? Many contemporary Confucians would say so. But then, how would those bland sages account for the fact that people are so devoid of humaneness if principle indeed is an innate gift of heaven? Perhaps they would back away from that ontological formulation. But then they would have abandoned the ancient Confucian commitments to heaven and the dao in favor of what in our time is little more than developmental psychology. Tu Weiming is faithful to the strong roots of the Confucian classics.

The potential complementarity of Confucianism and Christianity on matters of the ontology of the moral person and the goodness of creation, appearances of alienation notwithstanding, is epitomized in Zhang Zai's famous "Western Inscription," which begins:

> Heaven is my father and Earth is my mother, and even such a small creature as I finds an intimate place in their midst. Therefore that which fills the universe I regard as my body and that which directs the universe I consider as my nature. All people are my brothers and sisters, and all things are my companions. The great ruler (the emperor) is the eldest son of my parents (Heaven and Earth), and the great ministers are his stewards. Respect the aged—this is the way to treat them as elders should be treated. Show deep love toward the orphaned and the weak— this is the way to treat them as the young should be treated. The sage identifies his character with that of those who are tired, infirm, crippled, or sick; those who have no brothers or children, wives or husbands, are all my brothers who are in distress and have no one to turn to. When the time comes, to keep himself from harm—this is the care of a son. To rejoice in Heaven and to have no anxiety—this is filial piety at its purest. (in Chan 1963, 497)

The religious question for our time is how to recover this filial piety.

6

Motif Analysis East and West

6.1. Motif Analysis

The argument so far in defense of Confucianism for contemporary philosophy has identified Confucianism through some core texts and motifs of thought, except in the instance of citing Tu Weiming's contemporary writings. The purpose of this chapter is to explain this process. At the outset, however, it can be contrasted with two other common strategies for relating to traditions and claiming a legacy.

The most common, of course, is to do a detailed study of a particular thinker or text. This is a standard dissertation form in American Universities in philosophy, religious studies, history, and area studies departments.[1] The limitation of this form is that it supposes the reader is attuned to the cultural and philosophic assumptions of the subject text or author. Perhaps this is not a problem when writing for a learned Chinese audience about a Chinese thinker, or for learned Western scholars about a thinker such as Aristotle or Kant. Even in these cases, however, contemporary scholarship has been warning that the background assumptions and social situational factors need to be made much more explicit than traditional intracultural scholarship has been wont to do. When the project is to introduce historical thinkers and texts into a conversation in which their contextual culture has not been well understood, the detailed textual study approach is difficult. Perhaps such a study can be embedded within a much larger contextualizing historical discussion. Still, it will be hard for the audience to read the subject thinker or text in context. Such detailed studies surely need to be done in order for the arguments for ideas to be appreciated and assessed. But they make most sense only after the conversation within which the

107

readers address the text has been thoroughly leavened with the appropriate cultural understanding.

The other common way to relate to a tradition and claim an intellectual legacy is through philosophy of culture, focusing not on specific thinkers as much as on the cultures that contextualize them, using specific thinkers to illustrate and justify cultural generalizations. Jaspers's theory of "axial age" cultures, discussed briefly in chapter 8, is a classic example. Charles Taylor's (1989) magnificent *Sources of the Self* is a recent treatment of Western culture. But in the field of East Asian–Western studies, the remarkable trilogy by Roger T. Ames and David L. Hall (1987, 1995, 1998) has set the standard for cultural studies. Whatever specific criticisms scholars might have of their cultural generalizations, the massive wealth of their arguments and the imaginative genius of their comparisons will insure that the field is permanently changed and enriched by their work. Yet for the specific purpose of relating to a tradition so as to have resources and a legacy for addressing our own philosophic issues, the approach through philosophy of culture has limitations, even when carried through with such excellence as Hall and Ames display. Two limitations are important to mention here, both of which are different from the criticism made in section 3.3 to the effect that Hall and Ames impose external categories on the subject matter, a criticism of their extreme Aristotelian realism.

The first limitation is that its generalizations always allow of exceptions and this gets out of control when the purpose is to examine the culture for its philosophic worth or merit. Profound philosophies of culture have the excellence of making massive and stable generalizations. To be sure, the generalizations allow of exceptions, but the exceptions by their very exceptional character prove the rule. In this, Hall and Ames surely are right that, by and large, Chinese culture is shaped by holistic, correlational thinking with a minimum of interference by transcendent deities or determination by separable abstract principles, and the West by contrast has a lot of those things. The critical response to their work, however, has been to hunt for transcendent things in China and to show that many of the West's deepest philosophic and religious traditions do not meet their criteria of transcendence (see section 8.1). This response does not necessarily mean that their generalizations are not preponderantly true and stable in that sense. It means rather that for the purposes of looking evaluatively at the philosophic cultures, the exceptions might be more interesting. Philosophic merit might lie precisely in the act of rubbing against the grain of dominant cultural assumptions. Confucius certainly thought he was doing that. And perhaps the interest of the Neo-Confucians in principle (*li*) was a reaction against correlational habits of mind (Hall and Ames do not deny the Neo-Confucian concern for transcendent principle). At any rate, however well-grounded and stable the generalizations of a philosophy of culture, they obscure and hide the things that do not fit, and those things then are revealed and reconcealed as exceptions to the rule rather than as options on their own terms. Contemporary philosophers attempting to relate positively to those exceptions are thus shoe-horned into the genre of rooting for the underdog.

The second limitation is that the approach through philosophy of culture renders impossible any living identification with the culture except for the most conservative thinkers who continue the trajectory of a tradition without change. A Western thinker who lacks heavy-duty transcendence does not count as an heir to Western culture, for Hall and Ames; but if that thinker believes in linear causation, he or she could not count as Chinese. This situation is disastrous for a project such as Boston Confucianism which explicitly wants to employ certain thought-forms of Confucianism to address philosophic issues raised by conditions of modernity reflecting a Western origin. As a living philosophic project, it no more affirms all Chinese or Confucian philosophy than a Western philosopher would affirm the whole of the Western tradition with all its contradictions. Moreover, internal to the development of Boston Confucianism is debate over how to evaluate the Confucian tradition, for instance, the place of Xunzi relative to Mencius as expressed in the arguments made here repeatedly about the importance of ritual. Generalizations about the philosophic cultures of East Asia and the West, if pressed as definitive of those traditions as Hall and Ames do, kill those cultures. They make them museum pieces, not living traditions that might be extended in any number of excellent ways. And insofar as those traditions as museum pieces have authority, they marginalize, delegitimate, and dismiss the thinkers who do not adopt them in their generalized entirety. The result is to make the philosophic cultures and living philosophy external to one another. Yet living thought ought to be able to learn from its traditions.

The alternative approach to traditions proposed here, for the purpose of keeping them alive for contemporary thought, is motif analysis. A motif is an idea enshrined in a core text that is subject to explicit or implicit commentary by subsequent thinkers in the tradition. The motifs as variously interpreted also shape social and cultural behavior. The core texts for Confucianism that were defended in section 1.1 as relevant for the project of Confucianism in the Western branch of global culture are the writings of Confucius, Mencius, Xunzi, *The Great Learning* and *The Doctrine of the Mean.*

The core texts and motifs of world cultures are all particular, with highly diverse origins. Their metaphoric structures are unique. Even if motifs from different cultures could be shown to "say the same thing," the ways they say it are different, and the metaphoric shapes of the motifs would have different effects. A tradition is a historical line in which core texts and their motifs are commented on, interpreted, and reconstructed for application to changed historical situations. A tradition divides into competing schools with differing interpretations, reconstructions, and cultural embodiments. Moreover, the lines between traditions are fluid and changing and can be understood only through historical observation, not appeals to cultural essences. For instance, all the schools of Hinduism are united by giving positive interpretations of the Vedas and Upanisads, however much those interpretations contradict one another; Buddhism is defined in part by rejecting the authority of those texts, even when giving detailed commentary on them. Song Neo-Confucianism gave what it took to be the true ancient interpretation of the Four Books partly under the stimulus of a critical evaluation of the core texts and motifs of Daoism and Buddhism. New Confucianism and its Boston branch reinterpret those texts, and reconstruct their practical implications, for the world of late-modern global culture.

To *understand* a tradition is to follow out its historical lines of treatment of the core texts and motifs in varying historical circumstances, including the interactions with other traditions and their motifs. Boundary markers for traditions are thus merely useful tools for locating major historical moments. Perhaps Buddhism and Hinduism should be lumped together as "the religious tradition of South Asia," and Confucianism, Daoism, and Chinese Buddhism as "Chinese religion." By following the method of motif analysis, there is no need at all for generalizations about Chinese or Western culture as if they were wholes with exceptions. Rather, one follows the continuities of the motifs through the discontinuities of their interpretations.

To *participate* in a tradition is, among other things, to engage its core texts and their motifs so as to reinterpret them for one's own situation and recontruct their practical implications. To participate in a tradition is also to engage and reinterpret the history of those motifs' various interpretations, and the contexts in which they were expressed in cultural forms. This means that participation involves a reinterpretation and perhaps reconstruction of large measures of a tradition. Because we live in a culturally pluralistic situation, one's participation in even one tradition alone requires some interpretation and recon-structive evaluation of other traditions. Boston Confucianism involves positive reconstructions of what is good and bad in both the Confu-cian and Western cultural traditions. Moreover, it is vulnerable in our situation by not having developed thorough and critical engagements of the core texts and motifs of South Asia, except through the influence of Chinese Buddhism on Neo-Confucianism. The remainder of this chapter illustrates some of the logic of motif analysis.

6.2. Comparison

Participation in more than one tradition, as has characterized most interesting moments of cultural history, requires comparison. Com-parative philosophy is not a single-project enterprise. Comparison has many forms, each with strengths and limitations, and all need to be pursued. A word needs to be said first about comparison itself, and then about that part of comparison to be pursued here, comparison within motif analysis. Concerning comparison itself, an hypothesis shall be sketched here that has been developed elaborately elsewhere.[2]

Ideas can be defined in terms of their network meaning within semiotic systems. European semiotics is principally concerned with the codification of signs or ideas within such systems. Comparison of ideas in different systems is extremely problematic, however, unless the systems can be subsumed under a larger system. One way of viewing Ames and Hall's claim that Chinese and Western cultures are incommensurable is to take them to be talking about their very differ-ent semiotic systems, which indeed are not mutually interdefinable.

Another way of comparing ideas, however, is to see how they are used by interpreters or interpreting communities to engage reality. Here the ideas are defined in part by their respective semiotic systems, but comparison looks at how they work at interpretive engagement. Suppose one person learns to drive a car with Chinese instructions and with Chinese roadsigns, and another learns to drive with English words and signs. It would not take long for them driving together in either Beijing or Boston to make quite effective comparisons and trans-fers. Because philosophic ideas and religious symbols are means of engaging reality, their comparison is of this latter sort. Knowledge of the respective semiotic systems is required, but that is not the focus of comparison when the issue is comparative interpretation.

The questions to ask about comparing ideas in their interpretive use are whether they are about the same thing and whether they interpret it in the same respect. Chances are that ideas in different cultures refer to overlapping referents, dividing up the field of the subject matter with slightly different distinctions, but common enough to get along pragmatically in the real world. Chances are also that the respect in which the objects are interpreted are pretty much the same but not identical; the respect in which cultures interpret an object is what it construes to be important in the object, and pragmatic consid-erations enforce considerable realism on what it is important to pick up. Nevertheless, the metaphoric shape of signs, particularly core texts or basic motifs, mean that the contours of both commonly interpreted objects and the respects in which they are interpreted overlap but are not just the same. Comparison needs to sort out these commonalities and differences. A category for comparison is the more or less same respect in which the more or less same object can be interpreted. Ideas that are not about at least connectable objects cannot be compared, and ideas that interpret the same object in different respects cannot be compared with regard to their claims, only with regard to the respects in which they might be taken to stand for their objects.[3]

A full-fledged category for comparing cultures necessarily has two logical levels. One can be defined with some abstract precision, but is logically vague with respect to how it can be instantiated in the cultures it is aimed to compare. Logical vagueness means that the abstract category can be specified by mutually incompatible subtheories or categories; for instance, the vague category of a "theory of the self" can be specified by both Freudian and behaviorist subtheories. The abstract level takes its rise from fairly formal theoretical considerations, say, as part of a larger explanatory or descriptive theory, and it is aimed to identify a common referent and a common respect in which signs on other levels might interpret the referent. The other level con-sists in the various cultural instantiations or specifications. They enter the comparison in the symbols of their respective cultures and at this beginning point are not easily comparable with one another, if at all. Then they are translated into the terms of the abstract, theoretically formed, level, and in those terms they can be compared. Perhaps it is better to say that the terms of the abstract level are supplemented, filled in, and made more specific by having to be developed to trans-late all the nuances of the different cultural specifications.

The result is a historically thick comparative category with at least four moments as reference points. One moment is the compara-tive category as an abstraction within some formal theoretical back-ground. Another moment is the agglomeration of candidates to be compared, each expressed in the terms of its own context and brought to the comparison with the intent of phenomenological faithfulness to its uniqueness and roles within its own culture. The first moment can be called formal and the second phenomenological, if those terms are not taken too strictly.

The third moment is the process of translating each of the cultural phenomena to be compared into the language of the abstract category, representing each as a specification of the otherwise vague formal comparative category. This requires the expansion of the vocabulary of the abstract category to be able to express the details of each of the elements to be compared. That is, the vague abstraction is elaborated to be specified by each of the phenomena. The process of translation is a dialectical moving back and forth between the formal concerns of the abstraction and the phenomenological concerns for the integrity of the things compared. The translation moment is then superceded by the theoretical moment in which it is possible to understand the phenomena in summary connected fashion. Within this moment it is possible to tell whether two phenomena are different expressions of the same thing, overlapping but also expressive of differences, in contradiction or complementarity to one another. It is also possible, once the complete specifying language has been developed, to see whether a given culture has nothing that might count as a specification of the vague category: all that culture's specifications in the language of the comparative category involve denial or negation. This is the logical status of Ames and Hall's claim about transcendence (see sections 3.3 and 8.1): however the category of transcendence might be specified by Western philosophies, perhaps by Indian ones, and perhaps even by later Chinese philosophies, Confucius' philosophy denies any specification of transcendence.

This articulation of the complexities of comparison is too brief and abstract itself; it will be illustrated in the remainder of this book. Comparison, like nearly all philosophy, is nearly always in the middle. The moments distinguished are usually all presupposed at any point in the comparative process. Even to imagine comparing two things is to have some respect of comparison in the back of one's mind; that "respect of comparison" is an abstract and vague formal notion, even if only presupposed and that unconsciously. To imagine that things need comparison is to recognize, with whatever distortion, that they are different and exist in different contexts, such as the Chinese versus Western philosophic traditions. To attempt to translate the phenomena into language that expresses the respect of comparison presupposes all the other background and detailed comparisons involved in translation; translation requires a considerable hermeneutical circle. To take a summary theoretical perspective, drawing out comparative conclusions, requires sensitivity to the changes that have been wrought in the phenomena, and in the abstractions of the vague comparative category, changes that are fallible and might require another critical visit. No comparative project is wholly new but descends as a focusing or generalizing or analogizing of other comparisons, some of which are called into question in the comparison at hand.

Only one form of comparative philosophy fitting within that hypothesis, motif analysis, will be pursued here. The comparative concern in motif analysis is less with whether the motifs and the commentaries upon them are true than with how the various cultures' deep associations and resonances are shaped by them. The importance of this form of comparative philosophy comes from the fact that different cultures can use quite analogous philosophic expressions that have vastly different resonances underneath. These differences can be discerned only when it is possible to identify the differences in the ancient and perhaps subliminal motifs that provide the semantic contexts for the different cultures' expressions.

This chapter will elaborate and illustrate this proposal for motif analysis in four steps. The first is to give some examples of basic motifs in West, South, and East Asian cultures, indicating how each set shapes the three different cultures. The second is to indicate briefly how these basic motifs were differently developed in their respective cultures. Neither of these discussions will display more comparison than is necessary to indicate motif differences. The third step is to treat motifs as inventions of imagination and to show how they rest upon even deeper elements of cultural imagination; basic motifs are not the most fundamental imaginative structures. The fourth is to spell out some of the ways in which cultures build upon and modify motifs in the course of their interactions with other cultures.

For all this, the discussions in this chapter will not plumb deeply into the question of the respects in which the illustrative motifs compare. Cultural cataloguers can map the different motifs. Comparison needs to go beyond that surface to identify the common topic that different motifs interpret in the same respect, the abstract level of the comparative category. There are several approaches to this.

One, the most congenial to metaphysicians, is the dialectical: the tracing of an abstract dialectical conception that can be shown to underlie several different motifs in whole or part. Chapter 7 shall present a dialectical theory of being and then argue that the West, South, and East Asian traditions each have motifs for expressing all or part of the one dialectic.

A second is to construe motifs as ways by which a tradition schematizes something unsayable into something sayable, for instance, expressing the infinite in finite ways, and then comparing traditions' different ways of schematizing the same thing. Chapter 8 will discuss various ways by which traditions express the presence of heaven or the divine in the soul.

A third approach is to contrast two or more traditions on a common topic, showing how they respond differentially to a specific problem in that topic. Chapter 9 will trace Western and Confucian treatments of the self and explore how different they are with regard to the problem of self-deception.

A fourth approach to comparing traditions' motifs is dialogue among the traditions, exploring differences and similarities with questions and answers. Chapter 10 thus compares Confucianism and Christianity on several topics defined by their respective motifs on which they are assumed to be in serious disagreement, continuing the dialogue begun with Tu Weiming in chapter 5.

All these approaches go beyond "mere description" to some kind of normative claims to reflect participation in the traditions. The approach through dialectic supposes that the dialectic itself has some validity. The approach through symbolic schematization supposes the validity of an appropriate theory of schematism and of the correct identification of what is being schematized beyond what is simply present in the various symbols. The approach through juxtaposition of traditions regarding a specific problem supposes that both can be represented as genuinely engaging the problem. The approach through dialogue needs to respect the intentionality of all the partners to get at the truth.

6.3. Ancient Cultural Motifs and Their Development

Because this is a programmatic discussion, it cannot attempt any serious catalogue of ancient motifs. Rather the nature of motifs will be illustrated with examples of some of the most important ones from West Asia, South Asia, and East Asia, construing European civilization with its American colonies to be an appendage of West Asia.[4] Although the motifs discussed are very important, there is an arbitrariness in their selection, and many of their important neighbors and connections are ignored. Section 6.5 will examine a different but related set of motifs.

Two West Asian motifs stand out as singularly important down to the present day, the creation of the physical cosmos and the character of norms for human life that has the form or forms of a decree. The creation motif has several classic forms, especially the two creation stories in *Genesis* 1 and 2 and the assumptions about creation throughout the *Psalms*. Included within the creation of the cosmos is the creation of the human sphere with its conventions, as when Adam named the animals, and sociality. Hesiod too expressed myths of creation not so different from the Babylonian and Sumerian pre-Yahwist background of the Bible (see Anderson 1984).

West Asian civilizations also have built upon the motif that norms for human life resemble decrees. This motif is joined to the first in the Biblical images of God creating by speaking and laying down the law at the covenant occasions. The Greek gods in Homer and Hesiod also rule by decree. Decrees have many forms. One is the enjoining of a project or goal, e.g., to get out of Egypt, or to stay away from idols of goddesses. Another is the enjoining of a pattern of life, as in the Torah or Quran or normative folkways of a people; such patterns might be developments of ritual life even more ancient than the motifs, but they are often expressed as a code of laws or commandments. Yet another form of a decree is the enjoining of the development of a certain kind of character, "e.g., be loving, merciful, sophisticated, and steadfast. Goals, policies, codes, and virtues are typical Western forms of norms, all deriving from, or at least receiving reinforcement from, the motif of the kingly or divine decree.

The creation and decree motifs in West Asia together support a complex of motifs about the human condition that stress the appropriateness of celebratory thanksgiving for contingent existence and a particularly moral tilt to conceptions of human excellence and achievement.

South Asian civilizations share much with the West Asian because of some overlapping Aryan roots and extensive trade from very early times. Thus there are Vedic hymns and myths of the creation of the cosmos and also of kingly rule. But there are also important South Asian motifs of what can be called the True Self and of what might be called Immediate Identity. The motif of the True Self supposes a context in which people are tempted by some false self or selves, and possibly the most important expression of this motif is in the Samkhya sutras. According to the Samkhya philosophy, nature (*prakriti*) consists of three interweaving processes, an active hot principle (*rajas*), a slothful ballast principle (*tamas*), and a principle of subtle interpenetration and harmonization (*sattva*). But the True Self is a kind of pure consciousness (*purusha*), a pure witness to nature's doings. The temptation of most people is to allow the self to identify with part of nature, for instance, one's body or one's fortunes. The True Self is discovered through abstraction from attached involvements and the reestablishment of the consciousness as unmoved witness. This True Self motif is also expressed in the Upaniṣadic principle that atman (self) is Brahman and the Buddhist contention that liberation lies in nonattachment. Of course, there are many South Asian alternatives to the metaphysics in the Samkhya expression, often rejecting its strict dualism. Buddhism in most forms even goes so far as to deny the reality of the True Self; liberation involves the realization that there is no self to be bound to suffering. But the motif theme of the True Self remains even in Buddhism.

"Immediate identity" is not a very clear name for a motif, but it refers, for instance, to the statement of Krishna in the *Bhagavad-Gita* (2.47), "To action alone hast thou a right and never at all to its fruits; let not the fruits of action be thy motive" (in Radhakrishnan and Moore 1957, 110). Krishna's point for Arjuna is that his identity and worth consists in the accomplished and artful performance of his duty, irrespective of motive or consequences. There are special complications of this in the *Gita*, but the core of the motif is also expressed in the sense that the world is God's play, with no meaning outside that, and also in the Buddhist notion of *suchness*: things are merely such as they are. This motif is allied to that of the True Self, but lacks the latter's fixation on consciousness.

Together, the motifs of the True Self and Immediate Identity fund a larger cultural interpretation of the human condition as in need of liberation from ignorance by enlightenment. The ignorance has to do both with improper attachments of consciousness and with the wrong orientation of action. Enlightenment is described many ways and approached with diverse motifs.

The East Asian motifs to be lifted up here are the yin-yang cosmology and the Human Completion of Nature. The yin-yang cosmology is a strain in Chinese civilization that goes back far beyond any classic motif expression. Yet it is pervasively expressed in all the ancient philosophies of the Warring States period (Confucian and Daoist, as well as Moist, Logical, Legalist), the naturalistic schools, and most especially in the *Yijing*. The Yin-Yang school associated with Cou Yen (305 to 240 BCE) is by no means the first expression of the motif. Yang is activity or extension, and yin is the return to relaxation and home, and these traits are analogized across a wide variety of phenomena. The point to stress in the motif is that yin and yang are balancing elements with a problematic harmony. Too much yang and you can't go home again, like an army cut off from its base of supply or a person losing family because of competitiveness. Too much yin and nothing happens, with everything falling apart for want of the harmonizing activity of yang.

The motif of the Human Completion of Nature has two ways of being put, like yin and yang. The Daoists, for instance, in the *Daodejing* and the *Zuangzi*, put it the yin way, saying that true human life is as natural as possible with the least artificial interference from conventions and rituals: the attempt to supplement nature by human invention only renders human beings unnatural. The Confucians put it the yang way, for instance, in *The Analects* and *The Xunzi*, saying that what heaven and earth give human nature is merely biological and psychological potentials. In order for human nature to fulfill its own potential, it needs conventions and rituals.

The Yin-Yang and Human Completion of Nature motifs in East Asia combine to give civilizational importance to the claim that the human condition is to be obligated to attain attunement with the dao, both conforming to it and fulfilling it. East Asian civilization lacks the strong emphasis of West and South Asia on creation of the world. It shares with both a variety of expressions of the motif of norms by decree, in its references to the mandate of heaven and the ritual directives of the emperors. But it does not share with the West the sense that the decreed norms are external to people's inner nature and tendency; rather, they are to be attained by coming to terms with one's inner dao. East Asian civilizations share with the South Asian the thematic motifs that nature is composed of interweaving processes rather than integral things or substances; but the East Asian motifs rarely take nature's processes to be alien to the True Self or illusory, rather, as the self's inmost constituents.

By "motif" is meant an ancient idea, practice, or event that has a classical verbal articulation. The motif is the idea as articulated. A proper exposition of the points above should have quoted the creation stories from *Genesis*, the relevant portions of the *Bhagavad-Gita, Zhuangzi,* and *Xunzi*. For it is the texts themselves that are the subject of subsequent commentary and development. Furthermore, it is the textual expressions themselves that provide what is often most interesting and distinct about the motifs. For instance, the decrees of the depersonalized mandate of heaven are far removed from the decrees of jealous, loving Yahweh.

That ancient motifs are subject to subsequent commentaries is a simple and obvious point. The *Genesis* creation stories, especially the first, were embellished in the Christian New Testament in the prologue to *The Gospel of John,* and also in the baptism scenes for Jesus in all the gospels in which the water, spirit, and word conspire to create a new being. The Creation motif objectified the physical cosmos and contributed to the importance of "objective" science in the West. The motif of Norms as Decrees in its various expressions affected the development of Western judicial systems. Insofar as the decreeing king relates to others as citizens of his domain, human equality of citizens before the king's law comes to be prized. The expressions of decree as divinely ordained covenant flowered into social contract theory.

In South Asia the ancient motifs of the True Self and Immediate Identity were elaborated in a host of different ways. Vedanta in its nondualist and dualist versions is an obvious development of the True Self theme, and in fact its philosophic form consists in commentaries on rituals that themselves are supposed to embody the realization of the True Self. As mentioned, one of the ways in which Buddhism relates to the True Self motif is by denying the reality of the self in its doctrine of the "no-self," all the while advocating a practice of nonattachment very like that advocated in other South Asian traditions for realizing the reality of atman in Brahman. The Immediate Identity motif has been elaborated in interestingly diverse ways in subsequent theories of karma and reincarnation, in theories of action and duty, and in defenses of the caste system. It has had enormous theological significance in Ramanuja's theory of the world as the body of God.

In East Asia the Yin-Yang motifs have been carried down to and reinterpreted by contemporary thinkers, along with the Human Completion of Nature motif, through Daoist evolution into philosophy of nature and spirituality and through Confucian evolution in responses to Daoism and Buddhism into the highly personal project of becoming a sage in Neo-Confucianism. Chinese Marxism is such a peculiar thing to the Western mind, in part, because it has a yin-yang sense of material nature and a ritualized sense of the authority of the proletariat and its leaders.

In all these civilizations the interesting point in the tracing of motifs is the diversity of ways in which they are developed and responded to. Comparative philosophy can get behind apparent similarities and differences of propositional expressions by studying how thinkers and schools differentially react to the motifs. Furthermore, tracing the motifs through history gives a longitudinal density to our understanding of the significance of any given philosopher's language. We can apprehend it in terms of the dialectic of its inheritance of the motifs.

Lying behind this advocacy of attention to the history of motifs is a special claim about philosophic ideas as symbols. Contrary to what Cartesians vainly might have hoped, philosophic ideas are not structured by definitions but by complex processes of highlighting rules for integrating manifolds of meaning, as Kant would say, all set within a presupposed and probably fluid semantic context or background of meaningful ideas and practices. So long as philosophers come from the same community, sharing a common context, the content of that background can remain unexpressed and unconscious. The explicit rule-like characters of the ideas can be treated as if they were not mere shorthand for the culturally complex context-focus ensemble in which the philosophic idea or assertions consists. But when philosophy is dialogical, the contextual suppositions are essential parts of the ideas at stake. In reality, every philosophical idea is embedded in a dense symbol system with a history that can be taken for granted by thinkers who inherit it but that must be learned with careful differentiation by those who lack that heritage.

Furthermore, despite the pretensions of clarity and univocity in most philosophic traditions of West and South Asia, it is very hard to develop any seriously important ideas without compositing and compacting many symbol systems overlain on one another. Hegel's idea of the human self, for instance, draws upon a strain of development of the person created in the image of God, with appropriate symbol systems for that, and on combinations of strains of the self as normed by the ethical inspirations of Israel, Greece, the Celts, and the Germans. The self for Hegel arises out of symbol systems for the attainment of truth and error, for definition through families and the distinctions of private and public life, and for the obligations of political, religious, and cultural involvements. Dozens of symbol systems provide the background for Hegel's views, some of them rationally ordered to one another but many simply overlaid. The power of a philosophic idea in its concrete use is fed often as much by the contrasts and comminglings of different symbol systems in its contextual background as by clarity of the focused expressions of its rule-character. The bad price paid for seeming clarity in our time has often been loss of profundity; this is not because conceptual confusion gives a false impression of profundity but because profundity lies in the relevant, resonating background of the ideas, not only in their rule-like structures.

Tracing the history of motifs is thus a crucial ingredient for appreciating the power in alien philosophic ideas. We can feel the resonant power in many of our own ideas, even when we are committed to clarifying them into harmless abstractions. But the strange ideas of others seem empty, or worse, ready to be grafted onto our own heritage of motifs that might give them genuinely false profundity.

Of course, philosophy grows through dialogue, and different civilized heritages come to be shared. Furthermore, ideas can be transported from one civilizational set of symbols to another. But that growth and transportation are very dense processes, with changes resonating through many shifts in deep structure. Innocent of the traditions of ancient motifs, philosophical dialogue can only be superficial. The motifs mentioned here are only some of the most obvious shapers of civilizations of their sort.

6.4. Relations of Motifs to Deeper Imaginative Artifacts

Ancient motifs of civilization are only one kind of imaginative structure of interest to comparative philosophy. They are neither the most basic nor most ancient imaginative structures. Motifs of the kind mentioned here all arose during the axial age. That was a time when, as Ray L. Hart (1968) has shown, elementary ideas, practices, and events shaped the character of being human by attaining to verbal, indeed, soon literary, articulation. The motifs are important for how, in their verbal articulateness, in their literary expression, they shape civilizations. There are four levels of imagination *more basic* than motifs.

The first level is elementary space-time imagination. As Kant argued in one way and Whitehead in another more thorough way, human beings transmute the impingements of their environment and bodies into an experiential array with space-time characteristics.[5] For Kant, space and time are themselves forms of intuition, but spatio-temporal experience is constructed by several important synthesizing activities of the imagination. Probably all mammalian brains have a stratum of common space-time imaginative structure; for instance, unlike reptiles and amphibians they can mentally rotate objects in order to imagine a backside.

Human beings doubtless have imaginative structures sensitive to the specific characteristics of the human body, its reach, vision, hearing, and the field of pragmatically important environmental features. There may also be specifications of the spatiotemporal imaginative field that come from universal elements of sociality, of sexual attractions, parenting, cooperative defense, and food gathering. But cultures differ in these matters and at some levels they would differ in space-time imagination according to cultural differences. Peoples who live in buildings with right angles have a "carpentered" environment, in contrast to peoples whose dwellings are domes or tents (Heelan 1983). Motifs in the sense discussed here are imaginative structures that presuppose more elementary space-time imaginative structures. Some of the differences between philosophic cultures might arise at that more basic space-time imaginative level.

The second level, more elementary than the motifs but building upon space-time imagination, are archetypal imaginative structures of the sort that C. G. Jung and James Hillman have studied. Although they have made empirical claims that are not universally accepted, it is at least plausible that there are personified structures of fundamental human stances toward the world, possibly multiply—involved in any given individual. Whether genetically inherited or acquired through largely common elements of sociality, it makes sense that conditions of life span, of action and passion, of fortune and opportunity, of order and disorder, would evolve structures of imagination that are archetypal, or at least very general. Such structures would be more basic that the motifs of interest here and should be subject to empirical analysis. Whether these are common to all cultures or are diversified, such structures might lie behind the motifs and be of interest in setting philosophical comparisons.

The third level, perhaps more particular than archetypes but more basic than the motifs are pre-axial age mythic structures. Myths at this imaginative level have been studied by anthropologists and phenomenologists of religion such as Eliade. Although the myths lying at the primitive levels of various societies differ in content, they seem to have some common features. For instance, they seem to imagine the world as deeply organic, with many kinds of interpenetrating connections. The distinctions between self and world or self and other selves are not made sharply as they are at levels of culture affected by the civilizations of the axial age. Connections are not causal in the sense of Western scientific causation, or even of South Asian interweavings of processes or East Asian yin-yang interactions; rather, the connections are more like the consequences of concordance and discordance imagined in ritual performance with totemic and magical patterns. Mythic symbols are imagined to have nonsymbolic empirical consequences. This mythic matrix might lie deep in the psyche of every individual, overlaid but not erased by higher orders of causal understanding. Sophisticated civilizations might overlie such a mythic preconscious. Some have speculated that certain forms of schizophrenia are breakdowns of the higher patterns of connection and a return to behavior and consciousness within the mythic matrix. Whatever the empirical structure of the mythic matrix, it builds upon and presupposes space-time imaginative structures and perhaps also fundamental archetypes. The ancient motifs of civilizations overlie it.

There is a fourth level of premotif imaginative structure that needs to be specified as building upon the first three levels, namely, the content and practice of what the Confucians call ritual, in the sense of the conventions that are learned and rehearsed so as to make possible the playing of human roles in society. Although focus on the importance of rituals themselves is a Confucian motif, all societies have such rituals, even when not elevated to conscious importance. These ritual conventions lie on a spectrum running from physiological determinants through religious and court rituals (Neville 1995, chapter 7). A brief exposition of some of the main nodes of this spectrum will help set the motifs in context and add to the earlier discussions of ritual.

Human beings are born with underdetermined physiological capacities, as noted earlier. They can move their limbs, use their eyes, and eat, in motions crossing a vast domain of potential variation. But a given human being has to learn to walk at least one consistent way, and these ways are learned. The Chinese tend to walk with feet pointed straight ahead and moving the knees before the feet; exaggerated forms of this look to Westerners like shuffling. Westerners, by contrast, angle their feet out and fling their feet forward; exaggerated forms of this look to Chinese like the goose step. Westerners bend first at the hip, Chinese first at the waist. The cultural ways of determining physiologically underdetermined movements are not necessarily significant, only culturally specific. Without some cultural specificity people would move randomly and hence hardly at all.

The next node on the ritual spectrum is when these learned motions take on significance, that is, coded meanings in a cultural semiotic system. One way of walking can be assertive, another deferential, in one system, and those ways of walking can mean just the opposite in another system. Forms of eye contact that are respectful in one culture are brazen in another. Much cultural confusion comes from misreading significant body language.

Language itself and codes of gestures used for intentional communication are yet another node on the spectrum. Although language perhaps cannot be understood exhaustively as ritual performance, much of it can be understood that way. Language provides forms for doing what one intends. The forms themselves are underdetermined and have to be specifically performed with attention and wit. Performance needs to be learned and practiced; some people speak well and others poorly. Other considerations determine what to say and what forms to use, but the semiotic forms themselves are what make possible not only communication but all forms of cooperative, role-playing social life.

Social life itself is made possible by an even more determined element on the ritual spectrum, namely, role manners. Manners serve to integrate roles and to give people places in complex systems. They display authority and competences. Furthermore, their exercise is what gives nuance to complicated situations and allows people to respond with sensitivity and deference to the matters and persons at hand.

In addition to role manners there are etiquette manners. Every society has complex manners for greeting and departing, for conducting a communal meal, for doing business. Without ritualized manners of this sort, social interactions would have to be figured out from scratch each time, and there would rarely be enough time ever to figure out even elementary social commerce. Most people have experienced situations of meeting strangers when there is no known etiquette to handle what needs to be done. People who do know etiquette for other situations are often embarrassed at their lack of etiquette in the instance.

Social life is not a sequence of ritual forms on this spectrum but a compacted nest of them. Some rituals, particularly religious and court rituals, are aimed to polish, integrate, and perfect the other levels of ritual. Often they are structured with a transcendent reference to authority. These high-level explicit rituals are intended to epitomize and perfect ritual behavior. No rituals, even if well-practiced, substitute for the decisions of life, or even for the process of practicing them and becoming adept at adapting to the uniqueness of each situation. Nevertheless, the habitual practice of religious and court rituals is thought to effect a harmonization of all the other dimensions of ritual life. This is not so much an organization according to principle as it is a modeling of an ideal that draws its power from overlaid ritual levels.

The four levels of imaginative formation mentioned here as prior to or more primitive than motifs set a context of cultural life in which the motifs might make sense. Let us now consider layers of imaginative construction that build upon the motifs, thus further contextualizing them.

6.5. Motifs and Their Sequelae

The ancient motifs of the West, South, and East Asian civilizations took textual shape during the axial age. The ideas doubtless had earlier antecedents; the yin-yang ideas and myths of the creation of the cosmos date from millennia before the axial age. But it was during that period, from the seventh through the third centuries BCE that the classic verbal statements were articulated to which subsequent ages related.

Even within the axial age there was considerable development of the motifs. For instance, the creation myths in *Genesis* 1 and 2 are now in the form they received in the sixth century at the hands of the postexilic editors. But they are highly polished pieces and surely existed in various forms earlier. In their final editing, they were joined together, that is, thought of as two related creation stories. Yet they are clearly inconsistent, at least on the narrative level, which means presumably that they were construed as each having a point and also as balancing one another. Similarly, the Daoist and Confucianist expressions of the Yin-Yang and problematic Human Completion of Nature motifs are not easily made consistent. Sometimes in Chinese history, as for instance in the writings of Wang Bi in the early Wei-Chin period, these were mixed and mined for fruitful development. Other times, as in the rise of Neo-Confucianism in the Song, their differences were exaggerated or borrowed with distortions. But over time, the shifting interactions with the other have become integral to Daoism and Confucianism in any form.

The point is that civilizations do not keep their classic motifs pure but mix them with one another, not only in thinkers and commentators but in the interactions of their practical consequences. Or more accurately, the different motifs differentially affect critical culture-forming events and tasks, such as a migration or the fending off of invaders, the development of a monarchy or a different form of government, the incorporation of a new people into the nation, the establishment of institutions for education and the management of famine and disaster, the development of relations with neighboring peoples, and so forth. The adventures of the motifs interact with one another as they are differentially effective in shaping cultures' responses to history.

Jaroslav Krejci (1993) has argued that there are five basic paradigms of civilizational conceptions, rather like the background concepts of motifs, although not tied to classic expressions. His approach combines reference to motif ideas with the sort of generalization characteristic of philosophy of culture; though his approach shares the limitations of philosophy of culture for those interested in participation in traditions, his analysis illustrates the ways by which motifs interact. He cites the god-centered view of cuneiscript Mesopotamia, the death-centered view of Pharaonic Egypt, the human-centered view of classical Greece, the soul-centered view of India, and the rule-centered view of China. The axial-age development of these paradigms concerns their interactions. Ancient theocentrism related to the human sphere in the motifs of covenant in Judaism and in the battles over free choice in Zoroastrianism; Christianity developed both of these ideas in the motifs of the Son of God and then of a kind of ecclesiocentrism that tends to domesticate God in the church. Theocentrism encounters psychocentrism in classical gnosticism, in Mahayana Buddhism, and in the interactions of Chinese Buddhism and Daoism. Islam reinforces theocentrism but with an interpretation that theonomously defines a whole culture and mystical gnosticism. Krejci notes the integration of theocentrism and rule-centeredness, which he calls Cratocentrism, in Rome and the putative heirs of Rome. He also notes the reinterpretations and reinvigoration of earlier classical expressions in periodic revivals and renaissances. While his approach might be too simple and schematic, it helps underscore how the continually shifting patterns of civilization are, in considerable measure, reworkings of ancient motifs and their interactions.

In Western civilization, the creation motif has fostered a very strong sense for the world as a whole item that might be understood by science; the metaphysical conflict between materialism and idealism is not important here. In our century, Wittgenstein's claim that the world is all that is the case, Heidegger's question of Being, and Whitehead's cosmology, all suppose the cosmos to be a whole thing, which derives from the motif of its being something made: there is a difference between its existence and nonexistence, between reality and nothingness. This distinction is puzzling to the East and South Asian cultures for which the world is not totalized enough to have an ontological contrast. Totalization in this sense arises out of the resonances of the act or nonact of a creative will.

What the modern West has largely rejected in the creation motif, however, is the sensibility of an individual creator-God with a personal will. Thus for some late-modern Westerners the world is just there as a brute and alien fact. For others, the creator-God is reconstrued as a nonpersonal and nonindividual ground of being, to use Tillich's term, which leads to a creation-transcending mysticism. Those Westerners who do cling to a relatively nonmetaphorical belief in a personal God have difficulty relating this God to the impersonality of the created world, and often come to grief on issues of theodicy. The loss of the personal character of God has been devastating for the other West Asian motif mentioned, the sense that norms are decrees. Few people now believe there is a decreer, except perhaps a wholly arbitrary one. Hence, there is a great temptation to let norms slip into relativism. Philosophers such as Whitehead and Dewey who do develop an objectivist ground for norms do so by means of aesthetic motifs more closely allied to East Asia than by means of decree models.

The contemporary philosophic situation in East and South Asia is deeply affected by the spread of Western philosophy with Western imperialism. Indian philosophy was pushed into deep decline by the victories of the English and French in the eighteenth century. It was revived by a nationalist movement in the nineteenth and twentieth centuries, but that movement was led mainly by people such as Aurobindo, Gandhi, and Radhakrishnan who were educated according to the European system. East Asian philosophy encountered Western philosophy seriously in the nineteenth century through the allures of Western technology. Then China forcibly adopted Western Marxism in our own time. Currently there are revivals of older East and South Asian philosophies, with a strong sense of overcoming the effects of Western imperialism. But often these revivals are led by thinkers living outside East and South Asia who themselves, like Cheng Chungying, are deeply steeped in Western philosophy.

What is needful to know is how the traditions are interestingly different, how they compare with respect to fundamentally different ways of imaging the world, and how those images can be assessed critically. Without this it is impossible for any of us to appropriate the human heritages with responsibility and sophistication. No Western philosopher has to remain only a Western philosopher after coming to terms with philosophies from other civilizations.

The argument here has been a programmatic one, commending the comparative study of motifs in civilizations as part of comparative philosophy. This program itself rests on two sets of other philosophic claims that have been mentioned but not much developed. One set has to do with the nature of public philosophic discourse. Philosophy whose public is one tradition alone, such as the Western, is not really public in today's pluralistic culture but rather private and in-house. Following from this argument for philosophic publicity is the importance of sharing the contexts of the philosophic ideas of philosophers from cultures other than one's native home. It is not possible to interpret another philosopher without a grasp of the relevant background culture. There are many elements in the knowledge of knowing other cultures, and one of these is knowing how the various cultures compare. There are many kinds of comparison, and the one described and advocated here is comparison with respect to the ways cultures are shaped historically by ancient motifs.

The other set of philosophical theses at work here has to do with the nature of philosophical ideas. As Kant argued, ideas at one level are rules for integrating a manifold of other ideas or perceptions. The rule-like part of ideas can be defined in explicit discourse. But on other levels ideas are focal points against a background of other cultural elements, including the history of the development of the idea in relation to other ideas. To understand, much less judge, an idea requires knowing also its cultural background with the resonances that give it power.

A shifting, pluralistic cultural situation such as our own does not allow for easy focus on definitions. The essential connections of ideas with their cultural resonances cannot be assumed and is problematic. Philosophy in these times becomes shallow and culturally irrelevant if it insists on treating ideas as if their cultural backgrounds were understood and shared. Philosophy in our culturally pluralistic form must be far more lightfooted about moving through ideas with cultural assumptions. Perhaps it would be a good policy to treat every idea as something foreign and in the process of being transported to a new culture. Even the old ideas of our own putatively native traditions should be looked at as if they were something foreign, with their cultural assumptions newly made explicit in comparison with alternative cultural assumptions.

Needless to say, the project of Boston Confucianism supposes a background of comparative philosophy (and religious ideas) that allows for meaningful consideration of what texts are portable and relevant for contemporary problems. Moreover, it supposes some understanding of how the tradition itself is to be identified and related comparatively to the identities of other traditions, especially those of the West. This chapter has addressed directly the background issues taken for granted in chapter 1 and subsequent discussions.

7

Motifs of Being

7.1. The Trouble with Being

If Confucianism is to enter the world philosophic conversation, it needs to address questions that preoccupy that conversation even if they have not been its own explicit preoccupations. The argument was made in section 4.4 and elsewhere that Confucianism needs to address fundamental Western metaphysical questions such as the nature of being and value. The argument there was that pervasive moral issues such as the impact of science and technology on society, democracy and pluralism, and concerns for ecology require the addressing of those fundamental metaphysical topics. Certainly in the West such twentieth-century giants as Whitehead, Heidegger, and Dewey have addressed those topics for reason of their moral and cultural urgency. The Kyoto School of Buddhist philosophy has taken up those issues with explicit directness. But Confucianism is slow in this regard, despite the best efforts of metaphysicians such as Cheng Chungying.

Of course, those are Western topics—being, value, truth, and the rest. Ames and Hall (1998) would say they cannot be engaged out of the resources of the Confucian tradition. Yet although the rhetoric with which the issues have been raised here is Western, the problems and traditions' intellectual responses are not. The heart of the argument is that those problems are real and that all cultures have to face up to what is real, differing in their responses by differences among their basic motifs and other aspects of their imagination. This chapter will concentrate on the problem of being.

In cross-cultural perspective, the dialectic of being is in double trouble. We all know the one trouble that comes from the fact that being is not an object, or a genus, or a structure, or anything else within the world that characterizes beings. Because of this, philosophers have to approach being dialectically. There are many forms of dialectic, of which Plato's and Hegel's are perhaps the best known and William Desmond's one of the newest (Desmond 1987, 1990, 1995). They all have in common the need to start somewhere else and sidle up to a discussion of being to say things indirectly that cannot be said directly. The terms with which a dialectical argument begins themselves change in meaning, interpretation, and often reference, as the argument unfolds.[1] At the beginning, being looks like one thing, at the end another, and *beginning* and *ending* are relative terms. This is enough trouble to exasperate many philosophers about the very possibility of a dialectic of being.

This point can be stated more formally with a distinction between two terms of art. If we call the dialectic of being ontology, we should call the basic conception of the world from which the dialectic starts metaphysics. By metaphysics is meant the study of the defining characters of reality, of what it means to be determinate at all, to be something. Metaphysics is the study of what makes beings beings. Ontology as the dialectic of being starts from, or develops as its context, a metaphysical understanding of things and moves to an understanding of being (Neville 1968). But there are many different kinds of metaphysical systems, principles, and metaphors.[2]

The second trouble with the dialectic of being in cross-cultural perspective is now in view. The great philosophic cultures of the world, in East Asia, South Asia, and West Asia with its European appendage and American colonies, have radically different metaphysical motifs. Their metaphysical starting points are so different that we have to admit that the phrase, "dialectic of being," might have no significance at all outside the West. In the West, the diversity of metaphysical systems is largely a family matter. The systems were developed in conversation with one another and in critical reconstructive readings of earlier stages of intellectual history. But there is no comparable engagement across the world's philosophic cultures. From the fundamental motifs in ancient texts, on which nearly everyone in the respective different traditions comments, down to contemporary philosophers in those traditions, there is diversity to the point of incommensurateness. Even a little comparative philosophy makes plain the fact that the basic imagistic and conceptual structures with which a culture takes up and apprehends the world, are conventions and that the conventions of different cultures are different. Sometimes Western philosophers are shocked to discover that South and East Asian philosophers deal with many of the main problems of Western philosophy in terms and intellectual strategies radically different from the way Westerners think they *see* the world to be. We then realize that Western intellectual perceptions are conventions too, not fundamental intuitions but representations resident in conventional symbol systems. Perhaps the ultimately orienting notions in East and South Asian cultures are not those having to do with being at all, but with something else. Some thinkers respond to this situation with relativism, or with default nominalism (Hall 1994), both celebrating each culture in its own terms with a careful avoidance of comparison that might distort by interpreting one culture in terms of another. For a living philosophy to participate in two or more traditions, however, requires a contrary response.

The argument here is to defend two hypotheses. The first is that the great cultural-orienting notions, conventional though they are, nevertheless constitute ways by which people in those cultures engage reality. Just as limited signs within a cultural system are representations by means of which people engage nature and one another, so the cultural systems as large, roughly organized complexes, are representations for fundamental metaphysical engagement with reality. Without representations, we cannot engage.

The second hypothesis is that there is something like the dialectic of being in South and East Asian philosophies as well as in the West, despite the differences in conventional symbols. Indeed, all the great philosophic cultures are intensely diverse internally and each contains representatives of something like the main kinds of positions to be found in the others. This is not to say that there is a cross-cultural range of identical positions, any more than Duns Scotus and David Weissman are realists in the exact same sense, or that Ockham and David Hall are the exact same kind of nominalists. The second hypothesis will be defended by first reviewing the treatment of the question of being in Western philosophy, then presenting a thesis about the dialectic of being itself, as derived from the West and purified abstractly, and finally showing that this dialectic is expressed in crucial motifs from South and East Asia.

7.2. *Philosophy as Engagement*

The first hypothesis is that philosophic cultural conventions are ways of engaging reality. The hypothesis is important because of the very common mistake of inferring that there is no reference to reality beyond the semiotic system of signs. The mistake is made when people infer that just because all the objects referred to by signs themselves can be represented by other signs within the semiotic system, external reference is unnecessary. Signs are indeed defined within a semiotic system. Internal to the semiotic system, some other signs function as their referents and yet other signs interpret what they mean about their referents. Scholars can study the possible interpretations that can be made within the signs of a system, specifying the extensions of signs to possible referents and interpretants within the semiotic code. Not only linguistic systems but systems of artistic, musical, architectural, and other symbols can be analyzed and decoded. Perhaps we can even speak of whole cultures as having a system of conventional symbols, although the great cultures of West, South, and East Asia each entertain and are formed by varieties of loosely connected and sometimes discordant symbol systems. The philosophic conventions of the great cultures are assemblages, or hodgepodges, or families, of systems of philosophic categories and metaphors. Some contemporary thinkers believe that all we can do is to explore those systems and their rough connections. They believe that scholarly understanding is locked inside coded semiotic systems. To the extent that one system cannot responsibly be translated into another semiotic system, they draw the relativistic conclusion that the cultural codes are self-contained. Cultural codes might be compared in roughly general ways, according to differing tendencies, but not engaged with one another because that would threaten the integrity of the historically different conventional codes. When people say that "everything is a text," this is often the reason (Derrida 1976). This position is the *extensionalist fallacy* because it confuses the reality of interpretation with the extensional code of signs whose structure shapes interpretation (Neville 1996, chapter 2).

The truth is that the *intention* of interpretation is to use the *extensional* structure of signs to engage reality which might not be part of the sign system. From founding myths to the latest science and the daily news, a culture orients itself to reality by means of its assemblages of semiotic systems, which are taken to be icons of reality: reality is enough *like* the assertive structure of the cultural symbols as coded that those symbols guide engagement and are corrected through engagement's gives and takes.

The great cultures of the world, by which millions of people engage reality, are extraordinarily flexible in allowing reality to correct and realign the various sign systems they contain. Cultures constantly grow and contract, adapt to new circumstances, and advance strategies to ward off circumstances that would devalue something important in the culture. Far from cultures being comprehensive enclosed sign systems, they are dynamic interactions of local sign systems with one another as the realities of natural and social history move on. The cultures of West, South, and East Asia have different ancient motifs, but those motifs have been developed in countless ways since the ancient days, ways hardly consistent with one another but offering some purchase on engaging a part of reality that could not be engaged without the specific modification of the motifs as signs.

A technical way of making this point is to say that, in an interpretation, a sign has both extensional and intentional referents. The extensional referents are other signs within the sign system that are coded to be referred to by the meaning sign, and they help give the signs definite shape. The intentional referents are the real objects referred to by the interpreter with the meaning sign; the extensional referents ordinarily name the intentional referents. Thus the intentional interpretation does not use the sign by itself to interpret the reality but rather the sign in its symbolic code. Intentional interpretation takes reality to be rather like the structure of the code as such. The code as a symbol system is taken to be a partial icon of reality. But the iconic structure is only partial because we know that reality constantly corrects our sign systems.

We cannot engage things unless we have signs by which they can be interpreted in some respect. Cultures develop signs and sign systems so as to be able to engage things, and they change and improve their signs and sign systems in order better to engage things, with more nuance, more discrimination of the important from the trivial, more range and depth.

The question of the second hypothesis can now be framed. Do the philosophic cultures of East and South Asia have signs or systems of signs for engaging what the West engages with the signs of the dialectic of being? This question can be answered only partly and suggestively in the compass of a brief chapter. The parts to be addressed here are the following. First, the historical development of the dialectic of being in the West will be sketched. Then, in some detail, the outlines of a defensible statement of the dialectic of being will be argued, followed by some brief indications of some parallels in Indian philosophy which share the motifs of Indo-European culture with the West. Finally and at greater length, parallels in Chinese thought, which is quite different in many respects from Western, will be developed as bearing upon the project of Boston Confucianism.

7.3. Western Motifs for Being

The ancient motifs for the dialectic of being in the West came mainly from two sources, the Greek philosophic tradition and the Hebrew religious and theological traditions. There have been a vast number of different readings of those traditions and their interconnection, including some that take them to be hostile to one another. The reading which follows is selective as part of a normative reconstruction both of Christianity and Boston Confucianism. Its selectivity does not imply that it is indefensible, only reflective of a perspective that is being defended as a viable hypothesis.

The Greek contribution, beginning with the Pre-Socratics, was to associate the dialectic of being with the problem of the one and the many, with the problem of time and eternity, and with the problem of the relation of proximate causes to the conditions for causation (see, e.g., Brumbaugh 1961). But Heidegger was right about the Greek motifs: as soon as they got started on the dialectic of being, they tended to ruin it with deflections to questions of what things are or, in reaction, to a brute *that* contrasted with *what* (Heidegger 1959; Rosen 1993).

The Hebrew motifs, which combined with the Greek ones in Hellenistic Jewish and Christian thought, included, first, God as creator of the world; second, a symbolic understanding of God as supremely holy, whatever supremacy means (a point nicely formulated in Anselm's phrase, "that than which nothing greater can be conceived"); and third, a dialectical critique of idolatry. These Hebrew motifs need to be understood in terms of their historical development from anthropomorphic to transcendent and universalistic expressions. So God was early thought to be creator of powerful storms with military benefits for Israel, later to be creator of the entire cosmos. God was early thought to be better and more holy than the Egyptian gods, later to be more holy and supreme over whatever else you could imagine to exist. Idolatry early meant the worship of the wrong gods, later to be the worshipful identification of any finite thing with God. In all three cases there is an extraordinary dialectic of transcending whatever is in the purview as counting for the world. The Greek dialectic of unity, eternity, and the condition of conditions was not half so fierce as the Jewish dialectic of transcendence. When Philo and his early Christian followers expressed these ideas in the language of Greek philosophy, they inaugurated a Western family of versions of the dialectic of being according to which, roughly and vaguely speaking, being is the creator of the world and to be a thing with finite identity is to be created. There have been many accounts of creation, with distinctions of begetting, processing, creation of the material world, Neo-Platonic emanation, and the like. Generally, all the variants associate the source with the supremely holy, are suspicious of potential idolatry, treat creation as the source of both unity and diversity, distinguish the eternity of being from the temporality of the beings, and account for all causation within the world as grounded in the causation of the world.

Much has changed since the early centuries of the common era when Jewish, Christian, and Muslim philosophers worked out the families of the Western dialectic of being. Our sense of the cosmos is now far vaster, we understand causation differently, and after centuries of religious wars we are shamed by new depths of idolatry. But the dialectic of being can be given a new formulation that can be defended as true and symbolically engaging for our day.

7.4. The Dialectic of Being

Philosophical dialectic is a different genre from just about any genre of Confucian writing, and so what follows in this section seems an abrupt change from the kinds of argumentation preceding. Nevertheless, it will be argued that there is an implicit dialectic in Confucian thought rather like what is being expressed here in such a Western metaphysical way. The dialectic here is expressed with great abbreviation, with references to more complete expositions and defenses elsewhere. Impatient readers may speed ahead so long as they give the dialectical argument the benefit of the doubt!

Modern science has brought us to understand the world as anything that can be measured in any sense, and that anything determinate can be measured over against that with respect to which it is determinately different. So "the world," for us late-moderns, consists of all the things that are determinate at all and metaphysics, for us, needs to focus on what makes things determinate, on those principles or structures in which determinateness or "having identity" consists.[3]

The metaphysical hypothesis to be proposed here is that determinateness consists in being a harmony of essential and conditional features.[4] Conditional features are those by virtue of which a thing is related to something else with respect to which it is determinate. Essential ones are those by which it composes its conditional features into its own identity, giving itself position relative to other things. By "things" in this context is meant processes that relate to and mutually define one another: situations, events, enduring institutions and enduring individuals with natural and sometimes moral unity through time and change (Neville 1989, chapters 5, 6, 11, and 12). Without conditional features things would not be related to other things so as to be determinately different from them, and without essential features things would be nothing more than their potential relations, would lack the own-being of functioning as terms in the relations, and hence could not even be determinately related to other things. With essential features the metaphysical plurality and diversity of the world is expressed, each thing being uniquely itself, and with conditional features the metaphysical relationality of the world is expressed, each thing being determinate in part by reference to something else with respect to which it is different. To make this metaphysical hypothesis plausible and persuasive, it would be necessary to give a more complete account of actuality and possibility, of temporality, and a host of related issues.[5] Enough has been said here, however, to give a vague sense for where the dialectic of being might begin.

Consider the fact that two forms of togetherness are required for a metaphysical pluralism that acknowledges both the relatedness but also otherness of things. On the one hand is the togetherness of the conditional features, according to which things condition one another. Causation, temporal and spatial relations, and other contextualizing and relational elements are matters of the togetherness constituted by conditional features. But things themselves are *harmonies* of conditional and essential features. In order for the conditional features of different things to be together, the things themselves *with their essential features* must be together on a more basic level. Yet the essential features are not together conditionally. Their essential function is precisely what is not a function of other things. Things are other than one another only because each has essential features beyond the reach of the other, however much that togetherness is mediated by conditional features. Therefore, there must be a deeper context in which things in their essential otherness are together so as to make their mutual conditioning possible, an ontological context of mutual relevance (Neville 1968, chapter 3). Here is the point of transition from the metaphysics of determinateness to the ontology of being, and it is made through the question of the possibility of a plurality of related things.

In what could the ontological context of mutual relevance consist? What could provide such a context? In what sense could things be together in their essential otherness as well as their conditioning connections? The first thing to say is sweeping in its consequences, namely, that the ontological context cannot itself be anything determinate. For if it were determinate, then it would be related determinately to the other determinate things, in mutually conditioning relations, and that would require an even deeper ontological context in which the first ontological context could be together with them essentially. The suggestion of any determinate candidate for the ontological context of mutual relevance immediately falls into an infinite regress. Thus the ontological context cannot be "being as a determinate common property," nor "being as a superordinate totality," nor "being as a determinate dialectical power in the Hegelian sense," nor "being as God in the sense of a modally finite individual." This is but a rephrasing of the old point that makes being dialectical in the first place, namely, that it cannot be a thing itself, an object, a genus, or anything of that sort.[6]

But then what could the ontological context be if it is not determinate over against or in addition to the determinate things of the world? The hypothesis here is a reconstruction of the old doctrine of creation *ex nihilo*. The ontological context is *the act* of creation of all determinate things. Without the act of creation, there would be no determinate things, nothing. Thus the source of the creative act, prescinding from the creation itself, is wholly indeterminate, as required of the ontological context. The act of creation is a sheer making, an asymmetrical exercise of power that begins in nothing and terminates in the determinate things of the world. Space, time, and causal conditions are among the things created. The determinate things of the world are ontologically together by being made that way, relating according to their conditional features and enjoying essential differences that organize their conditions in different determinate identities with reference to one another. Although there are enormous complexities in understanding the relations among the temporal modes of past, present, and future, one clear point is that they are not together temporally. *Things in time* are together temporally, but the modes of time itself are not together temporally. They are together eternally within the act of creation (Neville 1993a).

Notice that the determinate nature of the act of creation is itself one of the products of the creative act. Without the creation, there would be nothing determinate. With the creation, that situation of utter nothingness is the source of determinate things, the creative act is productive of whatever is determinate, and the determinate world has just the diversity and just the unity it, in fact, exhibits. Here is the dialectical point about being. Given the creation, the three ideas in creation—source, act, and determinate product—are interdefined and symmetrically related to one another.[7] On the other hand, those very ideas in creation assert the asymmetry of making. Creation is making something new. It is not rearranging antecedent realities nor the giving of form to something that can take form, although both of those things happen within determinate processes. Creation expresses the maxim, "anything new, in respect of its novelty, comes from nothing," or its converse, "nothing new, in respect of its novelty, comes from anything." The maxim, "out of nothing, nothing comes," has very rare application in this world of novelty and change.

This dialectical notion of being as creation sustains at least three entry points of inquiry. Some philosophers focus on the determinate things whose being consists in being created. Spinoza's distinction between *natura naturans* and *natura naturata* is a classic expression, and Robert Corrington's ecstatic naturalism comes at being this way (1992, 1994, 1996, 1997). Other philosophers focus on the act of creation as in the principle of plenitude; Duns Scotus' primacy of divine will over divine nature is a classic expression, and William Desmond's treatment of being as plenitude and givingness makes the point in a contemporary way. Yet other Western philosophers focus on the source of the act, its fecund nothingness, the abyss from which all things freely arise; classical mystics such as Eckhart and Boehme make that point, as did Berdyaev earlier in our century.[8] But all entry points need to work around the whole dialectic of the asymmetry of the act of creation: determinate things are possible because they are created to be in conditional relation with one another while defined in their different integrities. Ecstatic contingency, infinite plenitude, the productive fire of nothingness are three interconnected ideas of one thesis: that things are created *ex nihilo*.

To be sure, the idea of creation *ex nihilo* is of Western origin, based on the rhetoric of causation, a rhetoric used differently in East Asia. But the concept here is very abstract, abstracting from most of the explicit Western connotations. It can be specified by those more concrete Western theories, but it is more abstract than they and can also be specified by their alternatives in other cultures, or at least so it will be argued shortly.

The idea of creation *ex nihilo* is also weird to most commonsense ways of thinking because it contravenes the ordinary thought that processes of change are rearrangements of antecedent elements. For practical purposes it is important to keep track of things during changes, and so the maxim, "out of nothing, nothing comes," serves to keep attention focused on rearrangement. Nevertheless, change cannot be merely rearrangement because an early phase of change has to have something new added to it in order for things to become any different. So in every change there is at least a modicum of sheer novelty, even if it is nothing more than new states following out the predictable inertia of antecedent forces, as in a deterministic system. In the case of creation *ex nihilo* there is nothing antecedent and the whole consequence is novel; that is the point of stressing *ex nihilo*. So though we are more accustomed to track elements in rearrangement, because every change involves some *ex nihilo* novelty, perhaps important novelty as in free decisions, and, no change is only rearrangement, our subliminal experience of novelty is as pervasive as that of rearrangement. Whereas most of us sense the novelty dimly, many poets and saints sense it vividly, and ontological creation *ex nihilo* has as much experiential analogy as do more customary rearrangement images.

7.5. South and East Asian Motifs for Being

In the West this dialectic of being has often associated creation with God, according to many conceptions of God—that of the nature romantics, that of the more traditional creation-oriented theologians, and that of the mystics. All of these, however, are a far cry from Deborah's God of storms (*Judges* 4–5) or Whitehead's (1929, Part 5) Great Companion, the Fellow Sufferer Who Understands. Judaism, Christianity, and Islam have entertained many conceptions of God that do not accord with the creation dialectic of being, or do so with fairly significant supplements. Nevertheless, in Judaism, Christianity, and Islam, that dialectic of being is not only to be found but has been prominent. The more interesting question is whether there are parallels in South and East Asian philosophic traditions.

The South Asian traditions arose from motifs as metaphorically connected with ontological use of causal notions, such as creation, as the West Asian traditions. A Vedic hymn to Visvakarman, whose name comes from the *kr* root, meaning work or making, (cf. Sanskrit *karma* and English *creation*), says the following:

> That which is earlier than this earth and heaven, before the
> Asuras and gods had being,
> What was the germ primeval which the waters received
> where all the gods were seen together?
> The waters, they received that germ primeval wherein the
> gods were gathered all together.
> It rested set upon the unborn's navel, that One wherein
> abide all things existing.
> Ye will not find him who produced these creatures: another
> thing hath risen up among you.
> Enwrapt in misty cloud, with lips that stammer, hymn-
> chanters wander and are discontented. (Radhakrishnan
> and Moore 1957, 18)

Then there is the famous Vedic hymn of creation:

> Non-being then existed not nor being:
> There was no air, nor sky that is beyond it.
> What was concealed? Wherein? In whose protection?
> Death then existed not nor life immortal;
> Of neither night nor day was any token.
> By its inherent force the One breathed windless:
> No other thing than that beyond existed.
> Darkness there was at first by darkness hidden;
> Without distinctive marks, this all was water.
> That which, becoming, by the void was covered,
> That One by force of heat came into being.
> Desire entered the One in the beginning:
> It was the earliest seed, of thought the product.
> The sages searching in their hearts with wisdom,
> Found out the bond of being in non-being.
> Their ray extended light across the darkness:
> But was the One above or was it under?
> Creative force was there, and fertile power:
> Below was energy, above was impulse.
> Who knows for certain? Who shall here declare it?
> Whence was it born, and whence came this creation?
> The gods were born after this world's creation:
> Then who can know from whence it has arisen?
> None knoweth whence creation has arisen;
> And whether he has or has not produced it:
> He who surveys it in the highest heaven,
> > He only knows, and haply he may know not.
> > (Radhakrishnan and Moore 1957, 23–24)

Those ancient motifs are not a complete expression of the dialectic of being in terms of creation, of course. And there were other motifs in India, particularly having to do with consciousness given an ontological interpretation, that have no close parallels in West Asian thought. Nevertheless, later South Asian thinkers did develop some very strong parallels to the creation dialectic of being. What is the distinction between Saguna and Nirguna Brahman if not a recognition of the point, on the one hand, that the source has the nature of being the source—in the Advaita position, the source of Isvara who creates a material world—and, on the other hand, that creation is wholly free play and the source has no nature in itself apart from its play, no determination at all? (Neville 1982, chapter 6)

The East Asian traditions, including the Confucian, do not give an ontological role to causation metaphors. East Asia thus constitutes a stronger test case for the thesis that the dialectic of being, interpreted in terms of creation *ex nihilo*, has proximate dialogue partners in cross-cultural perspective. This is not to say that East Asian philosophy does not have strong theories of causation. Everyone knows of the ancient yin-yang theory of the alternation of reciprocal tendencies. The sixty-four hexagrams of the *Yijing* represent, among other things, epitomes of causal structures. The East Asian conceptions of causation are somewhat different from those of the West, although the differences should not be exaggerated. The ancient Chinese understood regularity in nature as well as irregularity, and they imagined and built models of heavenly mechanics (see Major 1993; Needham 1956). But these causal conceptions were not the ones that they extended to ontological applications.

Some thinkers might conclude from this that the East Asians philosophers had no ontological interests, that being was not a problem for them. But the contrary is the case. There is an East Asian, indeed Confucian, version of the dialectic of being manifested in three topics: the conception of nature, the relation of being and nonbeing, and a sense of generativity. These three topics are all ideas for understanding the dao, and together they have something like the logic of the dialectic of being. To put the point another way, the dialectic of the dao is very like the dialectic of being.

For an East Asian conception of nature recall Xunzi's treatise on *tian*, variously translated nature or heaven (*Xunzi* 1994, chapter 17). Xunzi was one of the great Confucians of the pre-Han period but drew heavily from *The Daodejing* and *The Zhuangzi*, later classified as Daoist texts. For Xunzi, as previously noted, the natural world is a product of heaven and earth. Heaven is the principle of ordering things. It has its own dao, which is to impose or insinuate order or regularity into that which can take on order. Earth is the principle of material orderability; its dao is to take on order. Nature is their combination in processes that show various levels of regularity and irregularity. The regularity of the starry heavens is an emblem of heaven in Xunzi's philosophical sense, as the fecundity of the earth is an emblem of his earthy principle of orderability. The dao peculiar to the human, according to Xunzi, is ritual and sign-structured civilization which fulfills or allows the complete development of the elementary endowments from heaven and earth. The dao of the human needs integration with the daos peculiar to other products of nature, such as animals, crops, weather, topology, and the like. The harmony of all the specific or fulfilling processes is the cosmic dao, that in and by virtue of which things exist and against which one rubs when being stupid or wicked. With respect to the dialectic of being, all of nature, both the various and the integrated daos, are creatures of the conjunction of heaven and earth. This is a kind of ecstatic naturalism in the sense that the observable processes are taken to reflect their sources in heaven and earth. Yet heaven and earth by themselves, if they ever were by themselves, would be nothing. There would be no ordering of even the most purely regular things, such as stars, without stars being ready for circular motion. Like the Western dialectic of being, the East Asian supposes that the determinate things of nature are products of something that would be nothing if it were not to give rise to the natural dao.

Unlike the typical Western dialectic, influenced by monotheism, the East Asian posits two transcendent sources, not one. Prescinding from their combination to produce nature, this is inconsequential because two nothings or wholly indeterminate potentials are not different from one another. Regarded in combination they express two transcendental elements of nature, the propensity to harmonize and the receptivity to harmonization, like having essential features and conditional features.

The next East Asian idea to develop the notion of the dao as being, is its relation to non-being or nothingness. Laozi had written (in Chan 1963, chapter 40), "All things in the world come from being, and being comes from non-being." Wang Bi, the great third-century commentator, related this point to the problem of the one and the many. He argued that whereas the substance of things is being, the function of things is non-being, and function is prior to substance (in Chan 1963, 322–24). The one is the function of non-being in all things that unifies what otherwise are mere different products. This is not exactly the same as the dialectic of being sketched earlier because it gives priority to oneness over diversity. But it is like that dialectic in its expression of the one as both non-being and as the non-being present in the beings that rise from it. Wang strongly advocated the mystical path of tranquillity to penetrate to non-being in terms of which the dao can be grasped.

The eleventh-century Neo-Confucian thinker, Zhou Dunyi, developed the dialectic of non-being and being even further. He wrote, in his "Explanation of the Diagram of the Great Ultimate," already quoted in part:

The Ultimate of Non-being and also the Great Ultimate (T'ai-chi)! The Great Ultimate through movement generates yang. When its activity reaches its limit, it becomes tranquil. Through tranquillity the Great Ultimate generates yin. When tranquillity reaches its limit, activity begins again. So movement and tranquillity alternate and become the root of each other, giving rise to the distinction of yin and yang, and the two modes are thus established. By the transformations of yang and its union with yin, the Five Agents of Water, Fire, Wood, Metal, and Earth arise. When these five material forces are distributed in harmonious order, the four seasons run their course. The Five Agents constitute one system of yin and yang, and yin and yang constitute one Great Ultimate. The Great Ultimate is fundamentally the Non-ultimate. The Five Agents arise, each with its specific nature. When the reality of the Ultimate of Non-being and the essence of yin, yang, and the Five Agents come into mysterious union, integration ensues. Heaven constitutes the male element and Earth constitutes the female element. The interaction of these two material forces engenders and transforms the myriad things. The myriad things produce and reproduce, resulting in an unending transformation.[9]

Scholars have debated whether the first two ideas, the Ultimate of non-being and the Great Ultimate, are intended to be a correlated pair or an ordered sequence. Wing-tsit Chan translates them as a pair with the phrase "and also"; the Chinese words are simply *wu ji er tai ji*, literally, "negative ultimate great ultimate." Nevertheless, the fact that everything else in the paragraph cited is sequential—from Great Ultimate to yang to yin to alternation to the five elements to the ten thousand things, and then back down again to *wu ji*, the non-ultimate—suggests that Zhou Dunyi intended them as an ontological sequence. That is, he agreed with Wang Bi and Laozi that being comes from non-being and in turn gives rise to differentiation and everything else. If non-being were not to give rise to being and its sequels, it would be nothing; giving rise to them, it remains as the mysterious and unifying source in the ongoing process of nature. It may be noticed how Zhou developed and formularized Xunzi's conception of natural processes, although he and Wang Bi urged a mystical attentiveness to non-being in tranquillity that was alien to Xunzi.

The third idea in East Asian philosophy relevant to the dialectic of being is generativity. This was expressed anciently in such claims as Laozi's at the beginning of *The Daodejing* that the dao that cannot be named is the mother of the dao that can be named. That is, the dao expressed in the ongoing transformations of nature is the child of a deeper dao. That deeper nameless dao, of course, is *named* Mother in making that point, just as, in the Western rhetoric of the dialectic of being, the wholly indeterminate source is recognized as determinately the source of determinate things, in being called source.

There is in Chinese thought down through the Neo-Confucian period a double sense of causation or generation. One is the horizontal generation of the later from the earlier, and philosophic concerns about this are expressed in the yin-yang theory of transformations, in the analyses of harmonization relative to disorder, and in the moral concerns for destiny. The other is subtler and has to do with a vertical conception of the dao such that any thing, any change, is generated not only from its past but from an ontological ground that contains it incipiently. From this ground it takes form and flourishes and finally has a determined character that other things need to take into account. There is a strong sense of freshness and spontaneity that is not merely horizontal development but vertical generativity. Perhaps the most potent expression of this sense is in Zhu Xi's twelfth-century "Treatise on Jen" in which he attempts to use the notion of love or humaneness as the ontological character of the "mind of Heaven and Earth" which creates all things, especially the human sphere.

> The moral qualities of the mind of Heaven and Earth are four: origination, flourish, advantages, and firmness. And the principle of origination unites and controls them all. In their operation they constitute the course of the four seasons, and the vital force of spring permeates all. . . . Therefore in discussing the mind of Heaven and Earth, it is said "Great is Heaven, the originator!" and "Great is Earth, the originator." . . . In Heaven and Earth it is the mind to produce things infinitely. In man it is the mind to love people gently and to benefit things. (in Chan 1963, 594–95)

There is a plenitude in process that is not reducible to the movement from earlier to later. Everything arises from the depths of plenitude, and this is the dao.

The historical argument here is only fragmentary and imagistic. But it gives some support to the thesis that East Asian philosophy has something like the dialectic of being found in South Asian and more especially West Asian thought. Unlike the latter two, East Asian philosophy does not employ the causal metaphors of creation; instead, it inquires into the dynamic character of dao. But there is a deep structural parallel. Whereas the createdness in the determinate things in the Western model of creation *ex nihilo* is nicely expressed in the radical contingency articulated by what Robert Corrington calls ecstatic naturalism, Xunzi articulated an East Asian approach to the dao of nature in terms of the radical contingency of the material and human world on the principles of heaven and earth. Whereas the Western dialectic focuses on the mystical depths of non-being as the source of created determinate things, Laozi, Wang Bi, and Zhou Dunyi assert the origins of being in non-being and advocate the contemplative return to non-being as the One in the Many. Whereas the Western dialectic of the act of creation elaborates the theme of plenitude, as William Desmond does, East Asian philosophy develops the idea of ontologically originative generativity.[10]

The contextual purpose for this chapter is to show that Boston Confucianism can call upon both Chinese and Western roots to address the ontological question. None of this is to say that the abstract dialectic of being sketched here, even if fed by more concrete motifs from China and the West, is able to be fleshed out concretely and persuasively in our time. This is a critical creative task for contemporary philosophy to which Confucianism has a contribution to make. Or to put the point the other way, for Confucianism to be contemporary, it needs to be able to address the question of being positively or negatively.

8

Motifs of Transcendence

8.1. Transcendence as a Category

In his characterization of the axial age in *Way to Wisdom*, Karl Jaspers (1954, 100) wrote:

> The new element in this age is that man everywhere became aware of being as a whole, of himself and his limits. He experienced the horror of the world, and his own helplessness. He raised radical questions, approached the abyss in his drive for liberation and redemption. And in consciously apprehending his limits he set himself the highest aims. He experienced the absolute in the depth of selfhood and in the clarity of transcendence.

Note his citation of transcendence as a characteristic of all the cultures of the axial age. Moreover, it is in transcendence that the absolute is experienced with clarity, for Jaspers, just as the absolute is experienced in depth in selfhood. Now contrast Jaspers's claim with the following from David Hall and Roger Ames's *Thinking through Confucius* (1987, 12–13):

> Perhaps the most far-reaching of the uncommon assumptions underlying a coherent explication of the thinking of Confucius is that which precludes the existence of any transcendent being or Principle. This is the presumption of radical immanence.... [A]ttempts to articulate his doctrines by recourse to transcendent beings or principles have caused significant interpretive distortions. Employing the contrast between "transcendent" and "immanent" modes of thought will assist us materially in

147

demonstrating the inappropriateness of these sorts of transcendent interpretations.

Whereas Jaspers (1954, 99) asserts transcendence as a universal characteristic of the axial age, and specifically cites Confucius in this regard, Hall and Ames deny transcendence of Confucius and assert for Confucius a deliberately framed contrast, immanence. Was this a hasty overgeneralization on Jaspers's part, corrected now by Hall and Ames with their detailed scholarly understanding of Chinese philosophy? Does this difference reflect a deeper difference of philosophical projects, Jaspers's to find unifying elements of human civilizations and Hall and Ames's to stress both cultural differences and the dangers of biasing comparisons with categories from one side alone? Or is there genuine ambiguity about the meaning of transcendence, more than is commonly recognized in that notoriously ambiguous term?

These issues will be examined in five steps. First, it is necessary to say something about the formal notion of transcendence and deal directly with the powerful arguments of Hall and Ames. Second, the argument shall discuss some of the ways in which ancient Chinese, especially Confucian, thought exhibits and models transcendence, and third, it shall extend that to Neo-Confucianism. In both of the latter accounts, transcendence can be approached through considering how something important transcends the self and so defines the self. Fourth, the argument will switch the motif venue to Western Christianity and discuss God and the image of God in the soul as forms of transcendence, and then fifth, it will bring that to a historical parallel to the Neo-Confucians in the thought of John Wesley.

How shall we characterize transcendence as a formal abstract category, as a respect in which Chinese and Western philosophies can be compared? Hall and Ames (1987, 13) astutely recognize the need for such a characterization and provide the following:

> Strict transcendence may be understood as follows: a principle, *A*, is transcendent with respect to that, *B*, which it serves as principle if the meaning or import of *B* cannot be fully analyzed and explained without recourse to *A*, but the reverse is not true.

They cite and expand upon this characterization in *Thinking from the Han* (1998) which devotes three chapters to the denial of transcendence in early Confucianism; they do not deny that Neo-Confucianism introduced many transcendent elements, but they do deny that those came from originally Chinese motifs. One thing transcends another, on their view, if it is required for understanding the other, but the other is not required for understanding it. They illustrate this with the Christian creator God, the Platonic forms, the Aristotelian unmoved mover of Greek philosophy, the atoms of classical materialism that comprise the world but are unaffected themselves by that composition, and by existentialist notions of originating will, as in the will of the prince.

This abstract definition of transcendence is infelicitous for Hall and Ames's thesis about no transcendence in Confucian philosophy because heaven, earth, and dao are all transcendent in the strict sense. Those elements are known, of course, through what they do, and they are the founding principles of the processive cosmos rather neatly described by Hall and Ames (1998, especially chapter 9). One can say nothing about them apart from their functions in founding the cosmos, just as being, as the ontological ground of mutual contrasts, needs to be indeterminate save insofar as it creates the world (see section 7.4). No more than the creation *ex nihilo* theory do the ancient Chinese notions assert that there is some in-itself nature to them that gets expressed in their interactions in the world. Rather, it is the dependency that counts, the causal dependency, in various senses of causation (for instance, harmonizing, receiving harmony, and incipience). The Chinese thematic structure for this kind of notion is the *ti-yong*, substance-function, construction, articulated explicitly by Wang Bi, directly illustrating Hall and Ames's strict definition of transcendence: substance transcends function, though only known through it in cases such as heaven, earth, and dao. But there is transcendence in other important senses.

Ames and Hall's larger aim is to defend A. C. Graham's thesis that Chinese philosophy, at least its Confucian branch, is characterized by correlative thinking. Correlative thinking is to employ pairs, such as heaven and earth, or yin and yang, or triads, quartets, quintets, and so forth, to classify and describe phenomena; correlative thinking satisfies its urge for understanding when it classifies phenomena under the various elements of a correlative pattern (Graham 1989, e.g., 319). The Neo-Confucian philosopher Shao Yung brought correlative thinking to a fine science (Birdwhistell 1989). Correlative thinking is interesting, however, not in its definition of the correlates but in its disposition of a kind of intelligibility in the phenomena it classifies. The correlates themselves might be defined partly in terms of one another, as in the case of yin and yang, or in relative indifference to one another, as in the case of the Five Elements (water, fire, wood, metal, and earth). But in few if any cases would the correlates be wholly defined in terms of one another, and therefore, the correlates meet the strict definition of transcending one another, at least in some respect. Confucius' notions of heaven, earth, and dao are all used to help understand other things but themselves can only be illustrated in their functions in phenomena, not explained by phenomena or by one another.

Hall and Ames's strict definition is a little ambiguous because it seems to suggest that a transcendent principle can itself be wholly explained without recourse to what it transcends. Yet in all their examples—God, a Platonic form, the unmoved mover, a classical atom, a decisive will—the transcendent principle cannot be explained in itself, only in its explanatory function.

Irrespective of its helpfulness to their thesis about no transcendence in Confucius, Hall and Ames's strict definition of transcendence is problematic in another sense, namely, in that there are several other closely related senses of transcendence that it does not capture. For instance, transcendence almost literally means *goes beyond*. That can be taken in the sense of movement beyond specifiable borders, as when axial-age cultures identify the worldliness of the world and transcend that. Sometimes the transcendent is what you find when you transcend the borders, such as a Christian God beyond the world of determinations. Other times the transcendent is rather a perspective from which one can think of the world as such, as in Buddhist notions of emptiness or Buddha-mind. Transcendent here means place or perspective beyond borders, not a principle of explanation as in the Hall-Ames formula. Other times transcendence means change or growth beyond limits, as a moral person can transcend the limitations of his or her past, or transcend one moral stage for another. Mou Zong-san, the contemporary Chinese philosopher at whom Hall and Ames take great offense (1998, 222–30), uses transcendence in this sense, as do Tu Weiming, Ralph Waldo Emerson, and William James. There is a related sense of transcendence that refers to the capacity of consciousness to objectify itself and always step back to look at itself. This notion has popular roots in Kant, powerful development in Hegel, and contemporary currency in transcendental Thomist theologians such as Karl Rahner. Is there an abstract formulation of transcendence that allows for the comparison of potentially transcendent things in all these senses? They are not purely equivocal, because Rahner relates his notion of self-consciousness as transcendence to moral will and life and takes them to testify to the transcendent God who is the ultimate explanatory context of all potentially knowable things.

Suppose we say that a general definition of transcendence is that to which reference can be made, in any sense of reference, only by denying that the referent lies within the boundaries of a specifiable domain, whatever else is supposed or said about the referent. So the subject in self-consciousness is transcendent because it always lies outside the objects of consciousness. Moral transcendence is achievement beyond the potentials or restrictions previously given in a person's or group's character. A religious perspective is transcendent if it falls outside so as to objectify and look upon the world within which religious life is lived. A creator God is transcendent as not being among the creatures or a structure of the world created. An explanatory principle is transcendent if it is not itself among the things it explains or that explain one another.

We can specify this general notion of transcendence to the philosophic sphere by saying that transcendence is that to which reference can be made, in any sense of reference, only by denying that the referent lies within the boundaries of the world of phenomena, specified in some way or other, whatever else might be said about the referent. This definition catches pretty much what Jaspers meant by transcendence in his statement quoted at the beginning. That is, Jaspers meant to say, and said, that the various axial-age people came to recognize themselves and their world to be limited: Their individual consciousness is limited, their moral character and national history are limited, their knowledge is limited, and their physical cosmos is limited. As indicated in the initial quote from Jaspers, the limited in each sense has a serious depth or twist that makes reference beyond the limit. Thus Jaspers claimed that the axial-age cultures developed civilization-shaping representations of transcendent grounds of consciousness, transcendent moral ideals, transcendent historical purposes, transcendent truths, transcendent causes of the cosmos, transcendent perspectives on meaning, and transcendent explanations. The question Hall and Ames raise for Jaspers is whether his empirical generalization is universally true. If transcendence as defined above is a good abstract comparative category, and if the phenomenology of world religions is carried out attentively, and the translations with critical care, then we ought to be able to tell about Jaspers's generalization.

8.2. Transcendence in Ancient Confucianism

But the theme here is transcendence in Chinese philosophy relative to Western philosophy. The focus is not concerned to limit the investigation of Chinese philosophy to Confucius, as Hall and Ames did in their study. Although it is not possible here to investigate all senses of transcendence that have been mentioned, it is fruitful to focus on a sense of transcendence close to the center of Jaspers's concerns, namely, that the depths of the self are transcendent of individuals and connect to the transcendent source of the world. More specifically, the topic is to investigate as a comparative category the idea of *transcendence as it defines the self.*

Crucial ancient motifs shall be recalled, and then the argument will study in more detail the way the motifs were developed over a self-conscious philosophical process in a later period. In the Chinese case, the period is from the end of the Northern Song to the Ming dynasties, that is, from the Cheng brothers through Zhu Xi to Wang Yangming. In the European case, the period is early modernity from Descartes to Hume and Kant, but focused on John Wesley's theory of the self and transcendence, which he characterized as the problem of the fall and holiness.

The ancient Chinese assumptions about the self are based on the model of a spectrum from an inner pole or center to an outer pole of the ten thousand things of the world people share (for more detail, see section 9.3). Ranged along the spectrum are the physical properties of a person, the psychological characteristics, and acquired knowledge and skills. Furthermore, the spectrum contains the social roles in which a person interacts with others and with institutions, and also the rituals and language exercised in a shared community. Unlike West Asian senses of the self that emphasize self-reflexivity and various ways of defining the boundaries of the self, particularly with regard to guilt and responsibility, the East Asian senses emphasize the definition of persons in terms of their interactions and roles. To the extent we are our familial and social roles, our language and our speaking, we are to be understood not so much as individuals in ourselves but as contributors to larger realities. Often the family or the conversation is more important than the identities of the individuals within it. This is not to say that persons are viewed as abstractions in larger and more concrete wholes, as Hegelians might say. Rather, for East Asians a person becomes individuated through making relationships and exercises of social behavior, speech, and ritual more concrete, more nuanced, more meaningful on many levels. Persons differ because of their different bodies, their different social positions, and their different skills and accomplishments at concretizing their positions.

Regarding transcendence, what is of interest is the pole at the center of the self. The classic Confucian text, *The Doctrine of the*

Mean (*Zhong Yung*) already quoted in part, provides the elementary motif:

> Before the feelings of pleasure, anger, sorrow, and joy are aroused it is called equilibrium (*chung*, centrality, mean). When these feelings are aroused and each and all attain due measure and degree, it is called harmony. Equilibrium is the great foundation of the world, and harmony its universal path. When equilibrium and harmony are realized to the highest degree, Heaven and Earth will attain their proper order and all things will flourish. (in Chan 1963, 98)

The equilibrium is a still-point of readiness to respond to the ten thousand things. If the self were most truly that still-point, as some Buddhists believed, then the goal of life would be a meditative retreat to it. But the Confucians believed that life is defined by exercising one's relations, when the feelings are indeed aroused in perception and response. The good life, therefore, requires guiding one's interactions by the aesthetic, moral, or valuational sensitivities of the center, the mean in action, or harmony.

There is no good single English word to describe what is called valuational sensitivities. When the structure of the self is clear, or "sincere," as it is sometimes said, the ten thousand things are apprehended each with its own true nature and value. Things are appreciated without distortion. Moreover, the center is the source of one's responses to things, and when the self is sincere, appropriate actions flow back to the things with which one interacts. Mencius, in a text cited previously, provides the classic motif for valuational sensitivities in his famous remark about seeing a child about to fall into a well:

> Now, when men suddenly see a child about to fall into a well, they all have a feeling of alarm and distress, not to gain friendship with the child's parents, nor to seek the praise of their neighbors and friends, nor because they dislike the reputation [of lack of humanity if they did not rescure the child]. From such a case, we see that a man without the feeling of commiseration is not a man; a man without the feeling of shame and dislike is not a man; a man without the feeling of deference and compliance is not a man; and a man without the feeling of right and wrong is not a man. The feeling of commiseration is the beginning of humanity; the feeling of shame and dislike is the beginning of righteousness; the feeling of deference and compliance is

the beginning of propriety; and the feeling of right and wrong is the beginning of wisdom. Men have these Four Beginnings just as they have their four limbs. (Mencius 2A:6, in Chan 1963, 65)

For Mencius, the path to virtue consists in cultivation of the structures of self and society that allow the Four Beginnings a flourishing disposition throughout human activity. Without a well-trained body you would knock the child into the well trying to rescue it; without emotions freed from selfishness you would inhibit your impulse to help, or corrupt it with extra and false motives.

Although persons differ because of their different physical structures and social positions, the center is the same in everyone. This is the transcendent point. Before apprehending anything or responding in any way, before the feelings are aroused, the center is identical in everyone. *The Doctrine of the Mean* begins with the following statement quoted several times above: "What Heaven (*T'ien*, Nature) imparts to man is called human nature. To follow our nature is called the Way (Tao). Cultivating the Way is called education. The Way cannot be separated from us for a moment." (in Chan 1963, 98) Although the center is never without its position in each person, never by itself as Buddhists might hope, it is nevertheless the gift of heaven given to everyone such that, when made to flourish throughout one's life and a society's institutions, it is the manifestation of the dao. Xunzi differed from Mencius in believing that the Four Beginnings would not automatically develop if unobstructed. He thought that rituals and other conventional behaviors need to be taught positively for the heaven-given nature to find a properly human expression, a human dao. But he agreed with the basic motif that the center of all nature, including human nature, is heaven's dao of proper ordering.

8.3. Transcendence in Neo-Confucianism

The sources quoted so far are motifs from the pre-Han dynasty period. They are expressed mainly in the context of moral and religious philosophy. Skip ahead now to the Neo-Confucian period of the Song dynasty. Part of the difference in philosophical situations is that the Neo-Confucians had to respond to highly developed metaphysical thought introduced by Buddhism, and also sophisticated cosmology and metaphysics developed by some strands of Daoism. The Neo-Confucianists were concerned to be systematic and argue, and thus to look much more like Western philosophers than some of the ancient texts, although it cannot be said that Mencius and Xunzi failed to argue.

Cheng Hao, one of the greatest Neo-Confucian philosophers, transformed Mencius' category of *jen* or *ren* (humanity, sometimes translated love) into a metaphysical principle describing the character of what heaven imparts, that is, the center.

> The man of *jen* forms one body with all things without any dif-
> ferentiation. Righteousness, propriety, wisdom, and faithfulness
> are all expressions of *jen*. [One's duty] is to understand this prin-
> ciple (*li*) and preserve *jen* with sincerity and seriousness....
> Nothing can be equal to this Way (Tao, that is, *jen*). It is so vast
> that nothing can adequately explain it. All operations of the
> universe are our operations. (in Chan 1963, 523)

This is an extremely complex position. According to Cheng Hao, the same heaven-endowed mind that Mencius called the Four Beginnings is the ordering principle which heaven puts into all things. It is both valuationally sensitive and productive, the origin or generativity of things. Because the principle which defines the center of our minds is the same that defines all other things, in Hao's own special emphasis, by concentrating on cultivating our minds we are in unity and flowing harmony with the rest of the universe. All this is because of the transcendent heavenly principle in all things.

Cheng Hao's brother, Cheng Yi, agreed that "The mind of one man is one with the mind of Heaven and Earth. The Principle of one thing is one with the Principle of all things." (in Chan 1963, 551) But he was more concerned than Hao with the ongoing character of nature and human affairs and developed an extensive doctrine of "production and reproduction." Crucial to this doctrine was a distinction between principle and material force, *qi*. Principle is the source of ordering; it is what makes things harmonious. Material force is the actual world as ordered and in ongoing need of further ordering. Sometimes material force is associated with earth, as principle is with heaven. But often heaven and earth are lumped together with principle as the valuational ordering mind in and behind things, and material force is that which is ordered. Whereas Mencius and Xunzi had been concerned to develop the Four Beginnings into moral character, Cheng I's interest in ongoing production and reproduction led him to an interest in finding one's destiny.

Zhu Xi, the greatest of the Song Neo-Confucians, developed the ideas of the Cheng brothers and systematized them. In his rendition principle and material force become two elementary principles, one never without the other but neither to be reduced to the other. Because material force is always with us, and we always have *chi*-things to order, the primary human concern is to find and act in accord with principle. Zhu Xi also characterized principle as *ren*, love or what in the human sphere is humanity.

Whereas the Cheng brothers were contemporary with Anselm and Zhu Xi lived a century later with Abelard, the great Ming Neo-Confucian Wang Yangming was contemporary with Luther and like him intensified a subjective focus. Wang criticized Zhu Xi's distinction of principle from material force as too dualistic and insisted that principle is everything. The crucial point for Wang is the continuity of thought and action. Whereas most of the other Neo-Confucians were scholars, teachers, and administrators, Wang was most prominent as a military general. Impatient with the earlier advocacy of meditative quiet-sitting to gain clarity and contact with the inner mind or principle, Wang emphasized meditation in action, centeredness in battle as it were. Proper sagely discipline leads to instant expression of the principle in one's inmost heart, what he called "innate knowledge," in the actions of ordinary and extraordinary life (see Chan 1963, chapter 23). But even more than the Song philosophers he emphasized the transcendence of principle. Whereas his predecessors had emphasized the goodness of principle or *ren*, Wang said:

> In the original substance of the mind there is no distinction between good and evil. When the will becomes active, however, such distinction exists. The faculty of innate knowledge is to know good and evil. The investigation of things is to do good and remove evil. (in Chan 1963, 686–87)

There are many technical references in that quote, such as original substance, will, innate knowledge, and "the investigation of things" that cannot be spelled out here (see Ching 1976, Cua 1982, Tu 1976a). But they make the point of the continuity of the self in its definite positions and activities with the origin of all things that transcends even the distinction between good and evil. Always within the human sphere, we should be attentive to good and evil. But the mind with which we do this in itself transcends that distinction. It is the mind from which all things in the universe derive, and it is on that basis that

Wang developed his famous exposition of the ancient claim that to be humane is to be one body with the universe.

Transcendence was defined above as that to which reference can be made (in any sense of reference) only by denying that the referent lies within the boundaries of the world of phenomena (specified in some way or other), whatever else might be said about the referent. How has the Chinese tradition of transcendence and the self specified that abstract and vague definition? There are special nuances in each of the texts and thinkers mentioned. But a couple of general points can be made.

First, for the Confucian tradition from beginning to end the self is defined in terms of perceptions of, responses to, and interactions with the ten thousand things of the natural and social world. The transcendent in this context is what lies in the self beyond all the determinations of that definition. The center in *The Doctrine of the Mean* is the dao or mind of heaven before the feelings are aroused. The center is that readiness to respond to the child about to fall into the well but before the child is encountered and any response has begun, the Four Beginnings as incipient but not in motion. It is the Cheng brothers' mind of heaven but unexpressed in harmonious activity, principle as ready to order material force but not formed by the specific dispositions of material force. The center is Zhu Xi's *ren* as origination but not originating anything, the principle that is one but whose manifestations are many. The center is Wang's original substance of the mind prior to the will's distinction of good and evil. Although there is a rich variation in the Confucian and Neo-Confucian expositions of the character of the self and its relation to nature, there is a strong thread of continuity in the tradition regarding what lies at the center or heart of the self which transcends it.

Second, for the entire Confucian tradition, what is essential about the self is precisely the functioning within it of the transcendent center or principle. The hallmark of the Confucian sensibility regarding the human person is the readiness of virtue to tap into the normative responsiveness of the center. In the later thinkers, this center is given an explicitly ontological interpretation which develops the theme of the unity of the human capacity for profound perception and response, including social life, with the capacity of everything in the cosmos to be. What makes us human, according to the concepts and metaphors of this tradition, from its ancient motifs to developed metaphysics, is the immanence of transcendent heaven which gives us our inmost core and capacities for extensive harmony.

This exposition of some motifs in Confucian thought has answered at least some of the claims of Hall and Ames that there is no transcendence in this tradition until late. The presence of the transcendent in the self, however, is not the primary object of their antitranscendence attack. Rather, their motive seems mainly to be to protect Chinese thought from the imposition of Western categories, especially those they think are characteristic of Western theology. So the real issue is God, to which we must turn, leading the discussion to Western versions of the transcendent in the self, that is, the *imago dei* motif.

8.4. God and the Imago Dei

Section 7.4 argued that Western philosophic culture has given rise to a conception of God as the creator *ex nihilo*, the logical structure of which is derived from considerations of the dialectical problems of being and the one and the many. Being, or God, as the otherwise indeterminate creator of everything determinate transcends the determinations as indeterminate but is present in them as their creative ground. The focus in chapter 7 was less on God than on being, however, and now the argument is ready to make some comparative remarks about the development of the idea of God.

In most of the major religious traditions, there is a spectrum of images or ideas of the ultimate that range from the highly personified or anthropomorphic to the highly abstract, impersonal, principle-like, or negative. Perhaps the personified end of the spectrum took shape in the context of polytheism, although the axial-age religions had more holistic personifications as in the sky gods such as Indra, Yahweh, and Shang Di. For devotional purposes, personification seems to be very important indeed; there long must have been a bad consciousness about thinking of the sky god merely as the Big Guy in the Sky, for Buddhism developed devotions to Guanyin as a God-surrogate as Christians did for Jesus. The attempts to think universally and critically, and to avoid idolatry, probably pushed some transcendence dialectic similar to that sketched for being in section 7.4. Jesus could hold that God is both like a father and love; by the time of the earliest apologists (second century CE), Christians believed that God creates both form and matter (the historical origin of the *ex nihilo* doctrine). Origen and Augustine could claim that God creates time. For Thomas Aquinas God is the pure Act of Esse, allowing no internal distinctions and no external relations, more abstract (or more purely full) than which you cannot get. Tillich said God is beyond being and non-

being, the God beyond gods. Mystics have said that God is pure nothingness. Mahayana Buddhism has a similar direction on the spectrum,
with conceptions of the Buddha-mind, the Unconditioned, Nirvana
and suchness, and pure emptiness; Madhyamaka Buddhism denies
significance even to these metaphysical appellations. Confucianism
flourishes in a world of ghosts and spirits in which Shang Di has
protective and organizing work; but it also early rejected those anthropomorphic conceptions for a much more principled and personally
neutral conception of heaven, which in Neo-Confucianism was
identified with "principle" plain.

Most religions have this spectrum of images, and life according
to theose religion's ways employs those images in special places.
Irrespective of philosophical thinking about the ultimate, the practical presence of the ultimate in people's lives is appropriately symbolized by various images all along the spectrum, each in its place.
Perhaps the spectrum indicates a shift from popular to esoteric religion, with grades in between. Or perhaps it is a shift from devotional to universal philosophizing reflection. Or some combination
of these with others. One aspect of the spectrum is that the more
personalized images developed earlier and the less personalized
developed out of criticism of them and attempts to think of the ultimate universally.

A crucial point for understanding the history of religions is to
note from which place in the spectrum the religious tradition adopts
its primary rhetoric. The West Asian religions adopted their main rhetoric from the early personalized images, and so they represent God
primarily in the images of a person, a god. For these religions, Christian religious reflection is called "theology." The personified rhetoric is
sustained even when the theological points are that God creates time
and space and everything finite, and therefore cannot be a person
related to other persons in any ordinary sense. Protestant Christianity
has a particularly heavy commitment to personification language because the reformation emphasis on scripture was intended in part to
leap back over and delegitimate the much more philosophical language of medieval scholasticism. Biblical rhetoric pervades Christian
(and Jewish and Muslim) consciousness. Confucianism by direct contrast did not define itself in the personification language of Shangdi
but in the rhetoric of Confucius which depersonalized heaven, earth,
and the dao. Some residual personifying language, of course, remains
in the emphasis on heaven's mandate. But by and large the Confucian
rhetoric is impersonal and highly universalistic. Where Christianity

takes its dominant images from the personifying end of the spectrum, Confucianism takes its dominant images from the opposite impersonal end.

The difference in the locus of rhetoric does not mean that there has to be a crucial difference in the intellectual affirmations about the ultimate. Christian Neo-Platonic meditation on God as the One and its emanations is no more personal in content than Neo-Confucian meditation on the oneness of principle and its many manifestations. Nor is the Christian devotional encounter with Jesus in the garden with the roses much more personificatory than the Confucian encounter with Grandfather at the tablet. There might be vast differences in the ways the different rhetorics shape the soul, but that is not to say the intellectual commitments are that different.

One of the primary ways by which Christians have discussed the transcendence of God is through the idea of creation. In the modern period science has led us to think of the world as measurable, or at least determinate. This gives a new way of representing what the world is—the collection of determinate things, however they turn out to be related. Hall and Ames (1998) argue that the West is committed to the conception of a "single ordered cosmos." Surely some thinkers have believed that mathematics or the dialectic of history can wrap everything up in a single order, but that seems to be an exaggeration. We have seen that there are pockets of order with minimal connections between them so far as we can tell, and that even the definitions of things are multiply perspectival, a point well made by Whitehead (1929). But however tight or loose the orders of the world are in their connection, God can be conceived as creator of them and hence transcendent of any determination, save that derived from being creator. So to put the point the other way, to see what nature there is to the ultimate, or God, you have to look to what God creates.

With regard to the particular kind of transcendence focused in this chapter, the Christian tradition (and the Jewish and Muslim in slightly different senses using the same core text) says people are created in the image of God (*Genesis* 1:26–27). What is it that is most essentially human?—that gives a clue to God. What is most important in God that bears upon the human?—that is the *imago dei*. This is not an argument, or if it is, the argument is circular. It is rather a problematic around which Christians have thought out what essentially defines the soul and transcends it as normative for the soul. Very much like *The Doctrines of the Mean's* human nature imparted by heaven, what is definitive and normative for human nature is the divine image within it according to which it is created. Human nature is defined by its (dependent, created) relation to the transcendent.

8.5. John Wesley and the Image of God

The Western notions to be traced now as alternative specifications of transcendence are familiar in the context of *imago dei* theology and can be expressed briefly. There is little in the Chinese tradition quite as starkly creationistic as the account in *Genesis* of the creation of Adam and Eve by a transcendent creator (though see the creation myths in Girardot 1983). But the *imago dei* is a different matter, an ancient motif on which Western thinkers have commented down to the present day.

Thomas Altizer (1985) has pointed out that the distinctive Western conception of the self that reached is grandest expression in Hegel and was committed to an interiority and depth whose resources were exposed by Kierkegaard, Freud, Marx, and Nietzsche, took its rise from the phenomenon articulated by Saint Paul: the good I would, that I do not, and the evil I would not, that I do (see section 10.2). There is an inner contradiction, Paul said, that results from the fall or breaking of the image of God. The philosophical and theological traditions of the West have called upon many other ancient motifs to explicate this, for instance, Plato's idea of the Form of the Good and the difficulties of embodying it, and Aristotle's idea of God as the unmoved mover whom we can imitate only at a very distant remove. There is a rich variety of historical speculations about what the image of God is—reason, love, creativity, consciousness, responsibility, freedom, and the like.

For special insight, we can examine John Wesley's exposition of Adam's prefall state, when the image of God flourished in him, in contrast to the postfall stage of sin. Wesley is in many respects an arbitrary choice. But he was indeed a paradigmatic modern man like Wang Yangming, and very influential indeed in articulating the relation of human individuals and society to the transcendent. Furthermore, his characteristic emphasis on holiness, or attaining perfection, has many tantalizing similarities to the Confucian project of becoming a sage, a related topic to Confucian notions of the self sketched above.

Wesley said that there are three principal elements in the image of God: reason or the capacity to know, a moral will that loves as God loves, and freedom.[1] God has these traits infinitely, and they constitute divine holiness; human beings originally had them in finite fashion, and human holiness consists in that. Wesley distinguished two elements in knowledge, a kind of intuitive faculty that immediately and fully grasps both concepts and perceived things, and a faculty of comparison that allows for further inference. Wesley's description of Adam's original cognition is eloquent:

> His understanding was just; everything appeared to him according to its real nature. It never was betrayed into any mistake; whatever he perceived, he perceived as it was. He thought not at all of many things, but thought wrong of none. And as it was just, it was likewise clear. Truth and evidence went hand in hand, as nothing appeared in a false light, so neither in a glimmering one. Light and darkness there were, but no twilight. (Wesley 1987, 293–94)

As original human knowing is accurate and clear, it is also swift as spirit itself and capacious without limits; Wesley pointed out that Adam understood and named all the animals one after another. Those familiar with the relevant Confucian texts will recognize extraordinary similarity to the kind of innate knowledge sought by the sages, especially Wang. Wesley's own reflections arose out of the early modern reflections on the natural light of reason, as in Descartes's and in Locke's theory of original perception.

Wesley interpreted will as a combination of affections and cognition. Perfect will is to love, and true knowledge tells Adam what to do in order to love, just as God's holy behavior is loving and omniscient. Like the Confucian with clear character, Adam's affective center behaved lovingly toward all things. Unlike the Confucian stress on the responsiveness of the center to the values in the things encountered, Wesley's stress was on the loving beneficence of will, modeled on the long Christian tradition that God's loving being is the same as God's creating.

Adam's original freedom Wesley (1987, 295) interpreted as indifference. Knowing what's what and affectively disposed to love it for the better, it still was within Adam's freedom to do the good or not, just as it is in God's free power to create the world or not or to save fallen people or not. This bears a distant similarity to the Confucian notion of spontaneity, although there are important differences. Adam in fact did exercise his freedom to reject God's clearly understood command which he also loved as part of the covenant, and so fell. Like Saint Paul, Wesley knew that we can know the better and choose the worse.

But what Adam did in perfect freedom, according to Wesley, Saint Paul thought he did in bondage (see sections 5.1 and 5.2). Wesley gave a quaintly physicalist interpretation of the fall. The apple was poison and first corrupted the molecules of Adam's body so that he lost immortality. Wesley (1987, 297) said that an antidote taken quickly, from the Tree of Life, would have reversed the decay. Adam's knowledge became inaccurate with unclear distinctions; he slowed down mentally, made mistakes in inference, and could not hold much in mind. Adam's will lost its pure affection in love for God and the world and

> was now seized by legions of vile affections. Grief and anger and hatred and fear and shame, at once rushed in upon it; the whole train of earthly, sensual, and devlish passions fastened on and tore it in pieces. Nay, love itself, that ray of the Godhead, that balm of life, now became a torment. Its light being gone, it wandered about seeking rest and finding none; till at length, equally unable to subsist without any and to feel out its proper object, it reclined itself upon the painted trifles, the gilded poison of earthly enjoyments. (298)

Liberty too fled, as Adam was enslaved to his passions, his misplaced love now unable to find its true object. Adam had what Kant called a purely heteronomous will and unlike Kant's noumenal practical reasoner, had no capacity for choosing the good for only the right pure reasons. However quaint Wesley's poison theory, it accords with the modern notion that human beings are simply not up to perfect finite knowledge, will, and freedom because of their bodies and the habits of their society. Even Kant would say there is no freedom in the empirical sphere, and Wesley insisted that religion deal with empirical realities. Wesley's theory of justification and sanctification aimed to show how human beings might approach Adam's original perfection once again.

How does Wesley's approach, which represents so much of the modern Western thinking about transcendence, specify our original abstract vague definition? The sphere transcendence transcends is that of finite things in which the infinite holiness of God can only be imaged. Unlike many philosophical theologians in the West, Wesley did not speculate much about God's infinity. But he did say that the human image of God is only an image, not a shortened version. God's infinite knowledge is not merely knowledge of everything rather than only the things in the Garden Adam knew; God's infinite will is not merely loving everything, nor is God's infinite freedom total indiffer- ence. Rather, the image of God is a function of createdness, and God's infinity is as creator of beings who, among other things, image divin- ity Adam's way. For Wesley (1984, sermon 23), in development of an ancient Western motif, God is primarily creator and creation is God's infinite way of loving.

As for the Confucians, what makes people human for Wesley is the presence of the transcendent in their lives, individually and so- cially. That presence is the image of God, now broken and abused but still functional as an instant critic and a lure. Wesley's account of sanctification drew strongly from the Eastern Orthodox theory of *theosis* or "becoming God." Had he lived into the nineteenth century with its theories of evolution he would have had far more resources for the treatment of the physically and socially imperfect image of God as a lure and ideal. But he did hold that the Spirit of God functions even in the most corrupt people, if not always successfully, at least palpably in the sense of guilt. The Spirit of God reminds human beings of their transcendent definition.

As it is the transcendent creator who defines the human essence in the image of God, there is a continuity in human life, for Wesley, whereby the transcendent can be tapped and played out in actions. Although Wesley did not believe, with Wang Yangming, that God the creator (or the original substance of mind, that is, principle prior to finite positioning) is prior to the distinction between good and evil, he did hold that there is no break between the inmost stirrings of the human heart (in cognition, will, and freedom) and their expressions in action. This was Wang's theme of the continuity of knowledge and action. Like his contemporary, Jonathan Edwards, like his polemical opponents, the Roman Catholics, and like his successors, the pragma- tists, Wesley believed that the heart must show itself in actions. Hence the distinctive Methodist piety that refuses to separate personal holi- ness from moral action in society. Like Wang the general, Wesley or- ganized his troups for reforming the world and believed that increasing holiness is as holiness does.[2]

These remarks have tried to exhibit how the abstract vague com- parative category of "transcendence as defining the self" is made specific in two traditions with minimal contact. The treatment of the traditions has insisted on their own historical depth and variety, mov- ing from ancient motifs on which nearly every successor had to com- ment to some later systematic expressions. As a result of this discussion, it is possible to say how the Confucian tradition and the Christian down to Wesley relate with regard to the transcendent as defining the self, with both the transcendent and the self interpreted in their characteristic concepts and metaphors.

The discussion is incomplete, of course. Most obviously, both traditions regard the transcendent as definitive of the self because it is its source, and little has been said about the comparative senses in which those traditions would account for that sourcing. On the surface, heavenly principle is not the same as the creator God of West Asian religions, although functionally they are similar in regard to the comparison at hand. There is also much more to transcendence than its roles in defining the self that have been treated here. Moreover, the argument has not approached the sense in which Jaspers himself thought of transcendence as defining the self, namely, as the Encompassing that gives the possibility of meaning; Jaspers's theory owes much to Kant's epistemologizing of selfhood in the problem of meaning and objective truth, and that is another topic. Nevertheless, this discussion has illustrated a method of comparison that involves reading different traditions as specifications of vague categories they share in common.

9

Resources for a Conception of Selfhood

9.1. Problems with the Self

The self as an explicit topic is reminiscent of the concerns of existential philosophy in the earlier part of the twentieth century in Europe and many parts of Asia that encountered the West in its existentialist phase. As an implicit topic, however, the self is the concept at the bottom of many current debates, such as those over human rights, the relation of people to the environment, the claims of individuals versus groups, the importance of ethnic identity, and the relation of persons to the social systems such as the economic, political, and communicative within which they lie.

If Boston Confucianism is to be viable, that is, a contemporary philosophy that draws seriously on the Confucian tradition as well as Western thought to address the issues of late-modernity effectively, it needs to have a vigorous approach to the problems of selfhood. On the one hand, it needs to be able to register and honor what is profound and true in the West's struggles to understand personal identity. On the other hand, it needs to be able to reconstruct Confucian motifs for a viable conception of selfhood. Surely it ought to be possible to combine those two. One lesson of the previous chapter is that the self in both traditions is conceived to be defined in reference to a transcendent ultimate and normative reality.

Nevertheless, there are *prima facie* objections to any attempt to combine the two traditions. For all its internal difficulties, Western thought prides itself on understanding the self to be deep, to have a profound interiority. By contrast, Confucian conceptions of selfhood look superficial to Western eyes, too preoccupied with externals, too naive about the powers of education, too ready to excuse the obligations of

167

individual responsibility. For its part, Confucianism prides itself on the subtlety of its understanding of the process of attaining selfhood, of personal transformation, of achieving concreteness in human relations in ways that acknowledge the individual worths of people and things. By contrast, Western conceptions of selfhood seem too atomistic and individualistic to Confucian eyes, too inward-looking to be responsible, too selfish to serve the community, too ready to give the personal sphere an unrealistic priority over both nature and social institutions. So the problem for Boston Confucianism is to register Western profound interiority without selfish individualism together with Confucian subtlety of relational engagement without superficiality. The discussion of Tu Weiming's thought in chapter 5 was motivated in part by those concerns. The present chapter makes them explicit.

Western culture, indeed, has been accused often of excessive individualism, and this has been contrasted with the community-family orientation of Confucianism. Nevertheless, the heart of Song-Ming Neo-Confucianism was its emphasis on the self, with serious dialectical consideration of Buddhist and Daoist conceptions of the self. Perhaps Chinese culture did not treat the problem of the self thoroughly until the intervention of Buddhism. The Buddhist notion of reincarnation makes personal identity less a function of individuated relations with others and the environment and more a matter of an individual's own journey through time. The Neo-Confucians rejected what they saw as the selfishness of this turn, but in rejecting this had to develop their own notions of selfhood. Thus, the topic of the nature of the individual person is common to both the Western and Confucian (and Daoist) traditions and constitutes a good comparative focus for addressing issues of how those traditions might contribute to our philosophic conversation now. For the traditions say quite different things about the topic.

How shall the topic be approached in our context? This chapter will address the question of self-deception, that is, how a self can be in some contradiction to itself. For the Western traditions of philosophy and religion the hallmark of selfhood is the depth and isolation that come from the fact that it can be contradictory to itself at basic levels. Put in an extreme way, for Western thought a person who has not come to terms with his or her own self-deception is not yet a true self, still living in what Hegel called "dreaming innocence." And it would seem, on the other hand, that Confucians have understood the self as always to be a diaphanous entity essentially connected to the environment with only selfish blockages that muddy the water. These differences shall be traced here and shown to be more subtle than is commonly thought. Finally, some elementary categories will be introduced for a new conception of selfhood that draw upon the fundamental Confucian motifs but that are capable of registering the depths of soul characteristic of Western culture.

Construed in a narrow and uninteresting way, self-deception might be an impossibility, like affirming and denying a proposition in the same respects at the same time. In real life, however, there are many contexts in which we live with assumptions that we know at some level to be mistaken or misleading. These include psychological contexts, contexts determined by our sense of social realities, and contexts in which religious issues about the meaning of life are at stake. Self-deception is a common state of living in these contexts.

The structure of this chapter is, first, to introduce extreme notions of the self from Western culture, making the point about interior depth, contradiction, and self-deception in the most exaggerated possible ways. Of course, there are a great many Western conceptions of selfhood. Not all of them are plausible, and indeed, all are problematic. But the rhetorical force of considering the extreme ones will have the effect of saying that any Confucian conception that can register the extremes with regard to interiority can register that theme in the other conceptions. Next the chapter will review and reconstruct a Confucian conception of the self, pulling together many strands that already have been discussed in this book. Section 9.4 will elaborate a theory of how several senses of self-deception are registered within the Confucian motifs, relating these to the Western senses of self-deception. Finally, section 9.5 will introduce the categories of orientation and poise to define the contours of a new conception of selfhood based on Confucian motifs that still can register the depths of soul so important to the West.

9.2. The Self as Contradictory and Self-Deceived in Western Thought

The self in Western philosophy is an idea based explicitly on self-reference, the word deriving from the self-reflexive pronoun in English. Although the idea of self bears connotations of "person," "human being," "human nature," "soul," "spirit," "heart," "mind," "consciousness," "character," and "personality," among others, each of which has cognate words and ideas in nearly all languages, including Chinese and other East Asian tongues, it adds to all of these ideas that of self-reference or self-relation. Furthermore, there is also a sense that the self-reference involves embracing or overcoming some internal contradiction in identity.

This Western concept, the self, shall be described here in a few historically oriented remarks. Then it will be possible to articulate what the Confucian tradition exhibits instead, which can be called, somewhat oxymoronically, the Confucian conception of self. Although Chinese language has words or phrases for all or most of the kinds of self-reference or self-reflexiveness found in Western languages, including self-cultivation, self-deception, and selfishness, it does not have a summary word for person, human being, or individual personal character that itself is constructed so self-consciously out of self-reference itself.

Admittedly this is an initially dubious claim in light of the title of such distinguished works as Wm. Theodore de Bary's *Self and Society in Ming Thought* (1970), a volume to which de Bary contributed as well as edited. Yet in the writings of the various authors of that volume, "self" is nearly always used simply in its reflexive form, as in self-cultivation, self-criticism, and so forth, not as a noun substantive. One of the main themes of that book, and also of his *The Unfolding of Neo-Confucianism* (1975), is the development of individualism and heightening of subjectivity in Confucianism after Wang Yangming. But the noun substantive for that topic generally is human nature or character, not self. The only systematic use of the word "self" as a noun substantive is in Araki Kengo's essay in the latter volume on "Confucianism and Buddhism in the Late Ming" where it is attributed to Buddhist thought (de Bary 1975, 45, 59-60). That is not as oxymoronic as it seems because a no-self doctrine requires a heavy duty self doctrine to deny. The Neo-Confucians did develop a Confucian analogue to the Western conception of self; they did so out of ancient Confucian ideas, such as those contained in *The Doctrine of the Mean* and in *The Great Learning*, and their conception emphasized the self-cultivated responsibility of selfhood. Yet neither the early nor late Confucian conceptions of what I call self placed self-reference at the defining center.

Thomas J. J. Altizer (1980, 1985) has called attention to important origins of the Western notion of self in the ancient world, as mentioned in the previous chapter. One of these is the role of the divided will in Saint Paul whose classic statement, discussed in section 5.5, is the following:

> I do not understand my own actions. For I do not do what I want, but I do the very thing I hate. Now if I do what I do not want, I agree that the law is good. But in fact it is no longer I that do it, but sin that dwells within me. For I know that nothing good dwells within me, that is, in my flesh. I can will what is

right, but I cannot do it. For I do not do the good I want, but the
evil I do not want is what I do. Now if I do what I do not want,
it is no longer I that do it, but sin that dwells within me. So I find
it to be a law that when I want to do what is good, evil lies close
at hand. For I delight in the law of God in my inmost self, but
I see in my members another law at war with the law of my
mind, making me captive to the law of sin that dwells in my
members. (*Romans* 7:15–23)

Some thinkers leap to the conclusion that Paul was attacking the body
in favor of the soul, and indeed, that interpretation has been influential
in some parts of Christianity. But flesh here is a metaphor for a bit of
behavior that has a kind of autonomy of its own, a subroutine of life
that is harmful or wicked when taken out of the context of integrated
moral and spiritual behavior. Sexual passion, for instance, when running autonomously is lust, but when integrated into the wholeness of
personal and social life before God is the image of the greatest virtue,
love. The proper integrating principle is the law of God, or what Paul
elsewhere calls the mind of Christ, which is the person's own "inmost
self." As strongly as any Confucian devoted to principle (*li*) in the
heart (*xin*), Paul believed that God's law or loving intentionality is
innate to the mind.

But the mind does not automatically effect its good intentions.
Rather, the wholeness of human nature, according to Paul, includes
also the will which is always "close" to evil. The *problem* of human
nature is not the presence of the divine mind but the integration of
that mind with voluntary actions, especially vis-à-vis other people.
When one's will gives in to its subroutines and acts "in slavery to sin,"
then the authorship of the person over his or her own actions is lost:
sin itself, the subhuman passions with wicked consequences, becomes
the author. What is left of the person is merely the law of God which,
by itself, is hardly the person. From the standpoint of sensitivities to
the Buddhist dialectic about the no-self, the result of Paul's thought is
extraordinary. The normal human state for Paul is that the person is
bifurcated, indeed dissolved, into the innate law of God, on the one
hand, which functions now only as condemning judge, and the
nonpersonal acts of sin, on the other. In the standard state, for Paul,
there is *no* authentic or real self or personal authorship, only sinful
acts and divine judgment. Thus the problematic of salvation is to re-
unite these, the sin and the divine nature, in a responsible human
author. Contrary to Buddhism and nondual Vedanta, Paul's problematic of salvation is to achieve a self that is faithful to the divine principle

or law within and at the same time is effective in acting through bodily, social, and historical media that draw one always close to sin which ruins authentic responsibility.

Saint Augustine (*Confessions*, book 10) reconceptualized Paul's problem with an idea of soul combining memory of the past, alertness to the present, and will for the future, all of which add up to love. Furthermore, the human soul mirrors the divine soul, so that the wholeness of the human soul stands in reflective tandem with the wholeness of God. The individualism of Augustine in this move has not been entirely beneficial, and is in contradiction to the moral and communal strain within Christianity; the Cappadocian Fathers offered a better alternative for conceiving soul in interpersonal terms. But Augustine's idea has been more influential in the West. For him, sin consists in lying memory, faulty attention, and a bad will resulting from allowing the body to overwhelm the divine image within. But sin is not simply a falling away of the will with the loss of responsible authorship. It is a direct contradiction within the soul. Whereas Paul's soul dissolves away in bondage to sin, Augustine's becomes tortured in its self-contradiction, choosing to turn from that for which it most longs. Moreover, for Augustine, memory, attention, and will are all functions of consciousness, and the deepest hurt of sin is self-consciousness. From Augustine's theory arose the Western conception of the self as in guilty self-conscious self-contradiction to itself, struggling to let the divine image express itself throughout the arena of concrete action but unable to do so because turned away from God, unable to see the mirror (Vaught 1997).

Hegel made this point central to his whole philosophy, and he reversed the conceptual order of God and self. For Hegel, the self developing through unfolding self-contradictions becomes the model for God as Spirit unfolding through contradictions of nature and history. The self of Hegel's idealism is the result of overcoming negations. Some of these are external, and the grandeurs and pomposities of the bourgeois self and its religion of progress express this. Others of the negations are internal, rooted in the price paid in prior overcomings of negations. In both cases the self is what the self itself has made of itself in overcoming, or swallowing whole, the negations that had defined its previous oppositions. The Western self as the overcoming of self-contradiction is individualistic in the sense that its becoming is its own project. For Hegel, God's self requires the overcoming and internalizing of all externality. The human self might not internalize all other selves, but it surely internalizes all its relations to other selves so that they function as roles within it, and nothing more. The Hegelian self shows no deference, save to its own image in the other.

Kierkegaard (1955, 146) brought the point about the reflexivity of the self to its most abstract conclusion:

> Man is spirit. But what is spirit? Spirit is the self. But what is the self? The self is a relation which relates itself to its own self, or it is that in the relation [which accounts for it] that the relation relates itself to its own self; the self is not the relation but [consists in the fact] that the relation relates itself to its own self.

The Western self, at least in the heritage traced here, can have physical, social, and psychological structures. Yet all these are integrated by and subjugated to the problems of internal self-contradiction and self-consistency. The Western self is *deep* because it involves self-conscious reflection of reflection of reflection, down to the infinity of God conceived as equally deep. In its depths the Western self embraces, usually without clearing up, its own contradictions. Altizer in *Total Presence* (1980) accounts for the collapse of the large bourgeois ego as part of the death of God, the dialectical abandonment of the plausibility of the claim that God is a self-related, infinitely deep process of overcoming negations. The endpoint, Altizer says, is a kind of return to Buddhist silence regarding both divinity, which is now emptiness, and humanity, which is a historical surface on which the depths of human emotion are popularized by the universally accessible blues. If the Western self were ever to work it out that the law of God in the inmost mind automatically directed the will, the self would be bored.

Self-deception as understood in the West is deeply affected by the preoccupation with self-reflection and the containment of contradiction. The West has three main species of self-deception, or perhaps there are three main approaches to conceptualizing it.

The first is inner psychological self-deception of the sort thematized by dynamic psychoanalytic theory. Freud's version of this is that much behavior is directed by the unconscious, which is structured by a kind of primitive and selfish "primary process." The motivations of primary process are not entirely acceptable to the socially constructed superego that embodies norms of behavior thought to be essential to civilized social intercourse. The psyche has a censoring mechanism that renders the ideation of primary process unconscious, and its behaviors are hidden or deviously symbolized by the thought processes of the conscious ego. That the pretended conscious ideation of the ego is not the true ideation motivating and shaping behavior is revealed in dreams, slips of the tongue, and other imperfectly censored behaviors. The conscious content of mind is sometimes genuinely deceived about the real motivations behind behavior. For instance, when one acts so as to exercise control over another person, it might seem consciously that the motivation is to help the other person when, in fact, the primary process motive is anger or a competitive fear. Or one may consciously believe that the remarks and actions of a particular person are hostile and dangerous, when, in fact, the person is helpful or oblivious and one is unconsciously looking for signs that can be interpreted as hostile, as in paranoia.

In a more pervasive sense, most people have unconscious, or even conscious, needs to see the world in a certain way, and thus see selectively and with distortion. Almost all of us believe that others think about us more than they do and that they act to put us in a place advantageous to them. In fact, we generally overinterpret signs that might have a bearing upon our personal needs, especially psychological needs, and we generally underinterpret very important happenings that do not have much personal bearing upon us. Many self-deceptions are of this sort.

The second species of self-deception consists in the systematic distortions of the meanings and effects of social structures of the sort analyzed by Marxists and others concerned with ideology. According to Marx, people belong to social classes, as defined economically, and the competitive interests of their class shade the way they see everything. For instance, members of the capitalist class see the market of free price determination as an expression of human freedom and are deceived about the fact that people who are on wages, or even worse, those who simply have no connection with capital production, are not free at all to enter the market. Or a person raised in a particular religious tradition is deceived by the religion's ideology about what people in other traditions are experiencing. Self-deception in this second sense consists in being determined by the interests or prejudices of one's group, on the one hand, in contradiction to what one "ought" to believe, on the other hand. Because the person identifies with the group, perhaps unconsciously, as defining identity, this is truly the deception of the self by the self.

The third sense of self-deception in the West comes from an ignorance of the world combined with an ignorance of limits. Here is the heart of the tradition of tragedy. Oedipus was ignorant of his true parentage, and he was ignorant of how his status as king was limited by not being of a certain birth, and he deceived himself about his real status. Lear was ignorant of the powers of sin in his own kin, and he was ignorant of his capacity to command respect when he abandoned the responsibilities of rule, and he deceived himself about his life's possibilities and about his true friends.

More generally, we construct our worldview on the basis of a very limited vision of what is what, and the far deeper underlying forces sometimes break out of our domesticated expectations. We plan a life we think is possible but it is ruined by war, famine, or plague. We think that steady, well-intentioned behavior will be rewarded but discover belatedly that nature's rewards are distributed blindly. We think we are secure in certain people's affections or, to the contrary, are locked in bitter struggle, only to find that the forces that govern affection and contention shift the field in meaningless ways. Because the universe is infinitely complex in its causality, and our visions are only finite takes, our ignorance and self-sense are always somewhat self-deceiving.

Most forms of self-deception thematized in the West fall under one or a combination of these three heads. Each involves the self-reflexive embrace of some kind of contradiction in what constitutes the self's identity. The situation is different for the self as conceived within Confucianism.

9.3. The Self in Confucian Thought

The Confucians conceive the self to be a product of its own cultivation, just as much as does the Western tradition. For the Confucians, the attainment of true selfhood is a matter of becoming the responsible author of one's own character and actions. But the underlying model is different from that of the West. The following account is based not on the explicit doctrine of a single text but on a series of powerful motifs already discussed that have shaped each thinker in the multiplicity of Confucian strands.

According to *The Doctrine of the Mean*, as we have seen, the heaven-given human way is in a normative continuum of structured activities lying between two poles, *zhong* and *yung*. *Yung* means the ordinary world, the "ten thousand things" that constitute our environment and to which everyone must relate directly or indirectly. People's ordinary worlds differ by context and circumstance, by geographical location, historical place, and by one's associations. But everyone has an objective, ordinary world in which to live and with which to cope, and there is a great deal of commonality consisting of needs for nutrition, shelter, family, and social life. *Zhong* means centrality or equilibrium, "before the feelings of pleasure, anger, sorrow, and joy are aroused" (Chan 1963, 98). *Zhong* is the readiness to respond normatively to the various ten thousand ordinary things. Mencius, in his famous illustration of what he took to be a universal response to a child about to fall into a well, asserted that everyone whosoever has a readiness to respond to things appropriately; this readiness constitutes what he and the tradition have called the Four Beginnings of humanity, righteousness, propriety, and wisdom (*Mencius*, book 2A:6 in Chan 1963, 65; see the extraordinary discussion in Shun 1997).

The later Neo-Confucians developed this idea of *zhong*, or the incipience of right response in the Four Beginnings, into the doctrine of principle (*li*). Principle is the very essence of heaven, and it is identical in all human beings. But it is only the readiness to respond that is universal, the incipience of normative reaction: the actual situation to which each person has to respond is unique. We differ not in the principle in our heart but in that to which the principle must direct action, in the ordinary objective world of *yung*.

Human nature or the self in the Confucian tradition is not *zhong* by itself; one of the mistakes of Buddhism, according to the later Confucians, is meditatively to cultivate *zhong* by itself as if that were worth something. Rather, the self is *zhong* actually responding to the affairs of *yung* out of its developed nature. Not mere readiness but the habits of response constitute the self. The self consists of all the structures in a person that mediate the connections between that person's ordinary objective world and the *zhong* in that person ready to respond. So far, Saint Paul might not disagree.

These structures, for the Confucian tradition, include physical, cognitive, and emotional elements (to introduce some crude distinctions) and can be conceived as perceptive, on the one hand, and action-oriented, on the other—afferent and efferent. Moreover, those structures need to be educated or cultivated. As *The Doctrine of the Mean* says, "What Heaven (*T'ien*, Nature) imparts to man is called human nature. To follow our nature is called the Way (Tao). Cultivating the Way is called education" (in Chan 1963, 98). The body needs to be educated so that we perceive with sensitivity and discrimination and also so that we can act effectively on what we intend. A person who does not pay attention would not notice the child on the lip of the well, and a klutz would tumble into the well with the child while trying to save it. A person's cognitive skills need to be developed as well; it is one thing to understand the simple danger to the child at the well, another to understand the problems of economic competition; whereas the remedy for the child's situation does not need much learning, the remedy for economic problems does. Our emotions at any age can blind us to the true worths of the ten thousand things in our world to which we should respond appropriately; similarly, our emotions can bend our actions to selfish behavior even when we know what to do and are capable of it.

Two other points in the Confucian worldview need to be lifted up to understand this sense of self. First, as just mentioned, each thing or person in the world is viewed as having a nature with a specific worth. The appropriateness of a person's responses to things depends on identifying that worth and acting accordingly. The *zhong* or principle or Four Beginnings does not itself have a moral content but is a kind of aesthetic sensitivity to the value content of other things and an innate taste regarding how to honor those values. Because in any situation there are even more than "ten thousand things" that need to be honored at once, the actual exercising of *zhong* in the world is called "harmonizing," and it is what the great dao does on the cosmic scale.

Second, the Confucians were conscious from very early on of the fact that the structures of the self have the character of signs. They are habits (mainly socially constructed) of physical, cognitive, and emotional behavior that are learned like language. Most of the items among the ten thousand things that have elicited Confucian interest have been people and social structures. Physical habits of paying deference with eye contact, body posture, and appropriate performative speeches, as well as learning to ride and shoot the right way, to move efficiently, and to write beautiful characters, are important elements of physical education. Cognitive development is the acquisition of true concepts and effective speech for analysis and expression. The "truth" involved, according to Neo-Confucianists such as Zhu Xi, is not so much a matter of description but rather of learning to discern how the principle in other things expresses itself in the unique situation of the ordinary world of those things. Thus, Zhu Xi claimed that the investigation of things and the extension of knowledge consists in learning about principle. Principle itself is the same in all things but differently functioning in each thing because of that thing's perspective on the world (Chan 1963, 610ff.). The conceptual apparatus for discernment and expression, however, is a matter of habit, a function of signs. Similarly, emotions have no reality except in their exercise, and that exercise has the character of habit, of tendency, and is shaped by learned signs. The Confucians called the signs that make up an educated self "propriety" or "ritual" (*li*), focusing on a ceremonial paradigm. This is the point stressed in the previous chapters.[1] The paradigm is a good one, emphasizing as it does that the signs have to be learned and also that their essence lies in performance, not merely (or even) in symbolizing something else. Even explicitly cognitive signs, such as those in economic theory, have their truth in performance, which, for such cognitive signs, consists in actually expressing the economic realities—a sign from an alien language does not communicate and thus cannot perform so as to express a fact. The Confucians, as we have seen, knew that signs or ritual propriety are conventional but are to be judged by their performance. Cultures do things differently. But those cultures with no signs allowing for the exercise of friendship, filial affection, good care and nurture of the young, or promotion of the arts are culturally deficient, a point made earlier. A given person who has not learned the signs for performing the deeply human things is uneducated, deficient in the way. Moral reform is less changing people's intentions than changing the signs by means of which they perform their lives together.

The self, for the Confucian tradition, is the complex of sign-structured physical, cognitive, and emotional practices that relate the *zhong* in a person to that person's world. *The Doctrine of the Mean* calls the excellence or virtue of that relation "sincerity." The chief meaning of sincerity is a kind of clarity, or translucence, such that the true complicated nature and value of the ten thousand things is mediated to the *zhong* or heart, and the heart's aesthetically and morally right incipient response is unfolded in action to the things.

Confucians have by no means developed these motifs of the self all in the same way. Mencius, for instance, focused on the innate excellence of the heart and emphasized the negative side of unlearning bad ways of life more than the positive learning of higher structures. Confucius and Xunzi emphasized the importance of inventing and practicing the signs constituting ritual propriety. Neo-Confucianists rethought the motifs from a more speculative standpoint than characterized the ancient thinking. Zhou Dunyi, for instance, speculated that sincerity, the expression of *zhong* in action, is a function of material force. Zhang Zai interpreted sincerity in terms of the ordering of the different steps toward virtue in the classic *Great Learning*. Cheng Hao and Cheng Yi developed the theory of heaven and earth, principle and material force, as means to provide an intellectual context for the attainment of sincerity. Zhu Xi reinterpreted sincerity in terms of humanity (*jen*) to which he gave a metaphysical account that represents sincerity or humanity as a kind of cosmic generative principle that unfolds the self with "origination, flourish, advantages, and firmness." (Zhu Xi, "Treatise on Jen" in Chan 1963, 594). Wang Yangming deepened Mencius' emphasis with his theory of the heart-mind, and he focused more on the emotional and valuative elements of the self than on the cognitive to which he thought Zhu Xi was biased. Contemporary Confucianism can take great advantage of the pragmatic theories of habit and semiotics to develop a cross-cultural conception of ritual propriety, as discussed in sections 1.2 and 1.3.

Nevertheless, despite all these variations with contrary schools, the basic motifs for a Confucian conception of self are present throughout. None of them involves the doubling back of self-reference so as to mean the containment within the self of the contradictions of intent and performance, of self and other. Where contradictions arise, for the Confucian tradition, they should simply be educated out.

9.4. Self-Deception in Confucian Thought

Three forms of self-deception stand out as themes arising from the Confucian motifs. First is the form that arises from selfishness; second, that arising from inadequate habits, signs, and ritual propriety; and third, that arising from a misplacing of socially defined identity because of a lack of humanity (*ren*). These will be sketched in turn.

Selfishness is the core of human evil, in the Confucian account. Wang Yangming summed up a long tradition when he expressed the sincerity connecting one's heart-mind with the objective ordinary world as "manifesting the clear character" in "being one body with the world." He noted that Mencius' example of the child at the well might be criticized because a child is the same species as the adult, and seeing its danger could be an extended kind of selfishness. But we cringe from the suffering of animals about to be slaughtered, said Wang, and we have at least momentary pity at trees about to be felled; we even feel regret when we see tiles or stones shattered. Therefore, even if we were the butcher, the woodsman, or the demolition expert, we would feel momentary upset at destruction or pain.

> This means that even the mind of the small man necessarily has the humanity that forms one body with all. Such a mind is rooted in his Heaven-endowed nature, and is naturally intelligent, clear, and not beclouded. For this reason it is called the "clear character." Although the mind of the small man is divided and narrow, yet his humanity that forms one body can remain free from darkness to this degree. This is due to the fact that his mind has not yet been aroused by desires and obscured by selfishness. When it is aroused by desires and obscured by selfishness, compelled by greed for gain and fear of harm, and stirred by anger,

he will destroy things, kill members of his own species, and will do everything. . . . As soon as it is obscured by selfish desires, even the mind of the great man will be divided and narrow like that of the small man. Thus the learning of the great man consists entirely in getting rid of the obscuration of selfish desires in order by his own efforts to make manifest his clear character, so as to restore the condition of forming one body with Heaven, Earth, and the myriad things, a condition that is originally so, that is all. (in Chan 1963, 659–60)

Confucians have differed in what causes selfishness in the first place if everyone is initially endowed with the Way. Some, following Xunzi, have attributed it to lack of effort in developing good habits; others, following Mencius, have attributed it to having learned bad habits that should be unlearned. Some of the Neo-Confucians attributed it to the influence of material force through which heaven-endowed nature must work (Zhu Xi's "Treatise on Cheng Mingdao's *Discourse on Nature*," in Chan 1963, 598–99). For all of them, selfishness constructs or distorts the emotional and cognitive structures of the self, perhaps even the physical structures as in gluttony, so as to "obscure" what things really are and give too selfishly personal an orientation to desires. Wang's attack on desire as such illustrates some of the Buddhist influence on his thinking. But the point is one to which most others would subscribe: selfishness blocks responding to things according to the worth of dealing with them appropriately and instead gives people motives that subordinate that worth to personal benefit.

Yet because selfishness is the great evil in Confucian culture, there is a strong motive, stemming from selfishness itself, to rationalize selfish behavior as altruistic. Although contemporary Confucians can learn psychodynamic theory and use it to explain rationalization, there is nothing in Confucian culture itself that would seek out models of inner self-reflexive contradiction, such as primary process opposing the superego, with mechanisms of censorship and repression. Rather, Confucians would note that people tell themselves they are doing good, and redescribe their actions to make that convincing, when they really are acting selfishly. How easy it is to believe a weak or incomplete analysis when it makes us look good! The deep Confucian commitment to self-criticism reflects the tradition's recognition of this kind of self-deception. The long discipline of seriousness in watching and amending one's motives reflects the tradition's recognition of the power of selfish self-deception. The quotation from *The Doctrine of the Mean* quoted above continues:

What can be separated from us is not the Way. Therefore the superior man is cautious over what he does not see and apprehensive over what he does not hear. There is nothing more visible than what is hidden and nothing more manifest than what is subtle. Therefore the superior man is watchful over himself when he is alone. (in Chan 1963, 98)

The self-deception arising from inadequate signs and habits, from what Confucius would have called a breakdown in ritual propriety, is more complex than selfishness and it was Confucius' own preoccupation. Herbert Fingarette (1972, 11ff.) called attention to the importance of *li* as ritual propriety, employing the contemporary notion of the performative elements of symbolism to make the case. Contemporary pragmatism's semiotic theory is also helpful to understand the Confucian point.

The human realities of life, those over and above the realities to be understood in scientific or naturalistic terms, are those that consist in the exercise of habits structured by socially meaningful signs. To be a friend, for instance, is not to have a particular attitude about someone but to engage in activities with and for that person that constitute friendship, for instance talking, sharing experiences, rendering support, exposing one's vulnerability, and taking care of the person's welfare as equals might. Each of these activities is a tendency or habitual behavior shaped by its own signs. But together they add up to friendship because the abstract signs defining friendly behavior as such give each of the components a place and due proportion. A good culture has all the signs needed, signs that can be learned through ordinary experiences, for the prevalent practices of friendship and of the other human institutions that make for civilized living. A deficient barbarian culture is one that lacks the signs that can shape habits constituting the higher levels of civilized life. It does not matter what the signs are that can shape the habits, or what cultural semiotic system they belong to, so long as they make for the actual existence of civilization. Confucius' project from the beginning was to rediscover, revivify, or in desperation to invent, signs that could reverse the slide of his society into barbarism.

The possibility of self-deception deriving from inadequate signs and habits arises from the relation between relatively more or less vague levels of signs internal to some human excellence, such as friendship. A vague sign, and thus a vague habit, is one that allows several less vague instantiations to be mutually exclusive, or at least alternative to one another, and yet each is equally good. For instance, the vague habit of friendship requires some less vague habits having to do with greeting a friend; the greeting habits might consist in a bow, a handshake, a kiss on both cheeks, or a hug. A greeting habit that is entirely appropriate in one culture might have just the opposite meaning in another culture; a bow is an appropriate greeting in old-fashioned Chinese culture but would be interpreted as a distancing gesture in American culture. There are many other subhabits that go into friendship, having to do with how to talk, how to relate the friend to one's family, how to handle money, and so forth, in which alternative cultural forms might serve equally well in different cultures, but are mutually exclusive or counterproductive if combined in one culture. The institutions of friendship, family life, education, political life, cultural life, and many other dimensions of civilization are hierarchies of habits on habits, each level of which tolerates ambiguity below in a vague sense. But in any specific social situation, there must be a definite hierarchy of habits, with only certain ones tolerated by the higher levels of vague habits.

Self-deception arises when a higher level habit is operative but lacks a necessary subhabit. Thus people can believe they have friends and make a show of doing certain things with their friends, identifying themselves as a friend, but might lack crucial subhabits. They may have no way of greeting the friend that is not off-putting; they may have no way of relating the friend to their family, leaving things in confusion and divided affection; they may have no way of handling money with their friend. And so they are self-deceived about their friendship.

The kind of self-deception resulting from faulty signs and habits is learned when one learns one's society's semiotic. It may interact with the self-deception deriving from selfishness, of course, so that one's preoccupation with oneself affects the ability to relate to another as an equal. But the essential fact here is that the signs are at fault. American society places great emphasis on the care of children, but lacks crucial habits for the details of love, nurture, and education; American society is self-deceived about parenting, and so are many individual Americans. Western societies generally place great stock in democratic government, but often are inattentive to or ineffective in promoting the educational and economic conditions necessary for persons to participate in a large democratic system. Therefore, democracies are often self-deceived about how democratic they really are when certain groups, by their history, possess the subhabits necessary for democracy and others do not, thereby being disenfranchised. Examples of this sort can be multiplied like Jeremiads and are at the heart of the social critiques characteristic of Boston Confucianism.

In certain respects, the self-deceptions arising from faulty signs and habits parallel the self-deceptions arising from ideologies to which Marxists have given attention. But the Marxist analysis emphasizes a contradiction within the deceived self between underlying interests shaped by economic class membership and the ideological understanding of the situation that expresses acceptable values. The Confucian analysis lacks that preoccupation with contradiction. The problem for Confucians is not contradiction within the self but the absence or dysfunction of signs and habits that are supposed to be exercised for the higher level excellences to exist. The Confucian remedy is not the overcoming of contradiction in some kind of class struggle but rather the reshaping of the signs structuring the self in society. Among the signs that might need to be reshaped are those expressing differences in social class; Confucius, for instance, was an egalitarian educator in a time of aristocratic privilege. The Confucian emphasis is on the deconstruction of counterproductive habits and signs, and the recovery or invention of servicable habits and signs. Social criticism is the means to identify the problem areas.

The third form of self-deception, the misplacing of social identity because of a failure of humanity, has been the favorite target of Daoists within the Chinese tradition. Precisely because Confucians pay close attention to signs and exercise habits that are socially defined to establish status and relationships, they can deceive themselves about what really is going on and what values are at stake. Dressing according to one's station, greeting people with the style appropriate to the relation between one's own station and theirs, expecting recognition of one's authority and place, all these and other signs lend themselves to insufferable pomposity and abusive treatment of people who do not know or who disagree about the signs of status.

Within the Confucian tradition the emphasis on ritual *li*, on exercising the socially meaningful habits, has been tempered with a balancing emphasis on humanity (*ren*).[2] Humanity is the immediate giving of one's heart to others that adjusts the exercising of the socially significant habits into a due proportion. One need not always insist on wearing one's finery, or in being greeted properly, or in being recognized. The first stanza of Confucius' *Analects* includes the line, "Is one not a superior man if he does not feel hurt even though he is not recognized?" (in Chan 1963, 18).

Ren, not *li* as ritual propriety, became the central organizing category for the great Neo-Confucians such as the Cheng brothers and

Zhu Xi. As mentioned earlier, Zhu Xi provided a cosmological interpretation of humanity as the principle according to which things arise and flourish. In our own time, Confucians such as Cheng Chungying (1971, 1991), Antonio Cua (1978, 1982, 1985, 1996), and Tu Weiming (1976b, 1979, 1985, 1989) have elaborated both historical interpretations of *ren* and contemporary developments of it as a philosophical category. In one way or another, the contemporary accounts employ *ren* as humanity to shape and set the contours of Confucian social policy and the goals of personal education and cultivation. In Tu's theory (see sections 5.1 to 5.5), humanity is the norm by which to judge both social and personal structures; he interprets family relations as the core from that both personal structures and social structures develop, an ancient theme.

When humanity is missing or misunderstood, the development and exercise of civilizing signs and habits has no due proportion. Then the hierarchies of signs and symbols can become dysfunctional even when they are operative. You slap your friend on the back in greeting, you remember to send his child a birthday card, and you do not complain when he breaks your lawnmower, and still he makes you feel guilty as if you had not done something for him. He may be missing the openness and attentiveness of your heart that should shine in your eyes and temper your backslap, your avuncular role, and your neighborly forebearance. Even though all the behaviors of friendship seem to be operative, the heart is not in it. The heart can be absent from family duties, from community activities, and from service to high culture. In these cases, those civilized activities are hollow and not genuine. But because we understand those high human things from the signs and habits that constitute the exercising of them, we deceive ourselves. It seems we are doing the right thing, but affairs do not originate without compromise, they do not flourish with zest, the advantages that were suppose to accrue do not follow, and the definiteness of their actual practice dissolves into ambiguities. Origination, flourish, advantage, and definiteness are Zhu Xi's marks of *ren* (Chan 1963, 593–97). Sensing the problem, we deceive ourselves into redoubling the effort with better signs and habits, and that merely makes us pompous. The need is for humanity in the signs and habits.

Some rough parallel holds between the Confucian understanding of the self-deception that comes from a misplacing of status from want of humanity and the Western tragic sense of self-deception as in Oedipus and Lear. But in the latter, the self-deception involves an inner contradiction in how one relates to oneself as defined by situation and accomplishment. The contradiction is located in how one relates to oneself in peculiar ignorance. In the Confucian case there may be a misperception of self, such that one is subjected to comic ridicule or social criticism; but the problem is a lack of humanity that would put the signs and habits defining one's place in perspective. Failing that perspective, one can be both pompously ridiculous and morally abusive all the while thinking only of doing good.

In the comparisons here of Western and Confucian understandings of self-deception, nothing new has been said about the Western sense of self as being constituted by self-reflexivity containing contradiction. The point of this chapter has been to draw out a Confucian sense of self, a Confucian analogue for the Western notion, that does not depend on intensity of self-reflexivity or on the overcoming and containment of contradictions. Rather, Confucian motifs have been developed concerning the self as a structured continuum of signs and habits of physical, cognitive, and emotional behavior uniting the morally incipient heart, *zhong*, with the ordinary world of the ten thousand things, *yung*. This distinction between senses of selfhood has been used to explore differences between three senses of self-deception, concerning psychological, social, and status matters. Whereas the West approaches psychological self-deception through the psychodynamic theory of contradictory drives, the Confucian tradition sees it as a problem of selfishness. Whereas the West approaches social self-deception through ideology-theory of internalized class conflict, the Confucian tradition sees it as a problem of attaining adequate civilizing signs and habits. Whereas the West approaches self-deceptions of status with the understanding of tragic contradiction, the Confucian tradition understands it as a want of humanity.

In the contemporary world, both of these traditions have something to contribute. Situations of self-deception can be understood in terms of elements of both. No intellectual is only a Westerner or only a Confucian, except through culpable ignorance. Nevertheless, neither the motifs of the West nor those of Confucianism by themselves or even commingled are sufficient to provide an enlightening understanding of the self today. Thinkers are faced with a challenge to intellectual creativity. Charles Taylor (1989) has shown how a profound reinterpretation of the Western tradition can give a significant purchase on understanding the self and its values as defined by European modernity. But what about the issues of selfhood that arise from the interactions of the world's great cultures? How to understand the self in relation to ecological considerations? What can a universal conception of the self be for human rights theory when applied across very different cultures (de Bary 1998)? Taylor's topic—European culture from ancient times through modernism—does not treat these questions. Therefore, we need a broader base from which to start, say, that of Boston Confucianism.

9.5. The Self as Orientation and Poise

The final point here is to introduce some categories for understanding the self that arise from Confucian motifs traced above and that are capable of registering depths of soul, including Eastern and Western self-deceptions. Traditional Western conceptions are criticized for being too individualistic, which stems from the root metaphor of selves being substances that relate to others only as external other substances, or too inhuman and mechanical as in Marxist scientific materialism. Traditional East Asian conceptions are criticized for subordinating persons as merely instrumental to group welfare, and hence unable to appreciate human rights, or for dissolving persons into flows of nature that miss what is distinctive about human beings. This is not the place to rehearse or assess these criticisms, only to note that they and others suggest that some imagination is needed to reconceive the human self in community with others and nature. What follows is a suggestion for part of that project that derives from both Daoist and Confucian themes but most particularly from the conception in *The Doctrine of the Mean* discussed above, that the self is a structured continuum between a centered readiness to respond and the ten thousand things.

Let us suppose, by hypothesis, that the self is an organism, with a human biological endowment interacting with its environment according to acquired ritually shaped orientations, that is given human shape by the recursive structure of poise by which it harmonizes its orientations. This formula will now be explained, beginning with the notion of orientation.

Orientation is how a self comports itself or takes up a stance toward some level or dimension of reality. All specific actions take place within the habits formed by our orientations. Xunzi, as we have noted, pointed out that the rotation of the heavens is something about which we can do nothing but admire and contemplate relative to the scale of our own place in the universe. The rotation of the seasons, however, is something to which we orient ourselves by the dense tissue of activities involved in agricultural peasant culture, an orientation learned, often unconsciously, through imitation and direct participation in seasonal activities. In between, Xunzi noted, are irregular anomalies such as floods, droughts, and barbarians. Orientation to these irregularities is where good government comes in to plan ahead, offer emergency relief, and muster the defenses. Orientations are much more diverse than that, however. We have orientations to our families, and to each family member, and those orientations change as life progresses. We have orientations generally to our historical and political situation and specifically to our own economic welfare. We have orientations to our workplace and to the opportunities for leisure. Most intimately, we have orientations to our own bodies and to our particular careers.

Orientations are made up of learned ritual conventions. Most are picked up unconsciously as we are socialized into our culture's rituals. But some orientations are problematic, as when we cannot get along with our family or find the workplace intolerable for our personal needs. Other times, our culture might not have an orientation that it ought to be able to supply. For instance, we are only now becoming aware of the fact that human societies as well as individuals should have been oriented with greater respect to their natural environment. Who knows what else is important for human beings to be oriented toward but of which they are now innocent?

The point of an orientation is to discern the important or humanly relevant nature of its object and to comport human life appropriately toward it. The ritual structure of an orientation includes both the discernment and the comportment. Accurate discernment is itself a problem for finding adequate orientations, and appropriate comportment is another. But the most interesting problem from the standpoint of understanding the self is that the objects of orientation do not fit together well in the ways they are best discerned. We think about the cosmic realities, the rotations of the heavens, in the mathematical language of modern physics and the poetic language of the mystics. We are oriented to daily life in terms of the calendars of our jobs; only a few of us are farmers whose orientation is determined by the rotation of the seasons. We learn or invent highly determined semiotic systems for orientations to our families, other systems for orientations to civic duties, and still others for orientations to the historic position of our group. Orientations to our own bodies and careers involve different systems from all these.

The systems of signs by which we articulate all these different orientations might seem as if they were connectable by a super system, but they are not. Nineteenth-century Western science had the ideal of reducing all those orientations to the language of mathematical science, an ideal that blossomed and faded with the Encyclopedia of Unified Science movement. The attempt to impose any one language or system of signs on all destroys genuine orientation in those areas where the language blocks real discernment. The symbols of mathematical science only obfuscate the project of taking up an orientation on our mortality and the significance of our legacy to family and culture. The correlative thinking codified in the Han dynasty and again in Shao Yung was an ancient way of attempting to systematize different representative structures of orientations, no more successful nowadays than mathematical science. We live disjointed, fragmented lives because our orientations are not commensurate with one another. Or rather, persons inherit partly and partly work out for themselves patterns of harmonization of their orientations. The objects of orientation are often not static things but processes, such as one's growing family, or career, or historical position. So the patterns of harmonization need constantly to be shifted and accommodated to changes. Rather than speak of the structure of a self as a fixed pattern of harmonization, it is better to speak of a self as maintaining poise in balancing all together. The poise has a dynamic or fluid content, but it is always singular, singular and moving. The poise structure of a self is the constantly shifting patterns of its harmonizations and balancings of its orientations.

Suppose the self, then, is a continuum beginning from the inner center of responsiveness, that is, the intentionality of orientation, functioning specifically to take on orientations in body and mind to the near things of one's intimate body, to things and persons of direct contact such as family, friends, and coworkers, and then to social situation, historical place, nature, and the vast cosmos—the ten thousand things each with its own rhythm, dao, and discernible grain. The core inner responsiveness, Mencius' topic, might well be the same in us all insofar as it is by itself. But it is never by itself; it is always expressed in the orientations to our particular bodies and places in the universe, extending as far as our own particular perspective on the heavens. The orientations are all shaped by ritual conventions, Xunzi's topic.

In this conception of the self there is no fixed boundary of the self, as Western philosophy has supposed sometimes there must be. Rather, the boundaries are set in each instance by the nature of the things toward which a person is oriented. We are individual persons in orientation to the family within which we play specific roles relative to others. We are our family, however, insofar as the family plays a role in the larger community. We can say with Zhang Zai, "Heaven is my father and Earth is my mother, and even such a small creature as I finds an intimate place in their midst" (in Chan 1963, 497.) But we can also say with Wang Yangming, commenting on *The Great Learning*, that the great person, manifesting the clear character, forms "one body with Heaven, Earth, and the myriad things" (in Chan 1963, 660). It depends on what the orientation is toward.

In the theory of orientations, the boundaries of the self are functions of differing orientations, and the continuity of the self has to do not with an underlying fixed essence or character but with the history of the person's poise-efforts, with the ongoing shifting harmonization of the changing things to which the person must take up or correct orientations. How one is oriented, and how one relates that orientation to other orientations, is part of a person's unfolding essence.

But it is only part. Orientations set the conditions for specific actions but do not wholly determine them. People are essentially constituted in part also by the specific things they do and the moral character deriving from them. Life is filled both with specific actions and with the accidents for which no orientation is preparation (Neville 1995, chapter 8). Western philosophy has been rather good at defining the self in terms of specific actions and also in terms of the vicissitudes of accident and fate. It has not had good categories, however, for defining those elements of the self that consist in orientations to the ten thousand things and the processes of harmonizing those orientations. As a consequence it has not been able to articulate well the self's boundaries or many of its kinds of continuity. For this, the themes of orientation and poise that come from the Daoist and Confucian aesthetic, from the Confucian theory of ritual, and from the conception of the self in *The Doctrine of the Mean* are helpful additions. In this form they do not at all interfere with the Western scientific insights into the self that otherwise seem to delegitimate the prescientific Chinese conceptions.

The project of becoming a mature self, of becoming humane, to use Tu's words, thus always has three dimensions. The first is achieving proper orientations to the various realities that are relevant for one's changing age, place, social contexts, and historical situation. Orientations are personal habits that have something like a ritual form, making possible a dance with each relevant dimension of reality. They are learned in many combinations of ways, through being inherited, taught, developed through modifications, invented, or acquired through unique experience and struggle.

The second dimension is the continual quest for poise, for the balance to harmonize all of one's orientations at once. How one is poised needs constantly to change because most of the things toward which we are oriented change, because in the course of life we need to take up orientations to new things, because how we are oriented to any one thing might change for the better or worse, and because our orientations interact among one another and the interaction changes as all the other things change.

The third dimension is the actual history of a person's interactions. All interactions are shaped for better or worse by the person's orientations. But the orientations are not the same as what is done within them, the perceptions and responses to the ten thousand things. A person's moral character needs to be analyzed in all three dimensions: regarding orientations; evolving poise structure; and specific perceptions, responses, projects and personal history.

Does this conception of the self as involving orientations, poise, and specific acts look promising for Boston Confucianism? It is in strong continuity with the Confucian motifs. Furthermore, it easily gives expression to the various senses of self-deception highlighted for Confucianism in section 9.4. It can give clear expression to the kinds of contradictions noted so sharply in Western thought under the general rubric of having a poise structure that holds together two or more contradictory orientations to the same things, treating people according to primary process drives as well as ego and superego structures, having a doubled social consciousness as Marx described, having a tragic orientation toward life as if its limits were not real, and so forth.

Put another way, the self's self-consciousness arises when one realizes that the fault in a perceived bad relationship to something is a function of one's own orientation, not just the thing. Much of self-consciousness is the appreciation of the roles of one's own orientations to the structuring of relations and actions. More of self-consciouness consists in awareness of the particularities of one's poise structure, not just how one relates to one's family, to one's job, to one's civic duties, and to the stars, but how one relates each of those relations to one another. People with very similar orientations can harmonize them and keep them in poise in very different ways. And of course, part of self-consciousness is relating to the absolute particularity of one's perceptions and responses.

Defined this way, the self is under obligation to harmony in three senses. One's orientations ought to harmonize one's responses to the dimensions of reality to which one is oriented; a bad orientation misses or distorts what is important in its object. One's poise structure ought to harmonize one's orientations with one another in ongoing balanced ways: one's degree of personal integrity is largely a function of how one's orientations are kept in poise through the round of life. Finally, one needs to harmonize one's particular responses and actions with the relevant norms for their specific outcomes. In all three cases, the obliging norm is harmony. Harmony is made specific to those three different kinds of things to be harmonized. Neo-Confucians might say that principle is the general norm of harmony, one in itself but many insofar as there are many different things and kinds of things to be harmonized. Harmony transcends any set of conditions to be harmonized, and hence, the self is always looking to what transcends itself in order to achieve the appropriate harmonies required. Christians might say that orientations to things are ways of approaching those things with love, noting what is important about them and responding appropriately; poise is a way of loving oneself so as to achieve a high-level integration of life; right actions are a way of engaging the created world with respect to what ought to be done insofar as our actions can affect that; looking to God as creator of a world in which harmony is the norm for our partly free responses is a way of loving God, finally loving God as the fount of harmony itself, the harmony in which value consists.

These metaphoric specifications of the conception of self in terms of orientation and poise are only that—metaphoric specifications. But they resonate with the Confucian and Christian traditions.[3] The final question to ask in this chapter is whether this conception of the self augurs well for addressing some of the great contemporary problems that define the field for our living philosophy.

To highlight the definitive character of orientations for the self is to call attention to problems of relation and engagement. For instance, most societies and individuals do not have adequate orientations to the natural environment, as ecological issues demand, or adequate orientations to living in a pluralistic society. To point out the ritual character of orientations is to address the question of the social and semiotic factors in selfhood and make possible the ethical consideration of whether our social rituals are appropriate. To note that poise structures are essential features for defining individual identity is to be alert to differences among people who are very similar in the things to which they need to be oriented. It is also felicitous for lifting up the issues of consistency of cultural life under the conditions of late-modernity—how to relate to science, how to relate to economic systems, how to relate to power structures. By emphasizing (1) the relational character of personal existence in orientations, (2) the harmonizing character of individual life in poise, (3) the particular character of individuality in actions, and (4) the derivative character of all three from the principle or God who makes harmonious things possible and real, this theory of the self addresses the spiritual dimension of life: the deliberate effort to improve the human process of engaging ultimate reality truthfully by means of practices that shape the engagement with signs or religious symbols, that discern improved religious symbols for this purpose, that increase competence in the use of the symbols for engagement, and that foster the transformations of soul derivative from the engaging of ultimate reality with the symbols (see section 4.2).

10

Confucianism, Christianity, and Multiple Religious Identity

10.1. Engaging Problematic Cases

The hallmark of contemporary Confucianism as it contributes to the global philosophical discussion, especially in the West, is the belief that the principles and intellectual strategies of ancient Confucianism, which were in critical dialectical relation to ancient Chinese culture, are fruitful for a critical and dialectical analysis of contemporary cultures, most of which are not Chinese. Not all contemporary Confucians believe that Confucianism can be transplanted from its Chinese source to other soils such as late-modern, urban Western cultures of the sort to be found in present day Boston. The test of the hypothesis will be whether Confucianism is indeed useful on a global scale in the long run. This book has made several attempts to test it from many angles.

Chapter 1 presented arguments that Confucianism is indeed portable to non-Chinese contexts and illustrated some contributions it can make to philosophic issues of moral import in a city like Boston. That chapter stressed connections between Confucianism and Western philosophies, and chapter 4 raised issues of spiritual continuities. But there are also disconnections, incompatibilities, and incommensurabilities. Indeed, it was pointed out in section 4.6 that the imaginative structure of symbols in different spiritual traditions might hide very great differences because of the ways they affect the transformation of character. We are still rather far from having comparative categories that are subtle enough to detect similarities and differences in the ways symbols work in the soul (Neville 1996, chapter 5; 2000a, chapters 8–9, Appendix A; 2000c, chapters 7–10, Appendix A). This chapter

193

explores some problematic similarities and dissimilarities between Confucian and Christian motifs that seriously have affected the East Asian and Western philosophic cultures, respectively, generalizing many of the points introduced in the discussion of Tu Weiming in chapter 5. Of course, many other areas of comparison call for attention, but the religious have a centrality going back to the origins of modern Confucian-Western dialogue in the work of Matteo Ricci (Berthrong 1994).

This chapter will press questions bearing upon Christianity about four difficult cases of transporting Confucianism to a modern Western social context: about filial piety as a holy duty, about ritual propriety as it relates to Christian morality, about the kinds of objections a Confucian might have to a community constituted around elaborating the ministry and character of Jesus, and about what happens when someone wants to be a Confucian Christian or a Christian Confucian.

Obviously, these are related. Many thinkers have assumed, on the one hand, that filial piety requires the peculiarly dense family structure typical of East Asia, at least in some periods if not so much now, and on the other hand, that filial piety is a bit idolatrous to Christians. Many have assumed that Confucian ritual propriety goes far beyond religious rites, which by themselves might be analogous to Christian ceremonies, to constitute an artificial culture repugnant to a Christian appreciation of nature, and human nature, as created by God. Many also have assumed that Confucians must find the Christian doctrine of Jesus as the incarnation of God to be deeply mistaken because it supposes, on the one hand, too much transcendence in God and, on the other hand, too much immanence of divinity in Jesus. And many think that religions are exclusive.

The purpose here is to work through some of these problems with an eye to the flourishing of Boston Confucianism. The subject of analysis is not so much particular thinkers or texts in Confucianism and Christianity but rather elementary motifs that have shaped the respective traditions. Filial piety, ritual propriety, and incarnation are such basic motifs and have been given many specific interpretations; the analysis attempts to stand back and treat the general logic of the motifs.

10.2. Filial Piety as Holy Duty

Filial piety in the Confucian tradition, embodied as both ideal and practice in East Asian cultures, is a far more complicated phenomenon than will be indicated by the four traits to be discussed here. Nevertheless, these are among its most important traits, and each one allows for an engagement with Christianity.

The first is that filial piety is the virtue of being competent at honoring those who brought you into existence, most immediately your parents, then grandparents, and so forth. Piety toward teachers and mentors is a variant of this trait of filiality. The extension of honor backward in time is intimately related to your own extension forward in time. This trait of filial piety is a kind of deferring to the family processes of nature within which your own life has a duration and also a role contributing to something larger than itself. There is no contest with Christianity regarding the mutual affirmation of this trait, which is expressed as nicely as any Confucian statement by the fifth of the great commandments of the Torah: "Honor your father and your mother, so that your days may be long in the land that the Lord your God is giving you." (*Exodus* 20:12) Life is a gift, and it is given as part of a family. Honoring parents and family is honoring life itself.

The second trait of filial piety is that its institutions contribute to the social services that care for the elderly. In some social conditions, children's care of elderly parents is the only kind of care they can expect, and parents have as many children as they can in hope that enough will live long enough and remember their filial duty to provide for a comfortable old age. In modern societies West and East, however, conditions are far more diverse. There are retirement financial plans, both private and public, and in some circumstances elderly people prefer communities of their peers to life in a multigenerational household with small children. Modern medicine makes hospitals and doctors serious partners, if not senior partners, in caring for the health of the elderly. And the very great mobility of families in modern society makes intergenerational stability both rare and, alas, sometimes awkward. There is no reason to believe that Confucianism in the modern world, East or West, would or should be more committed to the actual care of the elderly than Christians would or should be. Because children are only one source of support for the elderly, individual family circumstances rather than institutionalized expectations are likely to be the most important factors in determining the care of the elderly.

The third trait of filial piety is a deeper matter than the first two, namely, that filial piety is part of a complex reciprocal relation in which one learns how to love, that is, how to be *ren*, humane. We met this in Tu Weiming's interpretation of *ren* (see section 5.4) and can summarize and elaborate the point briefly here. Beginning with infancy, in the ideal case, a child feels itself loved with a total caring love, a love that aligns the parent's face with the child's and smiles with no disguise, no dissimulation. A baby can be annoying, but never can a baby be your enemy, and therefore, a parent can love the baby without fear or defensiveness. Beginning parental love is purely open even when strained by fatigue. The Confucian virtue of sincerity as a kind of transparency of soul is easy for parents with infants. The parent loves with the expectation that the baby will receive the love at face value, for the baby has nothing else to do. As children grow and differentiate themselves, find roles, relate to the world, learn languages and signs, parental love also grows in complexity and difficulty. But ideally, a wise parent can continue to be truly sincere in love and teach the growing child how to receive love's complications. Just as the parent's love includes expectations for its reception by the children, so the children learn to accept love with expectations of continued trust in the parents and of roles and obligations for the children in returning that love. In the course of maturation, the development of mutual love between parents and children, with all the shifting dialectic of authority and freedom, fleshes out the complexities of love and caring that find instantiations, perhaps in attenuated ways, in all kinds of relations. Thus maturity in filial piety is the model required for loving a spouse, loving siblings, loving in more distant ways your neighbors, behaving humanely to the shopkeepers and other functionaries in your community, and also, of course, loving your own children. The pursuit of this ideal of filial piety as the nest for learning *ren* has pushed Confucian-influenced societies in East Asia to emphasize close family connections throughout extended families and to keep those families together.

Christianity is quite opposite on this point, as noted in section 5.4. Although Judaism is much like East Asian Confucianism in emphasizing personal identity in terms of family connections, Christianity separated itself out, from Pentecost on, by identifying with the widows and orphans, those without effective families. Jesus himself set the tone when he was teaching in a crowded house and his mother and siblings came up outside and asked to see him. Jesus replied, "Who is my mother, and who are my brothers?" And pointing to his disciples he said, "Here are my mother and my brothers! For whoever does the will of my Father in heaven is my brother and sister and mother." (*Matthew* 12:48–50) He said he came not "to bring peace, but a sword. For I have come to set a man against his father, and a daughter against her mother, and a daughter-in-law against her mother-in-law; and one's foes will be members of one's own household. Whoever loves father or mother more than me is not worthy of me, and whoever loves son or daughter more than me is not worthy of me." (*Matthew* 10:34–39) On another occasion a disciple asked Jesus' leave to go bury his father, but Jesus said, "Follow me, and let the dead bury their own dead." (*Matthew* 8:21–22) Can you imagine an East Asian Confucian saying those things? Less inflamatory but even more complicated is the story, as recorded by John, that, as he was hanging on the cross, Jesus told his mother to accept John as her son, and he told John to take Mary as his mother, reconstituting family caretaking responsibilities with an artificial, nonkinship family, when Jesus had living brothers.[1]

Jesus' point was not to do away with the symbolic power of family relations for the defining of love but rather to transfer them from the kinship family to a universal community now constituted under God as parent. All people on Earth, especially those susceptible to Jesus' message, are to be viewed as sisters and brothers and this view has prevailed in metaphors such as "the human family."

Jesus' view is quite different from Mozi's advocacy of universal love. For Mozi, family affection gets in the way of universal love; the model for universal love for him was mutual identification, rather like the Golden Rule (Chan 1963, 213–17). His argument for universal love was a kind of Hobbesian instrumental rationalism. For Jesus, on the other hand, universal love might very well be costly, surely dangerous when loving enemies, but commanded because all people are related as brothers and sisters, and all relate to God as the common parent.

Where do Christians say we learn love? Not regularly from our own parents because too many of us have broken families. Rather, we learn the meaning of the family metaphors from representations of God. Jesus used the God of Israel, the God who cared for people in history, to define what true parental love ought to be like. Of course, as we noted in section 5.4, the metaphor worked both ways: Jesus used the ordinary image of the benevolent father to subordinate the more common image of Yahweh as warrior king, but then used divine love to redefine the love that constitutes ideal family relations. Not even the most fortunate of us has a parent as good as God, but parental love has divine love as its model and ideal. For Christianity, one's kinship family ought to imitate the ideal that love God has for the world and that the covenanted people ought to have for one another. But if one does not have a kinship family, as so many do not, then one looks to the church for brothers and sisters and treats all people as if they were kin. The effect of this Christian position in most situations has been to emphasize the importance of kinship identity far less than it has been emphasized in Judaism or Confucianism. Families are important for those who have good ones or much property to inherit; but all is not lost for those who do not. Social and geographical mobility is less disrupting to Christian culture because people are less completely defined by family position than in many other cultures. Of course, there has been much historical variation regarding this point. A corollary of the Christian drift in this regard is that people have obligations toward their families even when the families are seriously dysfunctional, not the obligations of obedience and imitation characteristic of Confucianism, but of other kinds of care.

But unlike the Confucians, the Christians did not affirm love with distinctions based on kinship familial proximity. Rather, Christians gather into new families—churches—in which they voluntarily bond together with whoever else will take on the Christian way. Most churches would be expected to be internally varied, pluralistic as we say today, with rich and poor, educated and uneducated, slave and free, men and women, all worshiping together as a family and organizing social life around the family bonds created in the congregation. Paul's first letter to the Corinthians, from which the famous passage on love is taken, is mainly about how to organize such a reconstructed family in which Jesus is the eldest brother and all are children of God (see also *Romans* 8:29). To join such a church is to take possession of the rightful inheritance of all people as children of God. But most people fail to realize this and live like slaves or aliens within God's house or kingdom (*Romans* 8:14–17). So "love with distinctions" for Christians would mean parsing out the differences between caring for those within the Christian community and ministering to those outside it. In the history of Christianity these differences have taken many different forms, the most obvious of which is the difference between a largely Christianized culture with a state church and an alien culture where Christianity is a small movement.

The Christian way of learning love has a different logic from the Confucian, at least on the surface. For Christians, one does not learn love from parents particularly, but from saints. Saints here are those special people who do or say the right things so as to pass on the spark of Jesus' love which itself is the incarnation of divine love. There is an issue of lineage here, but not family lineage. The Christian lineage is from Jesus to his disciples to those whom they brought to love on down through the ages and across many various circumstances for loving. A saint need not be a particularly good or accomplished person, but someone who has caught the spark of love, whose breath carries the spirit that renews the soul. The Christian lineage of learning love passes through the church, not the family, although ideal childhood takes God-fearing parents as the first taste of church.

A skeptical secularist would point out that the Christian church has behaved as the ideal communicator of redeeming love rather than hypocricy, about as often as Confucian families have developed true *ren* rather than authoritarianism, which is to say, rarely. Or perhaps it is better to say that neither is often pure and completely successful but that both are very often partially successful. Further discussion of this point will be postponed until the fourth trait of Confucian filial piety has been explored.

The fourth trait is that filial piety is the taking on of the virtues of the ancestors. A filial person is one who learns the goodness and strength of character that his or her parents can teach. This is the obverse of the essential duty of parents, which is to make their children into good people. The most important filial accomplishment is to become so virtuous that your parents are given freedom from the obligation to make you more virtuous. Your parents have not done their duty and are bound by its obligations so long as you are not a person of full humanity, propriety, wisdom, and righteousness. Only by becoming good can you set your parents free so that they can grow old in peace and fulfillment. The ultimate failure in filial piety is to let your parents be failures in your own case.

Note that this is a transitive process. Your parents need to transfer their virtue to you, as theirs came from your grandparents. In the classical Confucian symbolism the line goes back to the great sage emperors whose virtue was perfect and who passed it on. Of course, the transitivity is sometimes blocked and often muddied, and a traditional Confucian project is to leap over generations of lapsed virtue to recover the virtue of the ancients (Tillman 1992; Berthrong 1998a, 97). This is a quite proper way to handle obvious failures in the transmission of virtue, and the equally obvious fact that most of us have parents with flaws we hope not to learn, while magnifying their virtues. Confucian political theory often has said that the distant emperor can be a model from which ordinary people learn virtue in a filial way. When the emperor perfects himself and loves his own immediate family, from the filial-like imitation by others, the whole realm can be renovated, according to *The Great Learning* (Chan 1963, 86–87).

Christianity has an unusually close analogue to this in its doctrine of the taking on of the mind of Christ, the imitation of Christ. In the Christian theory of the church, one of the predominant metaphors is that the church is the body of Christ animated by the Holy Spirit which forms and moves the body as the mind of Christ. In Aristotelian theology this metaphor attains considerable sophistication as the mind of Christ is like an agent-intellect for the corporate church. A variant on this metaphor, less given to hylomorphism and mind-body dualism, is that the church is the continuing resurrected body of Christ, continuing his life and ministry through the ages and into circumstances of which Jesus himself never dreamed. Because the church is historical, with a movement into this place, and then that place, with different actors in concert and sequence, the church as the body of Christ is quite particular according to this metaphor, something like a singular individual.

But for personal piety, especially popular piety, coming to have the mind of Christ, as Saint Paul advocated, means imitating the character and work of Jesus, adapting that to your own situation. Imitation, in part, requires taking on Jesus' several virtues in the sense of Aristotelian virtue ethics, but even more, it requires taking on a character in action, loving enemies, glorifying God while enduring such sufferings and persecutions as crucifixion, and keeping focus, faith, and fervor for the mission of reconciliation and the ignition of love. The point is that, for Christians, Jesus had the fullness of divinity as fit for human beings, and by becoming more Christ-like you become more divine in that humanly fit sense.

The attainment of virtue by taking on Christ's virtue is not all that different in form from the Confucian project of filial piety as taking on the virtue of parents, ultimately of the sages. The supposition of both is that there was appropriate perfection in the past, a perfection that applied not only to individuals but to individuals in their various relations with one another, with their institutions, and with nature. Through imitation it is possible for successors to the models themselves to come to perfect virtue, although the content of that virtue needs to be adapted to new circumstances. Both traditions characterize the state of failing in proper imitation as *selfishness*, in accordance with which people become diminished from the full human nature that would properly flesh out divinity or heavenly principle. Christianity insists more than Confucianism, at least on the surface, that self-centeredness is a kind of spiritual bondage from which a person can be freed only by encountering an effective demonstration of divine love directed at the person, either by taking Jesus' love to be so directed or by meeting it in one of the saints. Without resorting to Christianity's dramatic language of conversion, Confucianism motivates the small person to the path of sageliness by an encounter with *ren*, by being shown your parents' love which you have slighted and being filled with remorse or by encountering a person great in *ren*, such as Confucius, by suddenly understanding the model of the ancient sages, or by participating in a ritual the performance of which gives you a taste of *ren*. However you might be turned onto the path of the sage, or of Christian perfection, Confucianism and Christianity are in complete accord with what comes next, the method of attaining holiness or sageliness, namely, practice. Practice is the formation of habits that clear up your character so that the virtue of some previous concrete, particular person—your parents, the Great Emperors Shun or Yu, or Jesus—becomes appropriately embodied in your own life.

The preliminary upshot of this survey of the four traits of filial piety is that there are extraordinary parallels between Confucianism and Christianity so long as filial piety does not necessarily mean one's particular parents, and so long as the model of ancient heavenly established virtue is not necessarily Jesus. For both Confucians and Christians, the ancestral virtue is not to be copied as a pattern so much as reembodied in forms appropriate for one's own situation.

10.3. Ritual Propriety

The metaphoric significance of Confucian ritual propriety, discussed so frequently in earlier chapters, can be shown by analogy with the second creation story starting in *Genesis* 2. God, in that account, begins by creating a human being out of clay and water, and breathing the breath of life into it. Then God brings the person from that desert oasis to the Garden of Eden where nature already has been installed. After the human being has invented language and social conventions by naming the animals, and after discovering that the human being without a social mate is not a finished creation, in consequence of which Adam was divided so that there were male and female, God allows the first "truly human" action. The snake tempts Eve to eat the fruit of the tree of the knowledge of good and evil; she falls for it, and Adam joins her.

What in this complex metaphoric story constituted the fall of humankind? God had previously laid down the condition with Adam, who had told Eve, that they were not to eat the fruit of the tree of the knowledge of good and evil. This was a convention, with no justification in the nature of things. The snake represented pure nature. He told Eve the apple was beautiful, which she saw to be true, that it was not poisonous and would not bring death, and that it would make her and Adam more like God, a good thing, in being able to distinguish good from evil. Indeed, they were able to distinguish good from evil after eating the apple and thus shared in part of the divine nature. Moreover, there was nothing poisonous about the apple per se. The reason God made Adam and Eve mortal after the meal was not because of natural biological properties of the apple but because they had broken the convention, the covenant: they had forgotten their agreement with Yahweh and pretended that the natural things were the only real ones. But the covenant not to eat of that tree was an artificial agreement, not something in the ecology of the Garden and its magic plants. In this story there is God the divine agent, the snake as the symbol of pure nature, and the humans who were defined by their institutional arrangement with God in ways that cannot be registered in the natural viperous perspective alone. The humans forgot their covenantal, conventional, institutional definition and thus fell from grace.

There is an obvious analogy with ancient Confucianism. Humans are not human by heaven or creative principle alone, nor by earth or nature alone, nor by the two acting in concert, but by the development of institutions and conventions symbolized as ritual propriety. The way of the human, the human dao, is to bring natural endowments to fulfillment beyond anything entertained by natural order or receptivity, by natural endowment as constituted by heaven and earth in cooperation. The human dao requires the invention of culture, and it is for this reason that Confucians following Xunzi have long talked of the trinity of heaven, earth, and the human sphere shaped by ritual propriety.

What is ritual propriety but the very sort of thing Adam and Eve forgot, their covenant not to eat the fruit of those trees? The Chinese rituals differed in content but not in humanity-defining conventionality. The metaphors are different in many ways, but not in saying that the human does not achieve its own nature unless it goes beyond the snake's nature to the artifice of convention. Rituals, of course, do not themselves direct our intentional behavior. They do not tell us what political course to pursue, nor how to solve deep moral problems, nor what to enjoy in life, nor how to cope with floods and famine. Ritual behavior of itself does not give direction to life, which depends on circumstances and intentions. But rituals are the vehicles of social and personal living. Any significant, that is, sign-formed, behavior or meaning is ritually shaped. The content of life consists in doing things that are ritually shaped.

The ancient Confucians knew that without the knowledge and habitual practice of the rituals in which high civilization consists, the civilization cannot exist, as has been argued several times in these chapters. They complained that the rituals of the sage emperors had been neglected and forgotten. As a result, like barbarians they could cooperate in the hunt with rude rituals but could not run an intricate economy of production and trade; like barbarians they could be ruled by strongmen but could not have a peaceful empire where the regularities of nature could be celebrated and the irregularities coped with by dykes and granaries; like barbarians they could have children but, lacking the rituals of filiality, no civilized family life; like barbarians they could have colleages and rough lovers but no friends. Confucius, Mencius, and Xunzi saw the teaching and practice of high ritual as a revolutionary force to overcome militarism, banditry, and ineffective government. Commentators like Heiner Roetz (1993) who believe the emphasis on ritual in ancient Confucianism was conservative and that radical progress was for the Confucians to become Kantians surely have it backward: the Confucians were radical social critics who advocated ritual as a more powerful instrument of revolution and reform than military might.

Much of the excitement of contemporary Confucianism lies in analyzing our cultures in terms of the strengths and weaknesses of rituals at each point along the continuum of ritual behavior. The creativity called for by Confucianism addresses the problems of inventing rituals for pluralistic, mobile societies. In all this, Xunzi would point out that the rituals whose exercise constitutes civilization are the very things that enable the mind as ruler to bring our feelings and sensibilities to their fulfillment, shaping the inner grain of life so that our eyes, ears, nose, mouth, and body with their respective objects lead us to fulfilled desires, healthy aversions, excellent delights, rightly directed anger, truthful grief, and joy that harmonizes heaven and earth.

The second creation myth in *Genesis*, chapters 2 and 3, recognized that the human beings were not completely created until they had the conventions of language and their society together. *Genesis* recognized that the representation of nature as the sole guide of human life was the snake's trick: the conventions of the social relation between God and the humans, in which the humans were to tend the Garden and avoid certain foods, were the basis of truly fulfilled humanity. Since the fall, people are less than their original perfection. But *Genesis*, and the subsequent Judeo-Christian-Muslim tradition, has nothing like the subtlety of the Confucian analysis of ritual to understand what went wrong in the fall and what must be done to repair the covenant. Christianity has very much to learn in this regard with respect to the very heart of its analysis of the human condition as now lying in bondage to sin.

The original question above about ritual from the Christian standpoint is whether its elaborate Confucian form is an artificial construct repugnant to the Christian appreciation of God's creation of nature and human nature. The answer now should be a clear no. As surely as Xunzi, *Genesis* distinguishes between the regularities of nature in the sense of apples and snakes and the conventions that are needed to complete human nature. God teaches Adam the conventions of language by having him name the animals, and works on building a society until Adam is divided into male and female with a social order of home, work, and mutual pleasure and companionship. For Christianity the conventions that make up civilization are part of the original creation of human nature. There is a difference in cosmology, of course, in that for Confucianism nature is the product of the conjoining of the daos of earth and heaven, whereas for Christianity nature, including human nature, is the product of God. For Confucianism, the human dao of developing ritual is necessary for the interaction of heaven and earth to reach its own fulfillment. For *Genesis* also the creation of the garden and of the breathing clay human was not complete until the garden had a conventionally based social order to tend it. The conventional and artificial character of ritual in no way interferes with the Christian notion that God creates human nature: human nature is an artificial supplementation carried on by the God of nature in the other sense. Confucianism and Christianity are in complete agreement that the fall from original perfection consists in forgetting and neglecting the rituals of high civilization, and that sageliness or sanctification consists in their reestablishment and practice.

10.4. Jesus as Model

The third point of comparison is very brief, and concerns how Confucianism might relate to the Christian claim that a religious community should be oriented around embodying the character and work of Jesus. What this embodiment might be was discussed earlier in terms of the church and how it is analogous, in part, to the traits of filial piety having to do with learning to love and to be virtuous. Now the comparison should be focused around the Confucian problem of the relation between *ren* or humaneness, on the one hand, and ritual propriety, on the other. The problematic of filial piety was developed as the context for learning *ren*. The problematic of ritual propriety was developed in terms of the completion of human nature by civilization and right relation to nature and the divine. How are humaneness and ritual propriety related?

Ritual propriety, of course, takes a long time to learn, starting in infancy with learning to babble in the phonemes of the parents' language, as Aristotle pointed out. If one emphasizes the dense inter-weaving of rituals, becoming ritually competent requires great maturity. But rituals can be learned without any real humaneness, in which case they are hollow. On the other hand, Confucius asked (*Analects* 3.3, in Chan 1963, 24), if a person is not humane, what has the person to do with ceremonies or music? At best, use them for advantages. It is the humane person, the one awakened to true parental love and the need to reflect it back in filial piety, who will undertake to practice propriety. How does one become humane? Unlike ritual propriety, which must be learned laboriously, Confucius said (*Analects* 7.29, in Chan 1963, 33), "Is humanity far away? As soon as I want it, there it is right by me." Humaneness does not need to be learned the way ritual propriety does: it needs to be wanted. The problem with small people, even when they are adept at rituals, is that they do not want humaneness. Their wants are selfish. Of course, humaneness needs to be understood, and its complexities and depths perhaps are encountered best in a Confucian family or a truly effective church. But even when understood, the question with humaneness is whether you want it. If you do, you have it immediately to the extent of your understanding. How to live in society as a humane person remains to be problematic only insofar as it commits you to mastering the rituals of moral life and civilization, perfecting relationships with family, community, and friends.

This is strikingly analogous to the Christian configuration of liberating salvation or justification and holiness. The devotee is turned to the path of love and released from sin's bondage by encountering the divine love in some person or other and becoming inflamed by it, passing it on; this is justification or salvation. But then to live a holy life means taking on the character and work of Jesus in concert with others. That is a long process of reformation where bad habits change slowly and real confusions exist concerning what to do. Indeed, becoming holy is like trying to learn and practice ritual propriety in an age of degenerate rituals. The hope comes from the model of Jesus' character and work as adapted to one's own time. That character and work is the source of potential rituals for one's own time. Christians often have not been very good at adapting the first century Galilean representations of Jesus to their own situation. Partly that is because they lacked a sophisticated Confucian sense of what rituals are and how they function, frequently mistaking them for moral absolutes. Partly it is because the adaptation of civilizing rituals to new circumstances is extremely difficult: the actual rituals of Confucius' time would have little relevance to culture in Boston, and Boston Confucians need to be just as creative as Boston Christians, relative to the ancient models.

Now the Christian point about Jesus is that he is the source for Christians of both the love that liberates and makes one humane, and also the ritual propriety or holy habits of the heart that should civilize our time and bring it into proper relation with nature and the divine. Christians understand themselves to be freed from bondage to degenerate ways of life by the love of God expressed in Jesus and passed down the ages; they understand themselves to be engaged in the project of sanctification, which means learning to live in ways that reflect the original convenant and repair the damage done to original perfection. Those ways are mainly matters of ritual propriety, with rituals that need to be recovered or newly invented for new circumstances. To what would Confucians object in this Christian reference to Jesus?

The themes here have been: how to learn love, examining the models of filiality and the imitation of Christ; how to be civilized and rightly related to nature and the divine, examining the model of ritual propriety and its undeveloped analogue in *Genesis* 2; and how to be religious concretely in the sense of both loving and undertaking personal and social reform. These themes relate equally to the futures of Confucianism and Christianity and what they can learn from one another. And they bear powerfully upon the multiple religious identities of people who aim to be both Confucian and Christian.

10.5. Multiple Religious Identity

Because Confucianism has permeated a global society, some of its practitioners will come from non–East Asian traditions and will combine Confucianism with spiritual identities from elsewhere to form a "multiple religious identity."[2] How can one person be a Confucian and something else, say, a Christian? This is a return to the problem of Boston Confucianism with the prism focused on its spirituality. Because of spirituality's investment in ultimacy, which might be obscured in "mere philosophy," the spiritual problematic of Boston Confucianism increases the temperature. To be a Confucian and a Platonist at once might require fancy footwork, but your mother does not care. She cares a great deal if you claim to be a Confucian and a Christian.

A socially significant but spiritually superficial way to address the question is through the issue of religious *membership*. A person is a member of a spiritual tradition if membership is self-consciously affirmed and the person's spiritual practice is guided by the symbols and terms of the core texts and motifs of the tradition, however reconstituted for contemporary viability; it helps also if the person's membership is recognized by other members of the tradition, although isolation and heresy (a form of membership) are not uncommon.

With regard to traditions' attitudes toward multiple membership, the situation is diverse. Exclusivistic Christians who say all other religions are wrong or merely disguised forms of Christianity would not permit or take the time for the cultivation of Confucian spiritualty. But nonexclusivist Christians might look for spiritual sustenance wherever it might be found, and Confucianism is a good source. Christian identity is maintained by self-conscious participation in the Christian movement of reconciliation and worship begun by Jesus with his disciples and continuing down to practicing Christians today.

From the Confucian side, the whole issue of membership is just not very important. True, there was an existentialist theme in some Neo-Confucians who emphasized the importance of a defining decision to pursue the path of the sage; in our time, Tu Weiming has defended this position (see sections 5.1 to 5.3). But even here the point of the Confucian project is turning the self to the effort of spiritual perfection, not so much joining up to do it in a Confucian way, though that is supposed too. Efforts of the Song and Ming Neo-Confucians to distinguish their school from Buddhism and Daoism did indeed reflect a self-consciousness about a reconstituted Confucian school, but their main criticisms of the other schools had more to do with their failures to support adequate practice in personal, family, and public life than with primary doctrinal differences. The Confucian stress is not on whether one is in or out of the movement, although that is a question, but whether one is any good at it. Given the practical intentionality of Confucianism, the practical effort and accomplishment are more important than labels. Dai Zhen (1723–77) would have thought his contemporary John Wesley (1703–91) a profound Confucian sage if Wesley had been able to talk with him about *The Analects*. On the social level of membership, there is no difficulty being a member of the Confucian and Christian movements at once so long as they do not interfere conceptually and their practices reinforce and complement one another. Only the limits of time and energy need inhibit the efforts required to practice both spiritualities where they are different from one another.

On a spiritually profound level, of course, the issue is more complicated. The essential feature of spirituality is to engage the ultimate and this requires both appropriate symbols and competence at using the symbols to engage. The symbols of Confucianism and Christianity are quite different. Perhaps we can show clear similarities and differences at the intellectual level. But when the symbols are functioning within the soul in meditation and practice, they have very different imaginative structures. The Confucian symbols have only faint reminiscences of divine intentionality, little stronger that "the mandate of heaven," for instance (see section 8.4). By contrast, Christian symbols of the ultimate are redolent with intentionality even when the underlying metaphysical conception puts that aside apophatically (as in Thomas Aquinas or Tillich). The imaginative functioning of the different symbol systems in meditation, quiet-sitting, communal liturgies, and spiritually directed practices must be different: though both spiritual traditions emphasize self-examination, Confucians do not pray to anybody and Christians do not focus much reverence for ancestors other than Jesus.

There are several ways to understand the difference between spiritually significant symbologies. First, the traditions might simply be oriented to different ultimates, and it might be possible to defend a plurality of ultimates; in this case one can be a Confucian for some ultimate matters, a Christian for others. Second, the traditions might be oriented to the same thing as ultimate but interpret it in different respects, the Confucian picking up on the nonintentional aspects, for instance, and the Christian on the intentional ones; in this case multiple religious identity is a positive asset for a richer spiritual life. Or third, and most problematically, the traditions might agree on the ultimate orientation and interpret it in the same respect: do their different symbols for engaging mean that they disagree in their interpretations or that they are saying much the same thing in different ways? That is a serious scholarly question to which there is no full answer now because we lack clear and publicly justified comparative categories. But any person affirming multiple religious identities has to be ready to defend at least the compatibility if not the agreement and complementarity of the multiple traditions' symbols when they are about the same thing.

Now the defense of the consistency of a spiritual life lived actively through two or more spiritual traditions is not just an antiquarian project, the mere examination of the compatibility of traditional spiritual texts. On the contrary, it is an emotionally burning, forward-looking project. All the great spiritual traditions are facing the challenges of late-modernity, at least those posed by science, global morals, and ecology. Every religion needs to be reconstructed, or creatively extended, to address those challenges, and each would have to be reconstructed, even if it were alone in facing those challenges.

But they are not alone. The global interaction of religious traditions is yet another novelty of late-modernity, a challenge in itself to religious identity. The practical tests for the compatibility of spiritualities lie in the struggles they have together to call upon their traditional resources to address contemporary challenges. Highly intentional anthropomorphic Christian conceptions of God are just as much in need of deconstruction and reconstruction as Confucian conceptions of heaven above and the earth below. Modern science, the global moral situation, and ecology set a common agenda that differentially challenges the various traditions but unites them in the task of presenting symbols for spiritual engagement.

None of this guarantees in advance that the traditions are indeed compatible and that multiple religious identity might not be schizophrenic. Moreover, any reconstructive effort, even within a single tradition, is open to the charge that the reconstruction leaves out the most important parts of the tradition. But the proof of compatibility and illustration of its limitations come only in concrete lives, developed in conversation that is serious in the Confucian sense, and that is justified philosophically by reflection tolerably faithful to all sides. Boston Confucianism, especially in its members who are also Christians, is deeply committed to multiple religious identity, and to the serious and faithful conversation that can test its limits.

Notes

Preface

1. To be sure, the response is far more ancient. Both the early Buddhists and the Nestorian Christians represented important elements of Western thought to which Confucians had to respond. The 16th and 17th century Christian missions to China also brought Confucians in touch with European renaissance thought. But it was in the 19th century that science and other aspects of Western modernity came to be taken with great seriousness, as in the work of Kang Yuwei, for instance.

2. For a general interpretation of ancient Chinese philosophy as disputation regarding social criticism, see A. C. Graham 1989. For an interesting reinterpretation of Neo-Confucianism that treats it as a cultural and political movement as well as a philosophic one, see Hoyt Cleveland Tillman 1992; see especially his references to Wang Anshi.

3. One thinks particularly of Wing-tsit Chan, Cheng Chungying, Anthonio Cua, Liu Shuhsien, and Tu Weiming, among Chinese authors writing in English, and of Wm. Theodore de Bary among Western scholars. At a presentation of an early draft of this preface and chapter 1 at the Neo-Confucian Seminar at Columbia University, Professor de Bary pointed out that the development of Confucianism in America, in English, antedates its most recent flourish in Boston; Tu Weiming, for instance, had received some of his graduate education in the Columbia University program and others of Professor de Bary's students, such as Judith Berling and Rodney Taylor, did not think of themselves as Confucians for the very first time at the Berkeley conference.

4. Modern higher education in India was modelled on the British system, and many of the best students went to Britain to study. During the nineteenth century India saw a movement to recover the texts and ways of thought of its ancient past; but that movement failed to prevail against scientific education and has been limited to influence within Indian universities, hardly elsewhere; so far it has failed to become a serious participant in world philosophy, although it is influential in some forms of religious thought. Most African higher education is European oriented. Islamic higher education from

Gibralter to Jakarta is by no means of European origin, although Western science and technology are finding their way into the Muslim world; but Islamic philosophy has not yet entered the world-wide culture of philosophy in significant ways.

5. On the "three schools" or "three teachings" phenomenon, see Judith A. Berling, 1980, especially chapter 2. On the same point, with a discussion of modern multiple religious identity and another account of the 1991 Berkeley conference, which was hosted by Berling who was then dean of the Graduate Theological Union, see John H. Berthrong, 1994, chapter 2. For an introductory history of Confucianism including its recent entry into the modern world of the West, see Berthrong, (1998a).

6. For the other books of essays see Neville (1982, 1987a, and 1991a).

Chapter 1. The Short Happy Life of Boston Confucianism

1. With greater leisure of transplantation, I would include the *I Ching*, *The Book of Odes* and *The Book of Rites*.

2. I have analyzed the distinction between primary and secondary scripture, and its relation to tradition, in Neville (1991a, 36–46). An embarrassingly large number of citations and endnotes here are to this author's other works. Only in part a function of ego, in larger part it is a function of systematic philosophy that develops a concept from many different angles and contexts.

3. On Plato as a social revolutionary through education, see Brumbaugh (1962, 1982, 1989). For my comparison of Plato and Confucius, see Neville (1981, chapter 2), as well as chapter 9 here.

4. This compressed description of the Confucian model of the self reflects my own reading both of the ancient texts and of their interpretation by Neo-Confucians down to the present day such as Tu Weiming. For a more complete description with citations of relevant texts, see Neville (1987a, chapter 2, and 1991a, chapters 7 to 9).

5. Most notably, Tu Weiming (1979, 1985, 1989), Cheng Chungying (1990), Julia Ching (1976), and Antonio Cua (1982). Tu (1989) deals with intellectuals in China more than with Chinese philosophical principles for the West. Cheng's representations of Chinese thought for the West have been deeply influenced by the *Yijing*. See Cua and Ching for contemporary presentations of Wang Yangming's approach to humanity, the first in a moral, the second in a spiritual, mode.

6. See the extraordinarily profound description of this in Alexis de Tocqueville's *Democracy in America*, part 2, book 3.

7. Propriety not only has this moral function but also carries the moral to a religious dimension. Through civilization as embodied in the social prac-

tices shaped by proper ritual propriety, the domain of the human becomes equal to and a fulfillment of heaven and earth. See Robert Eno (1990), and Graham (1989, part 1, chapter 1).

8. Charles S. Peirce (1839–1914) was a philosopher, mathematician, and scientist; he was unsuccessful in holding academic appointments, was chronically ill with a painful neurological disease, and died in poverty. Nevertheless, he was a philosophical genius on a par with Kant. Charles Hartshorne and Paul Weiss published six volumes of his philosophical papers, *The Collected Papers of Charles Sanders Peirce*, and Arthur W. Burks edited two more. A new and more nearly complete edition is being published by Indiana University Press, but it is not yet far enough along to cover the major philosophical papers. A survey of Peirce's philosophy is to be found in Neville (1992, chapter 1). My own books developing pragmatism's theory of nature and signs are a trilogy called Axiology of Thinking, consisting of *Reconstruction of Thinking* (1981), *Recovery of the Measure* (1989), and *Normative Cultures* (1995).

9. John Dewey, also a classical pragmatist, did understand Peirce's theory. Nevertheless, Dewey toured China in 1919–20 lecturing on the elementary advantages of technology which he believed appropriate for China at that time (Dewey 1973). The unqualified praise of technology in these lectures contradicts the extremely nuanced and critical approach to technology in Dewey's books for English-speakers (e.g., 1981 or 1984) and that is required for an extension of Confucianism.

10. Whereas Rorty's development of pragmatism hauls the movement back to the modernist and postmodernist strands of late-modern thinking, I celebrate pragmatism's neat evasion of that dead end of philosophy (Neville 1992, introduction and chapter 1).

11. The sketch here of the pragmatic theory of signs as natural habits relating interpreters both to nature and to purposive intentions and intentionality is developed at length in Neville (1989 and 1995).

12. On the performative and illocutionary functions of language, see John Searle (1969) and also Fingarette (1972), who uses these notions to interpret ritual propriety.

13. Thus pragmatic semiotics rejects any functionalist approach to interpretation which sees a background as only an aggregate of connected individual interpretations. See Neville (1989, chapter 2).

14. For a careful elaboration of this, see Neville (1995, especially chapter 7).

15. William Theodore de Bary's development of Confucian studies and practice at Columbia University in New York has been longer lasting and more productive than any of us Confucians from Boston, even if he and his students Judith Berling, Rodney Taylor, and Mary Evelyn Tucker responded to the altar call in Berkeley. Liu Shuhsien and Cheng Chungying share the general program of Boston Confucianism with but brief connections with the City of Boston.

16. Ultimate concern is the defining point for religiousness according to Paul Tillich (1952), and in some respect, that must be right. I have argued that the marks of a religion are rituals that epitomize how people are supposed to relate to life, mythologies or cosmologies that symbolize the universe's character and limits, and spiritual practices aiming at improvement or perfection (see Neville 1991a, 156–63; Neville 1996, introduction and chapter 1; see also Eno 1990).

17. See, for instance, Judith Berling (1980).

18. For an extended discussion of the first encounter of Christianity with Confucianism, see Jonathan D. Spence (1983). For an account of the current status of the Confucian-Christian dialogue, see Berthrong (1994). In the long run, of course, Matteo Ricci won the argument.

Chapter 2. Confucianism on Culture

1. On the ways this was expressed in Chinese language, see Hansen (1983).

2. On primitiveness in Daoism, see Girardot (1983).

3. For a study of the historical diversity of Buddhism in China, see Ch'en (1964).

4. For a fine analysis of Xunzi's understanding of rituals, especially funeral rites, see Yearly (1995).

5. For an important discussion of the culture of virtue and courage that places the ancient Confucians in relation to Western thinking, see Yearly (1990).

6. Among the most important thinkers in this movement are John Berthrong, Cheng Chungying, Julia Ching, Antonio Cua, William Theodore de Bary, Liu Shuhsien, and Tu Weiming.

7. For the ancient Chinese conception of social justice, see Lee (1995).

Chapter 3. Confucianism in the Contemporary Situation

1. Academic philosophy in the United States and Great Britain has frequently, if not always, come to define itself as a special science among other sciences within the university and has thus drifted toward methods of self-definition and legitimation that distinguish it from other ways and topics of thought that once broadly fell under philosophy; see the various essays in Kasulis and Neville (1997), especially those of George Lucas, Jr., and George Allan. Rather than defining the public for philosophical discourse disciplinarily, many thinkers now are taking the definition from the scope of the problems that traditionally have fallen under philosophy in the West and China as well as elsewhere. Sometimes dismissed by academic philosophers, these public

intellectuals are quite clear that all the world's philosophic traditions are part of the dialogue. This point of view regarding public intellectuals is paradigmatically embodied in Confucianism and those influenced by it (see Tu Weiming 1989). On the importance of taking into account the philosophical traditions of the world's civilizations, see Samuel P. Huntington (1996).

2. For a wonderful account and translations of the Leibniz texts into English, see Ching and Oxtoby (1992).

3. Even more recent translations of parts of Zhu Xi's work have appeared, such as Gardner's in 1990.

4. It is interesting that, because neither Ivanhoe nor Yearley limits Western philosophy to the analytic tradition in the twentieth century, both are in departments of religious studies. Religious studies departments are often the locus of philosophy in America that is not analytical.

5. As I have argued with them in debate for years.

6. See his *Tai Chen's* Inquiry into Goodness (1971).

Chapter 4. Confucian Spirituality

1. Distinctions among various dimensions of life, or pervasive cultural enterprises, or perspectives on culture, such as art, religion, morality, science, and philosophy, are by no means new. Aristotle had a catalogue of them. With great influence Hegel structured his *Phenomenology of Spirit* according to them. In our time, Paul Weiss has developed a theory of such cultural enterprises and written separate books on several: the theory was first stated in *Modes of Being* (1958) and redone in *Creative Ventures* (1992). He studied politics in *Our Public Life* (1959) and *Toward a Perfected State* (1986), religion in *The God We Seek* (1964), ethics in *Man's Freedom* (1950), history in *History: Written and Lived* (1962), athletics in *Sport: A Philosophic Inquiry* (1969), and the arts in *The World of Art* (1961a), *Nine Basic Arts* (1961b), and *Cinematics* (1975). My own extended discussion of religion as a dimension of life in relation to others is in Neville (1987a, chapter 10).

2. See volume 38 of the *International Journal for Philosophy of Religion*, entitled *God, Reason and Religions: New Essays in the Philosophy of Religion*, a special retrospective twenty-fifth anniversary issue, edited by Eugene Thomas Long. See especially the essays by Robert P. Scharlemann, "Can Religion be Understood Philosophically?" and Neville, "Religions, Philosophies, and Philosophy of Religion." This issue is published separately as a book (Long 1995).

3. Whitehead (1926, 16–17) goes on: "It runs through three stages, if it evolves to its final satisfaction. It is the transition from God the void to God the enemy, and from God the enemy to God the companion. Thus religion is solitariness; and if you are never solitary, you are never religious. Collective enthusiasms, revivals, institutions, churches, rituals, bibles, codes of behaviour,

are the trappings of religion, its passing forms. They may be useful, or harmful; they may be authoritatively ordained, or merely temporary expedients. But the end of religion is beyond all this."

4. This part of the definition of religion picks up on anthropological and cultural studies. See, for instance, Driver (1991), Geertz (1973), or Turner (1969).

5. This part of the definition of religion is framed by considerations in sociology of knowledge (see Berger 1967) and picks up on studies of myth in phenomenology (for instance, van der Leeuw 1933, Eliade 1978–85), historical studies of religious ideas and their cultural assumptions, and theologies of various sorts including commentaries.

6. The literature in spirituality is not well focused. Streng's definition of religion starts from this point. See also Neville (1978, 1996, chapter 5).

7. For discussions of ultimacy, and religious symbols, and the iconicity of myths to reality, see Neville (1996). For a cross-cultural approach to ultimacy, see Neville (2000b).

8. For a brief discussion of the distinction between essential and conditional features, see Neville (1987b, 253–73). For a complete technical discussion, see Neville (1968, chapters 2 and 3).

9. See, for instance, Wayne Proudfoot (1985). On the other side, John E. Smith (1968) has defended what I would call an engagement theory of experience, deriving from pragmatism and its critique of British empiricism, that gets around the criticisms. Smith's own point is examined extensively in Kasulis and Neville (1997).

10. The distinction between transcendence in the sense of reference to an external God and immanent transcendence in the sense of transcending oneself was advocated by Mou Zong-san and is carried on by some of his students, including Tu Weiming (see Tu 1976b, chapter 5). Tu does not deny the transcendence of Principle, but insists that because it is what heaven implants in humanity, according to *The Doctrine of the Mean*, the transcendent is immanent. Christians would say the same thing about the immanence of God in grace and the *imago dei*. Tu does not deny that Principle is ultimate.

11. This is defined at much greater length in Neville (1996, chapter 2). The subhypothesis derives from the bearing of both sociology of knowledge and ontology or metaphysics on the understanding of religious or spiritual symbolism and is conditional in this sense.

12. See the further examination of this text in section 8.3.

13. There is scholarly debate as to whether in Zhou's line the Great Ultimate is supposed to proceed from the Ultimate of Non-being in some ontological sense, or just be reciprocal; see section 8.3. I discuss this in Neville (1991a, chapter 4).

14. See also chapter 10 in this book on this point.

15. This large claim is the thesis of Neville (1989), and is defended with respect to religious objects defined as finite-infinite contrasts in Neville (1996, chapter 7 and 2000c, chapter 8).

16. See Neville (1989). The entire pragmatic tradition, as well as that of process philosophy, supports a philosophy of nature that represents mentality as part of natural processes.

17. These qualifications are analyzed in detail in Neville (1989, chapter 4).

18. This interpretation of value theory and the deleterious roles of the fact-value distinction in modern Western philosophy is spelled out in Neville (1981, part 1).

19. From the Christian side the social connection is equally important, if problematic. H. Richard Niebuhr explored several models of personal-social transformation in *Christ and Culture* (1951).

20. For a sophisticated discussion of the ontology theme in reference to the reconstruction of Christian theology, with attendant epistemological considerations that would apply to any religious tradition, see Wildman and Richardson (1996, part 3). This text deals with the theological challenges of physical cosmology (Big Bang theory), chaos theory, quantum complementarity, information theory, molecular biology, and social genetics. See also Neville 2000b.

21. I have developed such a science-tolerant ontology, with a correlative epistemology and religious applications, in Neville (1968).

22. This has been argued in schematic fashion in Neville (1982, especially chapters 6 and 7). The varying ways by which a contemporary ontology can reconstruct Christian and Confucian traditional symbols is a major theme of Neville (1991a, especially chapters 3, 4, 8, and 9).

23. My own small claim to have made a contribution to the contemporary Confucian problematic rests principally not with interpretive works but with the three-volume monograph, Axiology of Thinking. The first volume (Neville 1981) gives an extended critical analysis of the European scientific fact-value distinction and its alternatives and presents a theory of imagination sketched in the text here.

24. The second volume of my Axiology of Thinking, *Recovery of the Measure* (1989) treats interpretation that does claim to be true and employs imagination to make claims or suppositions about reality.

25. The nature of theorizing is discussed at length in the first half of *Normative Cultures* (Neville 1995), the third volume of my Axiology of Thinking.

26. The topic of the second half of my *Normative Cultures* (1995).

27. Xunzi's text is chapter 17 in John Knoblock's *Xunzi* (1994, volume 3). See also Edward J. Machle (1993), whose interpretation I follow here.

Chapter 5. Tu Weiming's Confucianism

1. With Mary Evelyn Tucker he has edited the volume on Confucian spirituality for the World Spirituality Series (Tu and Tucker 1998). Like Cheng Chungying and Wu Kuangming (see sections 3.4 and 3.5), Tu is a contemporary American philosopher whose principal intellectual as well as ethnic roots are Chinese. Trained at Harvard University, where he now teaches in philosophy and intellectual history and is the director of the Harvard Yenching Institute, Tu's intellectual project is to develop the role of the Confucian intellectual in the contemporary world. His early work in many respects is an extension of the Confucian commentarial tradition. *Neo-Confucian Thought in Action: Wang Yang-ming's Youth (1472–1509)* is an intellectual biography of that great thinker in which Tu lays the groundwork for the claim associated with his teacher, Mou Zong-san, that the Mencian line of Confucianism comes down through Wang rather than Zhu Xi. *Centrality and Commonality: An Essay on Confucian Religiousness* (1976b) is a commentary on *The Doctrine of the Mean*, advocating it as of contemporary worth and interpreting it according to the Mencian emphasis on *ren*. *Humanity and Self-Cultivation: Essays in Confucian Thought*, (1979), *Confucian Thought: Selfhood as Creative Transformation* (1985), and *Way, Learning, and Politics: Essays on the Confucian Intellectual* (1989) all contain essays that are interpretive in genre but programatic in intent: the program is to lay out the task for a contemporary Confucian intellectual.

I have called Tu a philosopher, and that he is, but he is also an historian, an expert in social scientific analyses of the current situation, an administrator, and a deliberately active player in the formation of a political and intellectual conversation about contemporary global society. Whereas most contemporary Confucian (and Daoist) philosophers are content to live the academic life, Tu devotes much energy to the administrative shaping of a public community and discourse. He is in this respect a scholar-official. The writings most illustrative of this aspect of his career, perhaps, are his editing of two volumes of *Daedalus*, "The Living Tree: The Changing Meaning of Being Chinese Today" (1991) and "China in Transformation" (1993), volumes that bring together China experts from many fields.

2. Tu is not a philosopher of culture with an aesthetic bent, like Ames and Hall (see section 3.3). Nor is he a political philosopher with a particular program, like a liberal democrat or Marxist (though his sympathies are with liberal democracies). He is not a metaphysical or ethical theorist aiming to provide a speculative perspective on things. He honors all these things and engages in them from time to time, but they are not the focus of his project. His focus rather is on the creation of a global intellectual conversation that registers and reflects Confucian values.

3. My whole analysis of Augustine's fall and conversion owes much to Carl Vaught's (1997) "Theft and Conversion: Two Augustinian Confessions."

4. Chan (1963, 788–89). The list of more personal meanings of love in the preceding sentence also comes from this appendix on translating terms.

5. See the farewell discourses in *John* 13–17, particularly *John* 13:34–35: "I give you a new commandment, that you love one another. Just as I have loved you, you also should love one another. By this everyone will know that you are my disciples, if you have love for one another." Or *John* 15:9–10, "As the Father has loved me, so I have loved you; abide in my love. If you keep my commandments, you will abide in my love, just as I have kept my Father's commandments and abide in his love." And John 15:12–16 "This is my commandment, that you love one another as I have loved you. No one has greater love than this, to lay down one's life for one's friends. You are my friends if you do what I command you. I do not call you servants any longer, because the servant does not know what the master is doing; but I have called you friends, because I have made known to you everything that I have heard from my Father."

6. Before exploring this, however, a word should be said about words. Some Christian theologians have made much of the distinction between three Greek words for love: *eros*, *philia*, and *agape*. *Eros* takes its root meaning from sexual love and has been expanded to mean love of external things for what they can do for oneself, seeking union and fulfillment, and delighting in things for their own sake. *Philia* means friendship, mutual regard, and care for persons. *Agape* means love of something or someone out of the abundance of one's heart, regardless of the object's worth or even in spite of the unworthiness of the object; God's love of a sinful world is *agape*. The love Paul lauds in *1 Corinthians* 13 is *agape*, and some theologians such as Anders Nygren (1954) have defined it quite sternly as love of others without regard for self-satisfaction or delight and with the explicit intention of loving the unlovely. For these theologians, *agape* alone as other-regarding and not self-regarding is the paradigm of divine love to which people are called in imitation, not to *eros* or even *philia* insofar as it is a religious virtue.

But the emphasis on these distinctions is misleading. Rather, love is a polyvalent notion, and all three Greek words contribute to its metaphoric complexity. At the very end of *The Gospel of John*, Jesus asked Peter three times whether he loved him, and Peter answered three times that Jesus knows all things and, of course, knows that Peter loves him. Jesus' first question used *agape* and Peter answered with *philia*; Jesus' second question used *agape* and again Peter answered with *philia*. But Jesus' third question used *philia*, and Peter was sad because Jesus asked him three times whether he loved (*philia*) him and answered the third time with *philia*. On a superficial reading the words are interchangeable in this exchange. With a hermeneutics of suspicion, though, we might say that Jesus asked twice with a high-powered divine love in mind and finally gave up in frustration and merely asked Peter whether they were still friends. But the passage interweaves the themes of divine love and the friendship Jesus sought among the disciples and himself as emblematic of heavenly table fellowship; the setting after all was the breakfast Jesus cooked for the disciples after the resurrection. Although the word *eros* is not used in the New Testament, Christian thinkers quickly picked up the root metaphor of sexual love from *The Song of Songs* to describe people's love of God and the loving relationship between the Church and Christ its Bridegroom. Love has all these dimensions. Robert Johann (1966) has persuasively argued that, at least in the Thomistic line of Christianity, the opposition between other-regarding love and self-regarding love is overcome by the point that loving is itself the fulfillment of human nature, a point with which the Confucians agree.

In the Confucian case we have one word, *ren*, that has a range of meanings as wide as the three Greek words. There are other Chinese words for love, such as *ai* meaning sexual and romantic love, and *lo* meaning delight and taking satisfaction in something. These words do not function in the classic Confucian discussions of love as a cardinal virtue or ontological principle. But at least some of their main connotations are carried by *ren*. "Becoming one body with the world" is not without its sexual overtones.

7. This is one of the points of Diotema's speech in *The Symposium*.

Chapter 6. Motif Analysis East and West

1. Cheng Chung-ying's (1971) study of Dai Zhen, Tu Weiming's (1976a) study of Wang Yangming, Wu Kuangming's (1990) study of Zhuangzi, and Judith Berling's (1980) study of Lin Chao-en fall into this category. Lee Yearley's (1990) comparative study of Mencius and Aquinas exemplifies this approach in the comparative mode. The genius of these studies is that to a remarkable degree they do indeed introduce both thinkers and cultures into a conversation to which they are strange.

2. The theory of theories and comparison developed in my *Normative Cultures* (1995) has been used, and of course amended, by the Comparative Religious Ideas Project at Boston University. The three volumes coming out of that project (Neville 2000a, 2000b, and 2000c), detail the theory of comparison.

3. This discussion reflects Charles Peirce's claim that semiotics requires the analysis of signs in meaning systems, signs as having reference, and signs as functioning within interpretations that engage reality. See my analysis of this in Neville (1996, xix–xxiii).

4. These are not the only civilizations, of course. Other great native civilizations for which comparisons might be made include the African, Oceanic, and North, Central, and South American ones.

5. See Neville (1981, chapters 5 to 8).

Chapter 7. Motifs of Being

1. Most forms of dialectic are not only methods of philosophical analysis but assert that dialectic is constitutive of the realities it attempts to understand. Perhaps the Thomistic doctrine of the analogy of being is the best known version of constitutive dialectic. Hegel's version is to be found in his analysis of the relations among objective and subjective logic, and the logic of spirit, the "cunning of the notion." I have developed another version in Neville (1968, chapter 7).

2. Plato's image of dialectic as ascending a ladder of hypotheses stresses the hypothetical character of metaphysical principles; his elaborate discussion in the *Parmenides* shows how different metaphysical hypotheses give different results. See Robert S. Brumbaugh's (1961) masterful study, *Plato on the One*. Aristotle, by contrast, who used the word "dialectic" for something else, nevertheless thought his metaphysics of substances and causes was hardly a hypothesis but just the way things are, and his treatment of being is strictly linked to that view. Hegel shared Plato's recognition that there are many basic world hypotheses but found a way to relate them so as to have comprehensive version of the final way things are, which looks pluralistic from the outside. Desmond's metaxological metaphysics takes things to be defined ultimately in terms that are limited by opposing balances, so that the dialectic of being lies in the "between" of what can be said directly. My own metaphysical system is merely one hypothesis among many others, distinguished from them only by being better, according to arguments I'm not shy to give; readers should know that I smile when I say that. See my "Sketch of a System" (Neville 1987b). My claim is that this system is an appropriate extension of Confucianism for our time.

3. This historical and metaphysical claim is defended at length in Neville (1981, part 1).

4. This distinction was introduced in section 4.2 and is defended in Neville (1968, 1989).

5. The main topics of Neville (1989).

6. Justus Buchler's (1978) "On the Concept of 'The World,' " is one of the latest developments of this conclusion.

7. As Whitehead (1929, 21–22) might say, in analogy with what he said about creativity, many, and one constituting the Category of the Ultimate: the three elements of creation are not defined in terms of one another, but they cannot be defined without one another; to define one is to define all three.

8. This mystical stance is my own sensibility (see Neville 1993a).

9. Chan (1963, 463). I have substituted English words in some instances for words he left in the Chinese; Chan put the English words I use in parentheses, so the translation remains his.

10. I have not had the time here to discuss the attempts by Neo-Confucian thinkers, such as the Cheng brothers, Zhu Xi, and Wang Yangming, to integrate their symbols for nature, being and non-being, and generativity into a comprehensive, multiangled account of the dao. Nor have I discussed the efforts of contemporary New Confucians, such as Cheng Chungying, Mou Zong-san and Tu Weiming, to restate the Chinese points in Western terms. I hope to have stimulated interest in Westerners engaging contemporary heirs to East and South Asian philosophic traditions, however, by showing that the dialectic of being, so dear to Western hearts, has clear neighbors and variants in those traditions whose different metaphors and angles of vision might offer correction and light.

Chapter 8. *Motifs of Transcendence*

1. Wesley discusses the image of God in many of his sermons, but principally in numbers 5 (Wesley 1984) and 141 (Wesley 1987). I owe this interpretation of Wesley to the dissertation of Philip. R. Meadows (1997).

2. There are many complications of Wesley's doctrine of possible perfection in this life that are not expressed in my account. For a good general account, see Maddox (1994).

Chapter 9. *Resources for a Conception of Selfhood*

1. See also Neville (1995, chapter 7).

2. This is Fingarette's (1972) main point.

3. I have spelled them out elsewhere in much greater detail and with less metaphoric play (Neville 1991a, 1991b, 1993a, 1995, 1996).

Chapter 10. *Confucianism, Christianity, and Multiple Religious Identity*

1. There are scholarly problems with the identification of John as the Beloved Disciple and with the claim that Jesus had brothers. But the point of the story, regardless of its truth, is my point here.

2. I owe the phrase "multiple religious identity" to John Berthrong (1994, especially chapter 6, and 1999b).

Bibliography

Altizer, Thomas J. J. 1980. *Total Presence*. New York: Seabury.

———. 1985. *History as Apocalypse*. Albany: State University of New York Press.

Ames, Roger T. 1983. *The Art of Rulership: Studies in Ancient Chinese Political Thought*. Honolulu: Hawaii University Press.

———. 1987. With David L. Hall. *Thinking Through Confucius*. Albany: State University of New York Press.

———. 1989. Edited with J. Baird Callicott. *Nature in Asian Traditions of Thought: Essays in Environmental Philosophy*. Albany: State University of New York Press.

———. 1993. *Sun-tsu: The Art of Warfare: The First English Translation Incorporating the Recently Discovered Yin-Ch'ueh-Shan Texts*. New York: Ballantine.

———. 1995. With David L. Hall. *Anticipating China: Thinking Through the Narratives of Chinese and Western Culture*. Albany: State University of New York Press.

———. 1996. Edited with Wimal Dissanayake. *Self and Deception: A Cross-Cultural Philosophical Enquiry*. Albany: State University of New York Press.

———. 1998. With David L. Hall. *Thinking from the Han: Self, Truth, and Transcendence in Chinese and Western Culture*. Albany: State University of New York Press.

———. 1999. With David L. Hall. *The Democracy of the Dead: Dewey, Confucius, and the Hope for Democracy in China*. Chicago: Open Court.

Anderson, Bernard. W. 1984. *Creation in the Old Testament*. Philadelphia: Fortress.

Augustine. 1955. *The Confessions*. Albert Outler, translator. Philadelphia: Westminster.

Barraclough, Geoffrey. 1964. *Introduction to Modern History*. Great Britain: C. A. Watts. Harmondsworth, U.K.: Penguin, 1967.

Berger, Peter. 1967. *The Sacred Canopy: Elements of A Sociological Theory of Religion*. Garden City, N.Y.: Doubleday.

Berling, Judith A. 1980. *The Syncretic Religion of Lin Chao-en*. New York: Columbia University Press.

Berthrong, John H. 1994. *All under Heaven*. Albany: State University of New York Press.

———. 1998a. *Transformations of the Confucian Way*. Boulder, Colo.: Westview Press.

———. 1998b. Edited with Mary Evelyn Tucker. *Confucianism and Ecology: The Interrelation of Heaven, Earth, and Humans*. Cambridge, Mass.: Center for World Religions, Harvard University.

———. 1999a. *Concerning Creativity: A Comparison of Chu His, Whitehead, and Neville*. Albany: State University of New York Press.

———. 1999b. *The Divine Deli: Religious Identity in the North American Cultural Mosaic*. Mary Knoll, NY: Orbis Books.

Birdwhistell, Anne D. 1989. *Transition to Neo-Confucianism: Shao Yung on Knowledge and Symbols of Reality*. Stanford, Calif.: Stanford University Press.

Bol, Peter K. 1992. *"This Culture of Ours": Intellectual Transition in T'ang and Sung China*. Stanford, Calif.: Stanford University Press.

Bruce, J. Percy. 1923. *Chu Hsi and His Masters: An Introduction to Chu Hsi and the Sung School of Chinese Philosophy*. London: Probsthain.

Brumbaugh, Robert S. 1961. *Plato on the One*. New Haven, Conn.: Yale University Press.

———. 1962. *Plato for the Modern Age*. New York: Crowell-Collier.

———. 1982. *Whitehead, Process Philosophy, and Education*. Albany: State University of New York Press.

———. 1989. *Platonic Studies of Greek Philosophy: Form, Arts, Gadgets, and Hemlock*. Albany: State University of New York Press.

Buchler, Justus. 1978. "On the Concept of 'The World.' " *The Review of Metaphysics* 31/4 (June): 555–79.

Chan, Wing-tsit. 1963. *A Source Book in Chinese Philosophy*. Princeton: Princeton University Press.

———. 1989. *Chu Hsi: New Studies*. Honolulu: University of Hawaii Press.

Chang Chung-yuan. 1963. *Creativity and Taoism: A Study of Chinese Philosophy, Art, and Poetry*. New York: Julian Press. Reprint; New York: Harper, 1970.

———. 1975. *Tao: A New Way of Thinking: A Translation of the Tao Te Ching with an Introduction and Commentaries*. New York: Harper & Row.

Chapman, J. Harley. 1999. Edited with Nancy K. Frankenberry, *Interpreting Neville*. Albany: State University of New York Press.

———. 1999a. "Neville's Self in Time and Eternity," in Chapman and Frankenberry, 1999, pp. 111–24.

Ch'en, Kenneth. 1964. *Buddhism in China: A Historical Survey*. Princeton, N.J.: Princeton University Press.

Cheng Chung-ying. 1971. *Tai Chen's* Inquiry into Goodness: *A Translation of the Yuan Shan, with an Introductory Essay*. Honolulu: East-West Center Press.

———. 1991. *New Dimensions of Confucian and Neo-Confucian Philosophy*. Albany: State University of New York Press.

———. "On Neville's Understanding of Chinese Philosophy: Ontology of *Wu*, Cosmology of *Yi*, Normalogy of *Li*," in Chapman and Frankenberry, 1999, pp. 247–69.

Ching, Julia. 1976. *To Acquire Wisdom: The Way of Wang Yang-ming*. New York: Columbia University Press.

———. 1990. *Probing China's Soul: Religion, Politics, and Protest in the People's Republic.*. San Francisco: Harper & Row.

Ching, Julia, and Willard G. Oxtoby. 1992. *Moral Enlightenment: Leibniz and Wolff on China*. Institut Monumenta Serica. Nettel, Germany: Steyler.

Chu Hsi. See Zhu Xi.

Confucius. 1963 translation. *The Analects*, in Chan, 1963.

———. 1979. *The Analects*. Translated by D. C. Lau. Hong Kong: Chinese University Press.

Corrington, Robert S. 1992. *Nature and Spirit: An Essay in Ecstatic Naturalism*. New York: Fordham University Press.

———. 1994. *Ecstatic Naturalism: Signs of the World*. Bloomington: Indiana University Press.

———. 1996 *Nature's Self: Our Journey from Origin to Spirit*. Lanham, Md.: Rowman and Littlefield.

———. 1997. *Nature's Religion*. Lanham, Md.: Rowman and Littlefield.

Creel, Herrlee G. 1970. *What Is Taoism?* Chicago: University of Chicago Press.

Cua, Antony S. 1978. *Dimensions of Moral Creativity: Paradigms, Principles, and Ideals*. State College, Pa.: Pennsylvania State University Press.

———. 1982. *The Unity of Knowledge and Action: A Study of Wang Yang-ming's Moral Psychology*. Honolulu: The University Press of Hawaii.

———. 1985. *Ethical Argumentation: A Study in Hsun Tzu's Moral Epistemology.* Honolulu: University of Hawaii Press.

———. 1996. "A Confucian Perspective on Self-Deception," in Ames and Dissanayake, 1996.

———. 1998 *Moral Vision and Tradition: Essays in Chinese Ethics.* Washington, D.C.: The Catholic University of America Press. Studies in Philosophy and the History of Philosophy, volume 31.

de Bary, William Theodore. 1960. *Sources of Chinese Tradition,* two volumes. With Wing-tsit Chan and Burton Watson. New York: Columbia University Press.

———. 1970. *Self and Society in Ming Thought.* New York: Columbia University Press.

———. 1975. *The Unfolding of Neo-Confucianism.* New York: Columbia University Press.

———. 1983. *The Liberal Tradition in China.* Hong Kong: The Chinese University Press.

———. 1989. *The Message of the Mind in Neo-Confucianism.* New York: Columbia University Press.

———. 1991a. *The Trouble with Confucianism.* Cambridge: Harvard University Press.

———. 1991b. *Learning for Oneself: Essays on the Individual in Neo-Confucian Thought.* New York: Columbia University Press.

———. 1998. *Asian Values and Human Rights: A Confucian Communitarian Perspective.* Cambridge, Mass.: Harvard University Press.

Derrida, Jacques. 1976. *Of Grammatology.* Translated by Gayatri Chakravorty Spivak. Baltimore: Johns Hopkins University Press.

Desmond, William. 1987. *Desire, Dialectic, and Otherness: An Essay on Origins.* New Haven, Conn.: Yale University Press.

———. 1990. *Philosophy and Its Others: Ways of Being and Mind.* Albany: State University of New York Press.

———. 1995. *Being and the Between.* Albany: State University of New York Press.

Dewey, John. 1963. *Freedom and Culture.* New York: Capricorn. Originally published in 1939.

———. 1973. *Lectures in China, 1919–1920.* Edited and translated from the Chinese by Robert W. Clopton and Tsuin-Chen Ou. Honolulu: The University Press of Hawaii.

————. 1981. *Experience and Nature*. Edited by Jo Ann Boydston. In *John Dewey: The Later Works, 1925–1953*, volume 1: 1925. Carbondale, Ill.: Southern Illinois University Press. First edition, Chicago, London: Open Court Publishing Co., 1925. Second edition, New York: W. W. Norton, 1929.

————. 1984. *The Quest for Certainty*. Edited by Jo Ann Boydston. In *John Dewey: The Later Works, 1925–1953*, volume 4: 1929. Carbondale, Ill.: Southern Illinois University Press. Original edition, New York: Minton, Balch, and Company 1929.

Dilworth, David A. 1989. *Philosophy in World Perspective: A Comparative Hermeneutic of the Major Theories*. New Haven, Conn.: Yale University Press.

Driver, Tom. 1991. *The Magic of Ritual*. San Francisco: Harper.

Durkheim, Emile. 1915. *The Elementary Forms of the Religious Life*. Translated by Joseph Ward Swain. New York: Free Press, 1965.

Eliade, Mircea. 1978–85. *A History of Religious Ideas*, in three volumes. Chicago: University of Chicago Press.

Eno, Robert. 1990. *The Confucian Creation of Heaven: Philosophy and the Defense of Ritual Mastery*. Albany: State University of New York Press.

Fingarette, Herbert. 1972. *Confucius—The Secular as Sacred*. New York: Harper & Row.

Foucault, Michel. 1971. *The Order of Things: An Archaeology of the Human Sciences*. New York: Pantheon. Translator unnamed.

Frankenberry, Nancy K. 1999. Edited with J. Harley Chapman. *Interpreting Neville*. Albany: State University of New York Press.

————. 1999a. "On the Very Idea of Symbolic Meaning," in Chapman and Frankenberry, 1999, pp. 93–110.

Geertz, Clifford. 1973. *The Interpretation of Cultures*. New York: Basic Books.

Girardot, Norman. 1983. *Myth and Meaning in Early Taoism: The Theme of Chaos (hun-tun)*. Berkeley: University of California Press.

Graham, A. C. 1989. *Disputers of the Tao: Philosophical Argument in Ancient China*. LaSalle, Ill.: Open Court.

Hall, David. L. 1973. *The Civilization of Experience: A Whiteheadian Theory of Culture*. New York: Fordham University Press.

————. 1982a. *The Uncertain Phoenix: Adventures Toward a Post-Cultural Sensibility*. New York: Fordham University Press.

————. 1982b, *Eros and Irony: A Prelude to Philosophical Anarchism*. Albany: State University of New York Press.

------. 1987 *Thinking Through Confucius*. With Roger T. Ames. Albany: State University of New York Press.

------. 1994. *Richard Rorty: Prophet and Poet of the New Pragmatism*. Albany: State University of New York Press.

------. 1995. *Anticipating China: Thinking Through the Narratives of Chinese and Western Culture*. With Roger T. Ames. Albany: State University of New York Press.

------. 1998. With Roger T. Ames. *Thinking from the Han: Self, Truth, and Transcendence in Chinese and Western Culture*. Albany: State University of New York Press.

------. 1999. With Roger T. Ames. *The Democracy of the Dead: Dewey, Confucius, and the Hope for Democracy in China*. Chicago: Open Court.

Hansen, Chad. 1983. *Language and Logic in Ancient China*. Ann Arbor: University of Michigan Press.

------. 1992. *A Daoist Theory of Chinese Thought*. New York: Oxford University Press.

Hart, Ray L. 1968. *Unfinished Man and the Imagination*. New York: Herder and Herder.

Heelan, Patrick. 1983. *Space Perceptions and the Philosophy of Science*. Berkeley: University of California Press.

Heidegger, Martin. 1959. *Introduction to Metaphysics*. Translated by Ralph Manheim. New Haven: Yale Univesity Press.

Hobbes, Thomas. 1950. *Leviathan*. New York: Dutton, 1950. Originally published in 1651.

Hsun-tzu. See Xunzi.

Hume, David. 1779. *Dialogues concerning Natural Religion*. New York: Hafner, 1948.

Huntington, Samuel P. 1996. *The Clash of Civilizations and the Remaking of World Order*. New York: Simon and Schuster.

Ivanhoe, Philip J. 1990. *Ethics in the Confucian Tradition: The Thought of Mencius and Wang Yang-ming*. Atlanta: Scholars Press.

------. 1993. *Confucian Moral Self Cultivation*. New York: Peter Lang.

Jaspers, Karl. 1954. *Way to Wisdom: An Introduction to Philosophy*. Translated by Ralph Manheim. New Haven, Conn.: Yale University Press.

Johann, Robert. 1966. *The Meaning of Love*. Glen Rock, N.J.: Paulist Press.

Kasulis, Thomas P., and Robert C. Neville, editors. 1997. *The Recovery of Philosophy in America: Essays in Honor of John Edwin Smith*. Albany: State University of New York Press.

Kierkegaard, Soren. 1955. *Fear and Trembling*. Translated by Walter Lowrie, with *The Sickness Unto Death*. Garden City, N.Y.: Doubleday Anchor.

Knoblock, John. 1988. *Xunzi: A Translation and Study of the Complete Works*, volume 1, books 1–6; 1990, volume 2, books 7–16; 1994, volume 3, books 17–32. Stanford, Calif.: Stanford University Press

Kohn, Livia. 1989. *Taoist Meditation and Longevity Techniques*. Edited in cooperation with Yosinobu Sakade. Ann Arbor, Mich.: Center for Chinese Studies.

———. 1991. *Taoist Mystical Philosophy: The Scripture of Western Ascension*. Albany: State University of New York Press.

———. 1992. *Early Chinese Mysticism: Philosophy and Soteriology in the Taoist Tradition*. Princeton, N.J.: Princeton University Press.

———. 1993. *The Taoist Experience: An Anthology*. Albany: State University of New York Press.

Krejci, Jaroslav. 1993. Assisted by Anna Krejcova. *The Human Predicament: Its Changing Image: A Study in Comparative Religion and History*. London: St. Martin's Press.

Lagerwey, John. 1987. *Taoist Ritual in Chinese Society and History*. New York: Macmillan.

Lee, Thomas H. C. 1995. "The Idea of Social Justice in Ancient China," in *Social Justice in the Ancient World*, edited by K. D. Irani and Morris Silver. Westport, Conn.: Greenwood Press.

Liu, Shu-hsien. 1988. Edited with Robert E. Allinson, *Harmony and Strife: Contemporary Perspectives Easy and West*. Hong Kong: Chinese University Press.

———1989. "Postwar Neo-Confucian Philosophy: Its Development and Issues," in *Religious Issues and Interreligious Dialogues*, edited by Charles Wei-hsun Fu and Gerhard E. Spiegler. Westport, Conn.: Greenwood Press.

Long, Eugene Thomas, editor. 1995. *God, Reason and Religions: New Essays in the Philosophy of Religion*. Volume 18 in Studies in Philosophy and Religion. Dordrecht: Kluwer Academic Publishers.

Machle, Edward J. 1993. *Nature and Heaven in the Xunzi: A Study of the Tian Lun*. Albany: State University of New York Press.

Maddox, Randy L. 1994. *Responsible Grace: John Wesley's Practical Theology*. Nashville: Abingdon/Kingswood Books.

Major, John S. 1993. *Heaven and Earth in Han Thought: Chapters 3, 4, and 5 of the* Huainanzi. Albany: State University of New York Press.

Meadows, Philip R. 1997. *Sadhana and Salvation: Soteriology in Ramanaja and John Wesley*. Ph.D. dissertation, Cambridge University.

Milbank, John. 1990. *Theology and Social Theory: Beyond Secular Reason.* Oxford: Blackwell.

Moore, Charles A. 1957. *A Source Book in Indian Philosophy.* Edited with Sarvepalli Radhakrishnan. Princeton, N.J.: Princeton University Press.

Needham, Joseph. 1956. *Science and Civilization in China,* volume 2. Cambridge: Cambridge University Press.

Neville, Robert Cummings. 1968. *God the Creator: On the Transcendence and Presence of God.* Chicago: University of Chicago Press. SUNY Press Edition with a new Preface; Albany: State University of New York Press, 1992.

———. 1978. *Soldier, Sage, Saint.* New York: Fordham University Press.

———. 1981. *Reconstruction of Thinking.* Albany: State University of New York Press.

———. 1982. *The Tao and the Daimon.* Albany: State University of New York Press.

———. 1987a. *The Puritan Smile.* Albany: State University of New York Press.

———, editor. 1987b. *New Essays in Metaphysics.* Albany: State University of New York Press.

———. 1989. *Recovery of the Measure.* Albany: State University of New York Press.

———. 1991a. *Behind the Masks of God: An Essay toward Comparative Theology.* Albany: State University of New York Press. Translated into Chinese with an introduction by Chen Yanquan. Beijing, China: CASS, 1997.

———. 1991b. *A Theology Primer.* Albany: State University of New York Press.

———. 1992. *The Highroad around Modernism.* Albany: State University of New York Press.

———. 1993a. *Eternity and Time's Flow.* Albany: State University of New York Press.

———. 1993b. "Confucianism as a World Philosophy." Presidential Address for the 8th International Conference on Chinese Philosophy, Beijing, 1993. *Journal of Chinese Philosophy* 21(1994): 5–25.

———. 1995. *Normative Cultures.* Albany: State University of New York Press.

———. 1996. *The Truth of Broken Symbols.* Albany: State University of New York Press.

———. 1997. Edited with Thomas P. Kasulis. *The Recovery of Philosophy in America: Essays in Honor of John Edwin Smith.* Albany: State University of New York Press.

————, editor. 2000a. *The Human Condition*. Albany: State University of New York Press.

————, editor. 2000b. *Ultimate Realities*. Albany: State University of New York Press.

————, editor. 2000c. *Religious Truth*. Albany: State University of New York Press.

Niebuhr. H. Richard. 1951. *Christ and Culture*. New York: Harper and Brothers.

Nivison, David S. 1996. *The Ways of Confucianism: Investigations in Chinese Philosophy*. Edited with an introduction by Bryan W. Van Norden. LaSalle, Ill.: Open Court.

Northrop, F.S.C. 1946. *The Meeting of East and West*. New York: Macmillan.

Nygren, Anders. 1944. *Eros et Agapé*. Paris: Aubier.

Peirce, Charles Sanders. 1931–35. *The Collected Papers of Charles Sanders Peirce*. Edited by Charles Hartshorne and Paul Weiss. Volume 1, 1931; volume 2, 1932; volume 5, 1934; volume 6, 1935. Cambridge, Mass.: Harvard University Press.

Proudfoot, Wayne. 1985. *Religious Experience*. Berkeley: University of California Press.

Radhakrishnan, Sarvepalli, and Charles A. Moore, editors. 1957. *A Source Book in Indian Philosophy*. Princeton, N.J.: Princeton University Press.

Richardson, W. Mark. 1996. Edited with Wesley J. Wildman. *Religion and Science: History, Method, Dialogue*. New York: Routledge.

Robinet, Isabelle. 1993. *Taoist Meditation: The Mao-Shan Tradition of Great Purity*. Translated from the French edition of 1979 by Julian F. Pas and Norman J. Girardot. Albany: State University of New York Press.

Roetz, Heiner. 1993. *Confucian Ethics of the Axial Age*. Albany: State University of New York Press.

Rosen, Stanley. 1993. *The Question of Being: A Reversal of Heidegger*. New Haven, Conn.: Yale University Press.

Rorty, Richard. 1979. *Philosophy and the Mirror of Nature*. Princeton, N.J.: Princeton University Press.

————. 1982. *Consequences of Pragmatism*. Minneapolis: University of Minnesota Press.

Rouner, Leroy S. 1998. *Loneliness*. Notre Dame, Ind.: Notre Dame University Press.

Saussure, Ferdinand de. 1959. *Course in General Linguistics*. Translated by Wade Baskin, edited by Charles Bally and Albert Sechehaye in collaboration with Albert Riedlinger. New York: The Philosophical Library. (New York: McGraw Hill Paperback edition, 1966). Original edition compiled from notes by Charles Bally and Albert Sechehaye, in 1906 and 1911.

Searle, John. 1969. *Speech Acts*. Cambridge, U.K.: Cambridge University Press.

Shun, Kwong-Loi. 1997. *Mencius and Early Chinese Thought*. Stanford, Calif.: Stanford University Press.

Smart, Ninian. 1989. *The World's Religions*. Cambridge, U.K.: Cambridge University Press.

Smith, John E. 1968. *Experience and God*. New York: Oxford University Press.

———. 1978. *Purpose and Thought: The Meaning of Pragmatism*. New Haven, Conn.: Yale University Press.

Spence, Jonathan. 1983. *The Memory Palace of Matteo Ricci*. New York: Elisabeth Sifton/Penguin Books.

Streng, Frederick. 1985. *Understanding Religious Life*. Third edition. Belmont, Calif.: Wadsworth.

Taylor, Charles. 1989. *Sources of the Self: The Making of Modern Identity*. Cambridge, U.K.: Cambridge University Press.

Taylor, Rodney L. 1978. *The Cultivation of Sagehood as a Religious Goal in Neo-Confucianism: A Study of Selected Writings of Kao P'an-lung*. Missoula, Mont.: Scholars Press.

———. 1986. *The Way of Heaven: An Introduction to the Confucian Religious Life*. Leiden: Brill.

———. 1990. *The Religious Dimensions of Confucianism*. Albany: State University of New York Press.

Tillich, Paul. 1948. *The Shaking of the Foundations*. New York: Scribners.

———. 1952. *Systematic Theology, Volume 1*. Chicago: University of Chicago Press.

———. 1955. *The New Being*. New York: Scribners.

———. 1959. *Theology of Culture*. Edited by Robert C. Kimball. New York: Oxford University Press.

Tillman, Hoyt Cleveland. 1992. *Confucian Discourse and Chu Hsi's Ascendancy*. Honolulu: University of Hawaii Press.

Tu Weiming. 1976a. *Neo-Confucian Thought in Action: Wang Yang-ming's Youth (1472–1509)*. Berkeley: University of California Press.

———. 1976b; 1989. *Centrality and Commonality: An Essay on Confucian Religiousness*. Revised and enlarged edition (1989) of *Centrality and Commonality: An Essay on Chung-yung* (1976). Albany: State University of New York Press.

———. 1979. *Humanity and Self-Cultivation: Essays in Confucian Thought*. Berkeley, Calif.: Asian Humanities Press. Reissued with a new preface and a foreword by Robert Cummings Neville. Boston: Cheng and Tsui, 1999.

———. 1985. *Confucian Thought: Selfhood as Creative Transformation*. Albany: State University of New York Press.

———. 1989. *Way, Learning, and Politics: Essays on the Confucian Intellectual*. Singapore: Institute of East Asian Philosophies. Reprint edition, Albany: State University of New York Press, 1993.

———. 1991. "The Living Tree: The Changing Meaning of Being Chinese Today." *Daedalus* 120/2 (Spring).

———. 1993. "China in Transformation." *Daedalus* 122/2 (Spring).

———. 2001 (Forthcoming). *Confucian Spirituality*. Edited with Mary Evelyn Tucker. New York: Crossroad. Volume 11 of *World Spirituality: An Encyclopedic History of the Religious Quest*, edited by Ewert Cousins.

Tucker, Mary Evelyn. 1998a. Edited with John H. Berthrong. *Confucianism and Ecology: The Interrelation of Heaven, Earth, and Humans*. Cambridge, Mass.: Center for World Religions, Harvard University.

———. 2001 (Forthcoming). *Confucian Spirituality*. Edited with Tu Weiming. New York: Crossroad. Volume 11 of *World Spirituality: An Encyclopedic History of the Religious Quest*, edited by Ewert Cousins.

Turner, Victor. 1969. *The Ritual Process: Structure and Anti-Structure*. New York: Aldine.

Van der Leeuw, G. 1933. *Religion in Essence and Manifestation*. Translated by J. E. Turner with appendices to the Torchbook edition, incorporating the additions of the second German edition, edited by Hans H. Penner. New York: Harper and Row, 1963.

Van Ness, Peter H., editor. 1996. *Spirituality and the Secular Quest*. New York: Crossroad. Volume 22 of *World Spirituality: An Encyclopedic History of the Religious Quest*, edited by Ewert Cousins.

Vaught, Carl G. 1997. "Theft and Conversion: Two Augustinian Confessions," in Kasulis and Neville (1997).

Wang Pi. 1979. *Commentary on the* Lao Tzu. Translated by Ariane Rump in collaboration with Wing-tsit Chan. Monography 6 of the Society for Asian and Comparative Philosophy. Honolulu: University Press of Hawaii.

Wang Yang-ming. 1963 translation. *Instructions for Practical Living and Other Neo-Confucian Writings*. Translated with notes by Wing-tsit Chan. New York: Columbia University Press.

Watson, Walter. 1985. *The Architectonics of Meaning: Foundations of the New Pluralism*. Albany: State University of New York Press.

Weiss, Paul. 1950. *Man's Freedom*. New Haven, Conn.: Yale University Press.

———. 1958. *Modes of Being*. Carbondale, Ill.: Southern Illinois University Press.

————. 1959. *Our Public Life.* Bloomington, Ind.: Indiana University Press.

————. 1961a. *The World of Art.* Carbondale, Ill.: Southern Illinois University Press.

————. 1961b. *Nine Basic Arts.* Carbondale, Ill.: Southern Illinois University Press.

————. 1962. *History, Written and Lived.* Carbondale, Ill.: Southern Illinois University Press.

————. 1963. *Religion and Art.* Milwaukee: Marquette University Press.

————. 1964. *The God We Seek.* Carbondale, Ill.: Southern Illinois University Press.

————. 1969. *Sport, A Philosophic Inquiry.* Carbondale, Ill.: Southern Illinois University Press.

————. 1974. *Beyond All Appearances.* Carbondale, Ill.: Southern Illinois University Press.

————. 1975. *Cinematics.* Carbondale, Ill.: Southern Illinois University Press.

————. 1986. *Toward a Perfected State.* Albany: State University of New York Press.

————. 1992. *Creative Ventures.* Carbondale, Ill.: Southern Illinois University Press.

Wesley, John. 1984, volume 1, and 1987, volume 2. *The Works of John Wesley.* Edited by Albert Outler. Nashville: Abingdon Press.

Whitehead, Alfred North. 1926. *Religion in the Making.* New York: Macmillan.

————. 1929. *Process and Reality: An Essay in Cosmology.* New York: Macmillan. Corrected edition edited by David R. Griffin and Donald W. Sherburne, New York: Free Press, 1978.

Wiener, Philip P. 1958. *Selected Writings of Charles Sanders Peirce: Values in a Universe of Chance.* Garden City, N.Y.: Doubleday Anchor.

Wildman, Wesley J., and W. Mark Richardson, editors. 1996. *Religion and Science: History, Method, Dialogue.* New York: Routledge.

————. 1998a. *Fidelity with Plausibility: Modest Christologies in the Twentieth Century.* Albany: State University of New York Press.

————. 1998b. "In Praise of Loneliness." In Rouner, 1998, pp. 15–39.

Wu Kuangming. 1982. *Chuang Tzu: World Philosopher at Play.* Chico, CA: Scholars Press.

————. 1990. *The Butterfly as Companion: Meditations on the First Three Chapters of the* Chuang Tzu. Albany: State University of New York Press.

———. 1997. *On Chinese Body Thinking: A Cultural Hermeneutic*. Leiden: Brill.

———. 1998. *On the "Logic" of Togetherness—A Cultural Hermeneutic*. Leiden: Brill.

Yearley, Lee H. 1990. *Mencius and Aquinas: Theories of Virtue and Conceptions of Courage*. Albany: State University of New York Press.

———. 1995. *Facing Our Frailty: Comparative Religious Ethics and the Confucian Death Rituals*. Gross Memorial Lecture for 1995. Valparaiso, Ind.: Valparaiso University Press.

Zhu Xi. 1922 translation. *The Philosophy of Human Nature*. Translated with notes by J. Percy Bruce. London: Probsthain.

———. 1967 translation. *Reflections on Things at Hand*. Translated with commentary by Wing-tsit Chan. New York: Columbia University Press.

———. 1990 translation. *Learning to Be a Sage: Selections from the Conversations of Master Chu, Arranged Topically*. Translated with a commentary by Daniel K. Gardner. Berkeley: University of California Press.

———. 1991 translation. *Chu Hsi's Family Rituals: A Twelfth-Century Chinese Manual for the Performance of Cappings, Weddings, Funerals, and Ancestral Rites*. Translated and edited by Patricia Buckley Ebrey. Princeton: Princeton University Press.

Index

Abelard, 156
"Abiding in the highest good," 6, 82
Absolute, the, 57, 147; transcendent, 89
Abstractions, 48–49, 52–54, 120; in comparison, 111–15; in Enlightenment thought, 16, 80; people as, 152; to discover true self, 117
Absurdity, xix
Abuse, sexual, 23
Abyss, 138
Acceptance, 104
Act, creative, 137–39; of Esse, 69, 158
Action, 117, 119, 189; versus ritual, in ethics, 95; in structure of self, 176–77; spiritual, 73; spontaneous, 153
Adam, 116, 161–65, 201–02, 204. See also Eve
Adolescence, 99
Advantages, 144
Aesthetics, 47, 72, 77; of culture, 38–40
Affections, vile, in Adam, 163
Affiliation, 22
Africa, xxvi, 3, 58, 220; education in, 211
Agamemnon, as meat-brain interpreter, 71
Agape, 219
Agent-intellect, 200
Agriculture, 25
Ai (love), 220
Al-Ghazali, 60
Alienation, 87–88, 103–04; seriousness of, 90–91

Allan, George, 214
Altizer, Thomas, 161, 170–75
Altruism, 98
Ambiguity, 182
America, 130, 220; intellectual situation in, xiii; signs for friendship in, 182. See also Philosophy, American
American Academy of Religion, xxviii
American Association of Asian Studies, xxviii
American Philosophical Association, xxviii
Ames, Roger T., xxviii, xxxi, xxxiii–xxxiv, 34, 43, 47–50, 52, 54, 69, 108–09, 113, 129, 147–51, 160, 218
Analects, xiv, xxii, 3–8, 10, 33–34, 42, 97, 183, 205, 207
Analogy, in comparison, 114
Analysis, motifs for, 109–11; textual, 107
Anarchy, 45
Ancestors, 199–201, 208
Anger, 179–80; and self-deception, 174
Animals, named by Adam, 116, 162
Anselm, 60, 134, 156
Anthropocosmism, 68
Anthropology, 216
Anxiety, 105
Apologists, early Christian, 158
Apple, forbidden fruit, 201–02, 204
Appropriateness, 93–94; of habits, 182
Appropriation, of tradition, 4; of value, 71–73

237

Aquinas, Thomas, 46, 60, 69, 158, 208, 220
Arabic, xii
Archery, 25
Archetypes, in imagination, 122
Architecture, 132
Aristocracy, 40
Aristotle, xxi, 4, 43, 51, 70–71, 77, 107–08, 149, 161, 205, 215; categories of, 49–50; on dialectic, 221; ethics of, xix; as world philosopher, xxii
Aristotelianism, xxii, xxvii, 17; scholarly temperament in, 44
Arjuna, 117
Art, 13, 25, 50, 52, 132, 215; Buddhist, 33
Articulation, in imagination, 121
Artificiality, of culture, 30–33
Ascent, spiritual, 63
Asia, cultural assumptions of, 107; West, 152; West, South, East cultures of compared, 114–28
Assumptions, cultural, 48–50
Asuras, 139
Asymmetry, 48–50, 69, 137–38
Atman, 117, 119
Atom, 150
Augustine, xviii–xix, 43, 60, 89–91, 104, 219; on attention, 172; on self, 172
Aurobindo, 127
Authenticity, 9, 93; and love, 96
Authoritarianism, 199
Authority, and manners, 124; parental, 196
Authorship, of actions, 171; of self, 175
Axial Age, xv, xxix, 108, 121–22, 124–26, 151; defined by Jaspers, 147–48; religions, 158
Axiology, xvi, 75–79; of thinking, xvii, 77–79, 217

Babylon, myths of, 116
Background, assumptions in, 107; and foreground, 12–15
Balazs, Etienne, 85
Baptism, 118–19
Barbarians, 9–10, 29, 36, 81, 95, 100–01, 181, 186, 201–02

Barraclough, Geoffrey, xxv
Barth, Karl, 89
Battle, centeredness in, 156
Begetting, 134–35
Behavior, symbolically shaped, 102–03
Behaviorism, 112
Being, xxxi, 31, 50, 221; analogy of, 221; as creation, 138–39; as determinate, 137; dialectic of, 131, 133, 135–45, 58; as God, 137, 158–61; God beyond, 158–59; cultural models of, 130–31; motifs of, xvi, 114, 129–45; not an object or genus, 129–30; as plenitude, 138; as power, 137; question of, 126; as totality, 137
Bending, Chinese versus Western rituals of, 123
Benefits, social, 32
Berdyaev, Nicholas, 138
Berger, Peter, 58, 61, 65–66, 68, 77, 216
Berkeley, Confucian-Christian Dialogue Conference at, xiii, xxi–xxv, 211–13
Berling, Judith, xxiv, xxviii, 211–14, 220
Berry, Thomas, xxxv
Berthrong, John H., xxi, xxiv, xxviii, xxxiii–xxxv, 194, 199, 212, 214, 222
Bhagavad-Gita, 117–18
Bias, in use of categories, 60
Bible, 91; language of, in Protestantism, 159
Big Bang, 67, 75, 217
Big Guy in the Sky, as divine personification, 158
Biology, in Xunzi, 28–29
Birdwhistell, Anne, xxviii, 149
Blandness, in Confucianism, 84–88; of humanism, 75
Bloom, Irene, xxviii
Bodhisattva, vows of, 88–89
Body, human, and imagination, 121–22; language, 123; versus soul, in St. Paul, 171; as substance, 11; well-trained, 154
Boehme, Jacob, 138

Bol, Peter K., 43
Bondage, sin's, 163, 200, 203, 205–06
Book of Odes, 212
Book of Rites, 212
Boston Confucianism, xi–xix, xxi–
xxv, xxviii, xxxv, 1–2, 21, 55, 96,
104, 109–11, 128, 133–34, 145, 167–
68, 182, 186, 190, 194, 205–06, 209,
213; as a group in Boston, xxv;
north of the Charles and south of
the Charles, xxv; spirituality in,
206–09
Boston, xxi–xxii, xxiv; Confucians
from, 213; as ground for Confu-
cianism, 1–23, 183; primal culture
of, xxiv–xxv, xxx; driving in, 111;
rituals for, 205–06; University, 220
Bostonians, Irish-American, Chinese-
American, African-American, 16
Both-and, in Confucianism, 89
Brahman, 117, 119; Saguna and
Nirguna, 140; B.-Isvara, 75
Brahmins, Boston, distinguished
from Boston Confucians, xxi, 7
Bridegroom, Christ as, 220
Bridging, scholars of for Confucian
and Western philosophy, 43–47
Bruce, J. Percy, 43
Brumbaugh, Robert S., 212, 221
Buber, Martin, 89
Buchler, Justus, 221
Buddha-mind, 150, 159
Buddhism, xxiii, xxvi, xxx, 3, 11, 22,
42, 52, 70, 88–89, 110, 117, 119,
150, 154, 158, 168, 171, 176, 207,
211; Chinese, 26, 29–33, 51, 126,
214; Madhyamaka, 159;
Mahayana, 126–59; on self, 170
Burks, Arthur W., 213
Butterflies, 53

Calligraphy, 25
Canon, of scripture, 4
Cappadocian theologians, 172
Care, 103
Carpentry, and space-time imagina-
tion, 121–22
Carryover, in truth, 70–73; of the
ultimate, 79
Cassirer, Ernst, 48

Categories, 52; comparative, 112–15,
151–52, 164–65, 208; external, 108;
imposed, 49–50
Causation, 50, 134, 136; in Confu-
cianism, 141–45; in imagination,
122; in interpretation, 11–12; in
South Asian conceptions of Being,
139–40; in defining truth, 70–73
Celts, 120
Censorship, in psychoanalytic
theory, 173–74, 180
Center (*zhong*) and relationships
(*yung*), 94, 175–79, 185. *See also*
"Ten thousand things"
Center, of self, transcendent, 157–58
Ceremonies, 205. *See also* Ritual
Propriety
Ch'en, Kenneth, 214
Ch'ien Mu, xxvii
Chan, Wing-tsit, 8, 15, 19, 25–26, 30,
32, 26, 42–44, 66, 89, 96–97, 100,
105, 142–45, 154–55, 176, 178, 180–
81, 184, 188–89, 197, 205, 211, 219,
221
Chang Chungyuan, 13, 46–48, 52
Chang Tung-sun, xxvii
Change, xviii; not merely rearrange-
ment, 138–39; in self, 189–90;
social, xxii–xxiii
Chaos, 27–29, 33
Character, 116; authorship of, 175;
personal, 169–70
Charles River, dividing Boston
Confucians, xvi, xxv
Cheng Chungying, xxviii, xxxiii, 43,
47, 50–52, 54, 127, 129, 184, 211–
15, 218, 220–21
Cheng Hao, 3, 42, 76, 152, 155–57,
178, 180, 183–84
Cheng Yi, 3, 42, 152, 155–57, 178,
183–84, 221
Cheng-Zhu School, 76
Child, about to fall in well, 36, 153–
54, 157, 176, 179; of the dao, 144
Children, 99–102; of God, 101–02;
prodigal, 103
China, xv, xxvii–xxx, 2, 83, 126, 133,
212; contemporary Confucianism
in, 41–43; Dewey in, 213; language in, xi–xiii, 53, 169; and

China *(continued)*
  Marxism, 127; versus the West, in Hall and Ames, 108–09
Chinese Academy of Social Sciences, 57
Ching, Julia, 156, 212, 214–15
Choice, 85–88, 91, 96
Christ, body of, 199–200; imitation of, 199–200; mind of, 199–200; resurrected, 200. *See also* Jesus
Christianity, xxiii, xxx, 20, 22, 40, 58–59, 115, 126, 134–35, 139, 150, 158–65, 171, 191, 216–17, 219; compared with Confucianism, 194–209; Eastern Orthodox, 41, 164; exclusivism in, 207; on families, 196–99; and God, 69; and goodness of creation, 76; Jesus model for, 204–06; on learning love, 197–98; membership in, 206–09; Nestorian, 211; Roman Catholic, 164; as state church versus minority, 198; in tradition with Judaism and Islam, 203; in Tu Weiming, 88–91; understanding in, 8; Western, 148
Chung, Chai-sik, xxi
Church, as family, 197–98; as historical, 200
Circle, hermeneutical, 113–14
Civility, 15–16
Civilization, 10, 31, 40, 60, 95, 148, 204–05; Chinese, 117; paradigmatic conceptions for, 125–26; and habits, 181, 202–03; and ritual, 80, 93–95, 202–03; in social practices, 212–13; sophisticated, 122; of world society, xxix
Civilizations, 220; clash of, 78; dialogue among, xiv–xv
Clarity, 120; of heart, 35; of self, 178
Class, and self-deception, 174–75; class-conflict, 185
Classics, Confucian, xiv; textual expression of motifs, 125
Classification, 48
Clothes, putting on, as conversion, 91
Codes, 12; cultural, 132–33; of laws and commandments, 116

Collegiality, of Asian and Western Confucians, xxviii–xxix; and friendship, 18
Columbia University, xiii, 42, 211, 213; Seminar on Neo-Confucianism, 44, 211
Commentary, 118–20; on core texts and motifs, 110
Commiseration, 36–37, 97, 153–54
Commitment, existential, 57, 93, 96, 103; to the way of the sage, 88–91
Common sense, as philosophic ground, 51–52
Communalism, in Christianity, 172
Community, 8–9, 15–21, 57, 84, 152; fiduciary, 84, 91, 100; focus in, 73; in New Confucianism, 83–84; religious, 63; and conceptions of self, 167
Comparative Religious Ideas Project, 220
Comparison, xvi–xvii, 43–50, 60, 193–94; four moments in: formal, phenomenological, translational, theoretical, 112–15; motif analysis in, 114–15; of philosophies, 127–28; of semiotic theories in engagement, 111; theory of, xxxi, 111–15
Competence, of being civilized, 38–40
Comportment, 53–54
Concern, ultimate, 214
Concreteness, 48, 52–54; distorted by abstractions, 49
Confession, 91
Conformation, to principle, 88
Confucian-Christian Dialogue Conferences, xxi–xxv
Confucianism, xxiii–xxv, 12–15, 26, 29–33, 88, 109, 115, 117–19, 125, 159, 186, 213; on being and creation, 141–45; compared to Christianity, 194–209; contemporary, 41–54, 107, 193–94; philosophy of culture of, 26–40; in dialectical relation to culture, 193; in late-modern culture, 74–82; in East Asia versus the West, xi–xix; existential, xvii, 85–88; on grace, 90; on individuation, 73; on Jesus

as a model for virtue, 204–06;
membership in, xi–xii, xxi, 63,
206–09; motifs of self in, 185; on
nature, 204; from New York City,
213; normative philosophy in, 43,
47–54; piquant, 86–88; political
theory in, 199; as portable, 1–8;
and pragmatism, 11–15, 70–71;
project of, xi–xix; as public
philosophy, xxv–xxvii, 215; as
religion, 22, 57–62; rhetoric not
dialectical, 135; on ritual, 123, 202;
on the self, 167–69, 178–79; self-
deception in, 178–85; in global
society, 79–82; spirituality in, 57–
82; scholarly temperament in, 44;
scholarship on in Western
languages, 42–43; and transcendence, 147–51; and transformation, xii, 73; and ultimate reality,
68–74; values in, 84; virtues in,
97–98; and John Wesley, 164–65;
and Western philosophy, 104; and
world philosophy, xxvii–xxx, 107,
129. *See also* Neo-Confucianism
and New Confucianism
Confucius, xxii, 9, 13, 45, 49, 83,
108, 110, 113, 147–51, 178, 181,
183, 200–01, 203, 205, 212;
philosophy of culture of, 33–38;
as revolutionary, 34
Conscience, xviii–xix
Consciousness, 97, 169; pure, 116–
17; historical self-consciousness,
21
Contingency, 145
Continuity, 13; of innate nature with
external action, 37–38
Continuum, in self, 175–79, 186, 188
Contradiction, 168–75, 183, 185–86
Contrasts, finite-infinite, 217
Control, and self-deception, 174
Conventions, 6, 9, 94, 123, 130–31,
178, 187–88; in culture, 28, 40;
versus nature, 35; as perceptions,
131
Conversation, global, 50, 52, 55, 83–
84, 218
Conversion, 86, 88–91, 104, 200–01
Cooking, 25

Cooperation, and ritual, 203
Core, essential, in cross cultural
portability of Confucianism, 3–8;
of self, 82; spiritual, 63–69; texts
and motifs, 3, 63, 107, 108–11,
206–07
I Corinthians, 198
Correctness, 75
Correlative thinking, 48–50, 108,
149–50
Corrington, Robert, S., 138, 145
Corruption, 5–6
Cosmology, 61, 65, 126, 214; in Zhu
Xi, 184
Cosmos, creation of, 119; single-
ordered, 160
Cou Yen, 117
Court, imperial, 29; rituals, 124
Courtliness, 9
Cousins, Ewert, definition of
spirituality of, 62–69
Covenant, 197, 201–02; motifs of,
126
Cratocentrism, 126
Creation (divine), xviii–xix, 65–66,
96, 134–35, 149; in Christian
theology, 160–61; *ex nihilo*, 69,
137–39, 141, 145, 149, 158; as
good, 76; and love, 165; motifs of,
118, 124–25; stories in *Genesis*,
201, 203–04; Vedic hymn to, 140
Creativity (not divine), xviii–xix, 51,
87
Creator, indeterminate, 158
Creel, Herrlee G., 44
Critique, Confucian, of Western
(Boston) culture, 15–23
Crucifixion, 200
Cua, Antonio S., xxxii, 45, 156, 184,
211–12, 214
Cuisine, 48
Cultivation, of self, 37–38, 85–88; in
Daoism, 31–33
"Culturally obliged," xiii
Culture, Aryan, 116; created by
ritual propriety, 9–11; Chinese, not
distinguishing philosophy from
religion, 58–62; East and West
Asian compared, 152–54; as
fulfilling biology, in Xunzi, 28–29;

Culture *(continued)*
  global, 110; high and low, 25–26,
  30; indigenous, xxii; Indo-
  European, 133; killing of, 109; as
  liberating, 32; and nature, 25–29;
  non-East Asian, xxiii–xxv;
  peasant, 186; philosophy of, xxx,
  23, 25–40, 48–50, 52–54, 108, 218;
  religion in, 58–62; rituals of, as
  orientations, 187–88; scientific, 74–
  79; of urban West, 193; space-time
  imagination, differences in, 121–
  22; world, xi, xiv–xv

Dai Zhen, 3, 42, 45, 50, 207, 220
Dance, 25, 28, 32, 53, 189–90;
  biopsychic, 13; ritual as, 80
Dao, xxii, 28–29, 31, 33–38, 62, 66–
  67, 74, 76, 91, 93, 99, 105, 118,
  141–45, 150, 154–59, 176, 181, 204;
  departure from, how?, 36–37; as
  harmonizing, 177; in nature, 34–
  38; as transcendent, 149
Daodejing, 30, 44, 46, 141, 143
Daoism, xxii–xxiv, xxx, 3, 7, 11, 13–
  14, 22, 26–27, 29–34, 36, 39–40,
  43–44, 46–47, 51–54, 110, 117–19,
  125–26, 141, 154–55, 168, 186, 207,
  214, 218; as a ritualized religion,
  33
Daoxue Movement, 11
de Bary, William Theodore, xxiv,
  xxviii, 44, 170, 185–86, 211, 213–14
Deans, as scholar-officials, xxiv, 22–
  23
Death, 61; d.-centered civilizational
  motifs, 125–26
Deborah (from *Judges*), 139
Decrees, motifs of, 116–20, 126–27
Deference, xxvi–xxvii, 10, 18, 35–37,
  54, 153–54; in filial piety, 195
Definition, in philosophic ideas, 120
Deliberation, 14–15
Democracy, xv, 5, 79–82, 129, 182;
  liberal, 83–84, 218
Demystification, 32
Dependency, ontological, 149
Depth, in Western conception of
  self, 167, 173, 186–92
Derrida, Jacques, 132

Descartes, Rene, 7, 11, 46, 59, 76,
  120, 152
Description, 115, 177
Desire, 87–88
Desmond, William, 130, 138, 145, 221
Destiny, 144, 155; and deanship, xxiv
Destructiveness, xviii
Determinateness, 157; defined, 135–
  39; of world, 75
Determinism, 138–39
Devil, the, xix
Devotion, 158
Dewey, John, xv–xvi, 11–12, 38, 92,
  127, 129, 213
Dialectic, 114, 221; of Being, 129–31,
  133; in comparison, 113–15;
  between Confucianism and
  culture, xxii–xxv, 23; in Western
  conception of self, 173
Dialogue, Confucian-Christian, xi,
  194; interfaith, xxv, 115; in
  philosophy, 120–21
Diaspora, Chinese, xi–xiii, xxiv, 2, 8,
  21–22
Dignity, in death, 39; human, 16
Dilworth, David, 49
Dimensions, of life, 215; religious or
  transcendent, 63–74
Diotema, 220
Diplomacy, 58
Direction, spiritual, 63
Discernment, 5, 64–65, 77; a func-
  tion of orientation, 187
Discourse, bland, 84; community of,
  xi
Disenfranchisement, by failed
  habits, 182–83
Disputation, Chinese philosophy as,
  211
Diversity, 142; cultural, 16–21
Divinity, 200; in soul, 115. *See also*
  God, Gods
Doctrine of the Mean, xiv, 3–8, 26,
  36–38, 42, 66–67, 69–70, 75–76, 89,
  94, 97–98, 110, 152–54, 157, 160–
  61, 170, 176, 178, 180–01, 186, 189,
  216, 218; on selfhood, 175–79
Domination, xvi, 48
Dreams, 174; dreaming innocence,
  168

Dress, 183
Driver, Tom, 216
Dualism, body-mind, 200; in
    Samkhya, 117; in Zhu Xi and
    Wang Yangming, 156
Dung Zhungxu, 42
Durkheim, Emile, 61
Duty, 119; for Arjuna, 117
Dynamism, 87; of spirit, 63–64

Earth, 26–29, 62, 105, 150, 153–59,
    209; as Mother, 66, 188; as
    transcendent, 149. *See also* Trinity,
    of Heaven, Earth, and the Human
    and Material Force
East Asia, xxi, xxvi; as context for
    Confucianism, xi–xiii, 88–89; as
    context for philosophy, xi–xxv;
    culture of, 2–4; culture of in
    America, 17–23; culture of,
    primal, xxiii–xxiv; dialectic of
    being in, 133; and the West, 138
Ecclesiocentrism, 126
Eckhart, Meister, 138
Ecology, 52, 79–82, 129, 191, 209; as
    Confucian problem, 81–82; crisis
    in, 84
Economics, xxix, 39, 52, 82; habits
    for, 182; models of, xxvi
Ecumenism, xvi
Education, 22–23, 36; and the dao,
    154, 176
Edwards, Jonathan, xvi, 164
Egalitarianism, xxiv, 9, 16, 39, 99–
    100
Ego, author's, 212; in Freudian
    theory, 173–74; large bourgeois,
    173
Egypt, 5, 116, 125; gods of, 134
Elberfeld, Rolf, xxxii
Elderly, the, 20
Elements, five. *See* Five Elements
Eliade, Mircea, 122, 216
Elite, as philosophers, 58
Ellegate, Nancy, xxxiv
Emanation, 135
Embodiment, cultural, 110
Emerson, Ralph Waldo, xvi, 48,
    150
Emotion, 177–78

Emperors, 36, 99–100, 105; sage, 199;
    Shun and Yu, 201
Empiricism, British, 216
Emptiness, in Buddhism, 70, 150,
    159
Encompassing, Jaspers' category of,
    165
Encyclopedia of Unified Science, 187
Endowment, natural, of heaven and
    earth, 29, 202
Enemies, 200
Engagement, 54, 64–65, 79, 111, 216;
    defined, 131–33; a function of
    imagination, 77; philosophy as,
    131–33; defining the self, 70–74; of
    world with poise, 191–92
Enjoyments, earthly, gilded poison
    of, 163
Enlightenment, 9, 16, 39, 45, 59;
    Buddhist, 32–33, 117; European,
    xv, xxiv, 7, 71, 79–80
Enlightenment Project, in Tu
    Weiming, 72, 83–84
Enmity, 23
Eno, Robert, 33, 213–14
Environment, xxix, 36, 121; as a
    problem, xv, 74, 79–82; ritual
    aspect of, 187; and conceptions of
    self, 167
Epictetus, 43
Epistemology, 47, 59; in defining
    spirituality, 70
Equality, 79–82; in friendship, 181;
    of opportunity, 16
Equilibrium, 92, 153, 175
Eros, 98, 219
Essence, 189
Essentialism, circumvented in
    theory of harmony, 64
Eternity, 134–35; as togetherness of
    modes of time, 137–38
Ethics, xix, 47–48, 51–52, 72, 129;
    Aristotelian, 200; and Chinese
    semiotics, 39; contemporary, 50–
    52; global, 74–82; and orientation,
    191; and ritual, 45; Western, 96
Ethnicity, xxvi; and conceptions of
    self, 167; and Confucianism, xxi–
    xxv
Etiquette, as ritual, 124

Europe, xxvi, 130, 212; with American colonies, as appendage of West Asia, 115; philosophy of, compared with Chinese by Hall and Ames, 47–50
Eve, 161, 201–02. *See also* Adam
Evil, xviii–xix, 22–23, 171; in Confucianism and Christianity compared, 102–05
Evolution, 164
Examination system, 17
Excellence, 116
Exclusivism, in Christianity, 207; among religions, 194
Existentialism, 149; in commitment, 57; in Confucianism of Tu Weiming, 84–88; on the self, 167
Exodus, 195
Experience, engagement theory of, 216; spiritual or religious, 63–69
Explanation, 50
Explanation of the Diagram of the Great Ultimate, 142–43
Extension, of meanings and signs, 132–33
Externality, in Hegel, 172–73
Externalization, 92–93
Extirpation, of selfish desires, 87–88, 91
Eye contact, as semiotic, 123

Fact/value distinction, 12–13, 76, 217
Faith, 104
Fall, the, 152, 201–03
Fallacy, extensionalist, 132
Fallibility, 77
Familiarity, false, 49
Family, 15–21, 25, 29, 31, 33, 84, 92, 98, 152, 175, 182, 184, 205; broken, 101, 197–98; of God, 102; and individuality, 188; intergenerational, 195; non-kinship, 197; orientation to, 187; structure of, in Boston Confucianism, 19–21; universal, 197
Fang Fu-kuan, xxvii
"Farewell Discourses," Jesus, in John's *Gospel*, 219

Farming, 58, 187
Father, 105; as motif for God, 158
Fazang, 42
Features, of harmony, essential and conditional, 64, 135–39
Feelings, arousal of, 176; in Xunzi, 27–29
Feminism, xxiii–xxiv
Feng Youlan, xv, 42
Fiduciary community. *See* Community
Filiality. *See* Piety, filial
Fingarette, Herbert, xii, xxviii, 8–11, 45, 84, 181, 213, 222
Finite/infinite contrast, defined, 65–69
Firmness, 144
"Five Elements" (or "Five Agents"), 48, 66, 74–75, 143, 150
"Five Relations," 15, 25, 100
Fixation, 86–88; in Xunzi and Tu Weiming, 93–94
Flesh, in St. Paul, 170–71
Flourish, 144
Folkways, 116
Form, 158; in Aristotelian definition of truth, 71–72; of the Good, 161; Platonic, 149–50
"Forming one body with heaven, earth, and the myriad things." *See also* "One body . . ."
Foucault, Michel, 46–47
Foundationalism, 47, 59
Founding element, of world, 65–69
"Four Beginnings," xvii, 36–37, 77, 88, 97, 154–55, 157, 176–77
"Four Books," xiv, 3, 110
"Four Causes," 49
Fragmentation, 93
Freedom, xix, 126; in Adam, 161–64; learned, 196; for parents, 199–201; and poise, 191; and self-deception, 174
Freud, Sigmund, 90, 112, 161, 173–74
Friendship, xxii, 4, 9, 13–23, 29, 33, 84, 98; and ritual, 203; in self-deception, 181–82
Fu, Charles Weishun, 47

Fuller, Steve, xxxii
Function, defines transcendent things, 149–51. *See also* Substance-function distinction
Functionalism, 213
Funerals, 32, 214

Gandhi, 127
Garden, 81, 203; of Eden, 164, 201–02; Jesus in, devotion of, 160
Gardner, Daniel K., 215
Geertz, Clifford, 216
General, military, 156, 164
Generalization, and exceptions, 108–09
Generativity, 141–45, 155, 178
Genesis, 116, 118, 125, 161–65
Gesture, 13
Ghosts, 159
Gibralter, 212
Girardot, Norman, 44, 161, 214
Global society, 79–82
Gnosticism, 126
God, xvii–xix, 69, 97, 134–35, 148, 150–51, 158–65, 171, 200, 203, 209, 216; beyond gods, 159; body of, 119; many candidates for conceiving, 161; creating by decree, 116–20; as creator, 126, 160–61; as Father, 101–02, 197–98; prior to the distinction of good and evil, 164; image of, 89, 98, 148, 158–65, 172, 216, 222; in Hegel, 172–73; law of, 171; personal, 126; of storms, 134, 139; turning from and toward, 90–91, 103–04; in Whitehead, 139, 215–16. *See also* Creation (divine) *and* Creator
God-centered civilizational motifs, 125–26
Gods, 140, 108
Golden Rule, 197
Good, and evil, transcended, 156; "g. that I would I do not," in St. Paul, 161–62, 171
Government, 6, 14, 29, 31, 22, 186–87; as human endowment in Xunzi, 28–29; good, in Legalism, 32; versus strongman, 9

Grace, xviii–xix, 86, 104
Graduate Theological Union, 212
Graham, A. C., 19, 32, 48, 149–50, 211, 213
"Great Commandment," of Jesus, 97
Great Learning, The, xiv, 3–8, 42, 92, 110, 170, 178, 188, 199
"Great Transformation," (*dahua*), xix
"Great Ultimate," 66–68, 73, 143
Greece, ancient, 4–5, 120, 126, 134; foundational to Western culture, 48; gods of, 116; language for philosophy, xii, 43; philosophy of as portable, xxii
Greeting, rituals for, 124
Ground of Being, 69, 75. *See also* God *and* Ultimacy
Guanyin, 158
Guilt, 152, 184
Guo Xiang, 42
Guru, xiv, 72

Habits, 15–16, 22, 33–38, 177, 179–85, 213; bad, 180; changing, 205; ideas as, 12–15; in self-deception, 181–83; of selfishness, 87–88
Hall, David L. xii, xxviii, xxxi, xxxiii–xxxiv, 34, 39, 43, 47–50, 52, 54, 69, 108–09, 113, 129, 131, 147–51, 158, 161, 218
Han Feizi, 31–32
Han Yu, 42
Handshakes, 182
Hansen, Chad, 31, 53, 214
Harmonization, 34–35, 76, 177, 188; of technology and culture, 40
Harmony, xvii–xix, xxii–xxiv, 9–11, 27–29, 48–49, 136–39, 149, 155, 157–58; cosmic, 70; of essential and conditional sub-hypotheses in hypotheses about spirituality, 64; of heaven and earth, 66–67; of life, 33–38; in Neo-Confucianism, 64; in self, 190–92; yin-yang in, 117–18
Hart, Ray L., 121
Hartshorne, Charles, 213
Harvard University, xiii, 1–2, 42, 218
Harvard Yenching Institute, 218

Hats, ceremonial, 10
Health, of elderly, 195
Heart (xin), xviii, 90–91, 103, 169,
    171; heavenly principle in, 87–88;
    same in all people, 176; in ritual,
    184; of self, 5; in Wang Yangming,
    178–79
Heaven (or heavenly principle; *see
    also* Principle), xviii, 26, 36, 57–58,
    62, 85, 93, 105, 115, 140, 150, 153–
    59, 176; and Earth, 66, 69, 188 in
    modern science, 74–75; engen-
    ders, the human completes, xix;
    gift of, 104; mandate of, 208;
    mind of, 155–57; in soul, as
    divine image, 160–61; transcen-
    dent, 149 157–58; in Xunzi, 81,
    141–42
Heavens, the, 186–87; models of in
    China, 141; orientation to, 190
Heelan, Patrick, 122
Hegel, G. W. F., xv, 54, 120, 130,
    137, 150, 152, 161, 168, 172–73,
    215, 221
Heidegger, Martin, 9, 46, 51, 89, 126,
    129, 134
Hemingway, Ernest, xxi
Heresy, 207
Hermeneutics, 50, 60, 113–14; in
    Confucian studies, xi–xiv;
    cultural, 53–54
Heroism, 40
Hesiod, 116
Hexagrams, sixty-four of the *Yijing*,
    141
Hierarchies, of habits, 182
Hillman, James, 122
Hinduism, xxvi, 110
History of religions, 60, 62–63
History, 27; dialectic of, 160; of
    motifs, 120–21
Ho Yen, 42
Hobbes, Thomas, 7, 33–34, 59, 76,
    197
Holiness, 40, 89, 134, 152, 164–65,
    200–01; in Christianity, 73, 76
Holism, in Chinese thought, 108
Holy Spirit, 199–200
Home, 117
Homer, 116

Homogeneity, 15–16
Hong Kong, xi, xxi, xxiv, xxvii, 41
Hsiung Shih-li, xxvii
Hu Shi, xv, xxvii
Huainanzi, 42
Huisi, 42
Human being, created, 201
Human Completion of Nature,
    motifs of, 117–19, 125
Human condition, 116
Human nature, as evil, 102; as
    good, 6, 35–38; and ritual, 92–96;
    as selfish, 37–38; socially defined,
    98
Human rights, 44, 47, 185–86; and
    conception of self, 167
Human sphere, versus cosmic, 25–
    39
Human-centered civilization, motifs
    of, 125–26
Humaneness (*ren*), xxv, 16, 35–38,
    83, 102, 144, 204–06; as love, in
    Tu Weiming, 96–102. *See also ren
    translated as* Humanity *and* Love
Human-heartedness. *See* Humane-
    ness
Humanism, xv, xvii, 74
Humanity (*ren*), xii–xiii, 4, 8–11, 25,
    36, 75, 91, 153–54, 176, 178, 183–
    85, 195, 199–201, 218; in Cheng
    Hao, 155–57; not far away, 205;
    defined as poise, 82; for Tu
    Weiming, 84, 92–96. *See also ren
    translated as* Humaneness *and*
    Love
Hume, David, 7, 59–60, 152
Hundun (Hun-tun), xxxiii
Hunting, 61
Huntington, Samuel P., xxvi, 215
Hylomorphism, 200
Hypocrisy, 15
Hypotheses, 221; concerning
    comparison, 111–15; about
    harmony, 135–39; defining
    spirituality, 62–79

Iconicity, 132–33, 216; as form of
    reference, 61
Ideal, versus actual, 76
Idealism, in Hegel, 172

Identity, defined, 135–39; finite, 134–35; moral, 78, multiple religious, xxiv, xxx, 22, 206–09, 222; personal, 82, 167

Ideology, 183; of modern science, 77; and self-deception, 174–75

Idolatry, 134–35, 158; and filiality, 194

Image of God, *see* God, image of

Imagination, xvii, 46, 61–62, 77–79, 217; archetypes in, 122–23; deep structures of, 121–25; in motifs, 114;

Imitation, 199–200; in families, 198

Immanence, in Confucianism, 147–51; and transcendence, 69

Immediate Identity, motif of, 117, 119

Imperialism, xxvii, 127

Importance, 71–73; in orientation, 187, 190–91; and triviality, 54

Incarnation, 194

Incommensurability, of Chinese and Western cultures, 111

Indeterminacy, 144; in ontological ground of mutual contrasts, 149. *See also* Being, dialectic of

India, xxv, xxx, 3, 41, 58, 126, 140; education in 211, philosophy of, xxxv

Individualism, xiv, 73, 186; in Augustine, 172; in ethics, 95; in conceptions of self, 167–68

Individuals, enduring, 135–36

Individuation, 73, 152

Indra, 158

Ineffability, 115

Infants, and love, 195–96

Infatuation, 18

Infinity, in God, 163–164; in self and God, 173

Influence, political, 100

Informality, 18

Inheritance, of property, 197–98

"Innate knowledge in action," *Liang-zhi*, 87–88, 156

Innate love, 98

Institutions, 80, 154, 202; as defining self, 73

Instrumentalism, 39, 92

Integration, spiritual, 64–74

Integrity, in comparison, 113; personal, as poise, 190

Intellectuals, 212; Confucian, 83, 218; public, 214–15

Intelligibility, in correlative thinking, 149–50

Intention, versus extension, 132–33

Intentionality, 11–12, 77, 86–87, 171, 188, 213; divine, in Confucianism and Christianity, 208

Interaction, among cultures about motifs, 114

Interiority, of self, 161, 167–75

Internalization, in Hegel, 172–73

International Society for Chinese Philosophy, xxviii, 50

Internet, xxvi, xxix

Interpretation, xvii, 70–73, 77–79, 130, 217; in comparison, 112–15; of Confucianism to the West, 43–47; defined, 132–33; pragmatic theory of, 11–15; in self-deception, 174

Intimacy, 105; cosmic, 66, 74

Intuition, forms of, 121

Investigation of things, 156, 177

Irony, 52–53; of convention, 38–40

Islam, xii, xxiii, xxvi, xxx, 22, 41, 58, 126, 135, 139, 159–60, 203; higher education in, 211–12; on religious membership, 63

Israel, 120, 134

Isvara, 140

Ivanhoe, P. J., xxviii, 45, 215

Jakarta, 212

James, William, xvi, 11, 150

Japan, xii, xv, xxx, 2

Jaspers, Karl, 108, 147–48, 151–52, 165

Jeremiads, 183

Jeremiah, 34

Jesus, 20, 91, 97, 101, 103, 118–19, 158, 196–98, 206, 208, 219–20; as elder brother, 198; character of taken on, 205; and Confucianism, 194; as model of virtue, 204–06. *See also* Christ

Jobs, orientation to, 187–90

Johann, Robert, 220
John, disciple of Jesus, 197, 222
John, Gospel of, 118
Journal for Chinese Philosophy,
    xxviii, 50
Journey, spiritual, 63–69
Judaism, 20, 22, 126, 134–35, 139,
    159–60, 197, 203; on families, 196
Judgment, 77; on self, 171
Jung, C. G., 122
Justice, 5, 36; distributive, xv, xxix,
    31–32, 74, 79–82; global, 209; and
    ritual, 80

Kang Yuwei, 42, 211
Kang, Ouyang, xxxii
Kant, 7, 11, 51, 59, 71, 107, 120–21,
    150, 152, 163, 165, 213; and
    Confucianism, 203; manifold in,
    128
Kantianism, 21
Karma, 119, 139
Kasulis, Thomas P., 214, 216
Kengo, Araki, 170
Kierkegaard, Soren, xix, 52, 54, 86,
    89, 161; definition of self in, 173
Kingdom, of God, 103–04
Kinship relations, in Christianity, 20,
    101
Klutz, falling into well with child,
    176
Knight of Faith, xix
Knoblock, John, 27, 37, 218
Knowledge, 50; in Confucian action,
    176–77; intuitive versus compara-
    tive in Wesley, 162; sociology of,
    216; of value and fact, 77–79
Kohn, Livia, 33, 44
Korea, xii, xv, xxi, xxx, 2
Krejci, Jaroslav, 125–26
Kreuzer, Johann, xxxii
Krishna, 117
Kyoto School of Buddhism, 129

Labor of the notion, Hegelian, 54
Lagerway, John, 33, 44
Lamentation, 4–5
Language, 26, 123–24, 152, 213; as
    conventional ritual, 10; East
    Asian, 169; and self, 177–79

Laozi, xxii, 30, 42, 142–45
Late modernity, xv–xvi, xxix, 16–17,
    94–96; facticity in, 126
Latin, 43
Lau, D. C., 97
Lear, 175, 184
Learning, 4; of ritual versus
    humanity, 205; of signs, 177–78
Lee, Thomas H. C., 214
Legacy, in tradition, 107–11
Legalism (as a school of Chinese
    philosophy), 3, 26–27, 29–33, 42,
    117
Leibniz, G., 7, 41–42, 215
Leisure, orientation to, 187
Li. See Propriety *and* Ritual, *espe-
    cially* Ritual, propriety
Li Ao, 42
Liang Shu-ming, xxvii
Liberal arts, xiv
Liberation, and no-self doctrine,
    117
Liezi, 42
Life, philosophic, 25; solitary, poor,
    nasty, brutish, and short, 33
Limits, of Christian compatibility
    with Confucianism, 209
Lin Chao-en, 220
Literati, Confucian, xiii–xiv, 38
Liturgy, 59, 208
Liu Shuhsien, xxxiii, 47, 211, 213–14
Lo (love), 220
Locke, John, 7, 59
Logic, 21, in Hegel, 221
Logical School in China, 117
Lomanov, Alexander, xxxiii
Long, Eugene Thomas, 215
Love (often a translation of *ren*), 13,
    18, 96–102, 191, 204–06; in Adam,
    162; blocked by alienation, 102–
    05; in Augustine, 172; in Chinese
    vocabulary, 220; Christian, 9;
    in Christianity and Confucian-
    ism compared, 96–102; l. with
    distinctions, xxiv, 79, 100, 198;
    divine, 171; according to Jesus,
    219; learning to, 195–201, from
    saints rather than parents, 198;
    liberating, 206; ranges of mean-
    ing in Christianity and Confu-

cianism, 96–97; as motif for God, 158; parental, 99–102; as principle, 156; redeeming, 199; universal, 32

Lu Xiangshan, 3, 42

Lucas, George, Jr., 214

Lust, 91, 171

Luther, Martin, 156

Lu-Wang School, 76

Ma I-fu, xxvii

Machle, Edward J., 27, 218

Maddox, Randy, 222

Magic, 122

Maimonides, 60

Major, John, 141

Mammals, 121

Mandate of heaven, 118

Manifesting the clear character, 6, 73, 79, 179, 188–89

Manifold, in Kant, 120, 128

Mann, Mark H. Grear, xxxiv

Manners, 9

Manners, as ritual node, 124

Manners, Miss, 95

Mao Zedong, xxvii

Marcel, Gabriel, 89

Mark (gospel of), 20

Marx, Karl, 161, 174–75, 190

Marxism, xxii, xxvii, 38, 83, 183, 186, 218; Chinese, 119

Mary, mother of Jesus, 197

Material force (translation of *qi*), 68, 155, 157, 178; in Zhu Xi, 156–57

Materialism, 149

Mathematics, 42, 160; in orientation, 187–88

Matrix, mythic, 122–23

Matter, 158

Maturity, 103; in filial piety, 196

Maxims, on novelty, 137–38

May Fourth Movement, xv, xxvii

McKeon, Richard, 49

Meadows, Philip R., 222

Meaning, 130; and culture, 71; of life, xv, xxix

Meaninglessness, in self-deception, 175

Medicine, 48

Meditation, 31, 156, 208; and contemplative way of life, xiii–xiv; in self-cultivation, 176

Membership, in Confucianism and Christianity, 206–09; religious, 63, 207

Memory, in Augustine, 172; bitter, 23

Mencius, xiv, xvi–xvii, xxii, xxv, 3–8, 25–26, 42, 45–46, 77, 88, 94, 97–98, 100, 109–10, 154–55, 176, 178–79, 180, 188, 203, 218, 220; philosophy of culture in, 33–38; project of, xviii, 51; on selfishness, 102; tradition of, 93

Mentality, a naturalistic account of, 217

Mercy, 103

Meritocracy, 17, 39, 79–80

Mesopotamia, 125

Metabolism, 30–31

Metaphor, 52–54, 71, 110, 112; of spirituality, 63–69

Metaphysics, 47, 52, 94–95, 136, 208, 216; comparison in, 114–15; contemporary Confucian, 50–52, 68–69, 129; in Daoism, 31; defined, 130; hypothesis in, 221; metaxological, 221; moral, xvii, 51–52, 77; Neo-Confucian, 178; Plato's, 5

Methodism, 164

Methodology, xxxi

Milbank, John, 61

Military issues, xxix, 213

Mind, 50, 169; in Aristotle, 71; m.-body distinction, 70–71; in Cheng Yi; integrated with action, 171; original substance of, 156; of small and large people, 102–03, 179–80; as substance, 11; in Xunzi, 27–29

"Mind of Heaven and Earth," 144

Minford, John, xxxii

Ministry, 103

Minorities, 16

Mirroring, 71

Missionaries, 41

Missions, Christian, 211

Model, for love, 103

Modernism, 213

Modernity, 7, 211; late, 167, 191, 208–09
Moism, xxiv, 3, 19, 26–27, 29–33, 100–02, 117. *See also* Mozi
Money, in friendship, 182
Monotheism, 69, 75, 142
Moore, Charles A., 117, 139–40
Moral identity, 78
Moral realism, 76
Morality, 50, 77, 215; transcendence in, 150–51
Mother, 105; as dao, 144
Motifs, xvi–xvii, xxxi, 4–8, 107–28, 133; ancient, 164; for Being in South and East Asia, 139–45; Christian and Confucian compared, 194–209; for God-centered civilizations, 125–26; mixed, 125–28; of self in Confucianism, 178–85; of self in Confucianism compared with West, 190–91
Mou Zongsan, xvii, xxvii, 37, 51–52, 77, 150, 216, 218, 221
Mover, Unmoved, 149–50, 161
Mozi, 42, 79, 197. *See also* Moism
Multiculturalism, xxiii
Music, 25, 32, 72, 132, 205
Mysticism, 126, 139, 142, 145, 159, 187, 221
Myth, 61, 68, 77, 214, 216; in imagination, 122–23

Narrative, 48, 61, 125
Nationalism, in India, 127
Natura naturans and *naturata*, 138
Natural law, 42
Naturalism, 32, 70–73, 138; ecstatic, 142, 145; in self, 186
Nature, 6, 11, 217, 221; creation of, 204; in Confucianism, 141; and culture, 27–29; human, 86, 89, 161, 170, in Axial Age religions, 147, as heaven-endowed, 179–89; philosophy of, 51–52, 119; as value-laden, 77–79
Needham, Joseph, 42, 141
Negation, in Hegel, 172–73
Neo-Confucianism, xiv, xxiii, xxxiv, 11, 27, 37–38, 51, 64, 76, 85–86, 97–98, 108–10, 119, 125, 142–43,
148–50, 160, 168, 177, 191, 207, 211–12, 222; as interpretive perspective on Confucianism, 43–44; Leibniz on, 41–42; and principle, 176; on self-deception, 183–85; transcendence in, 154–58
Neo-Platonism, 69, 135, 160
Neo-Pragmatism, 11, 47
Nestorianism, 211
Neurophysiology, 72
Neville, Beth, xxxiv
Neville, Leonora, xxxiv
Neville, Naomi, xxxiv
New Being, 103, 119
New Confucianism, xv–xvii, xxviii, 51, 110; in Tu Weiming, 83
New Testament, 97, 118, 220
Niebuhr, H. Richard, 217
Nietzsche, Frederich, 48, 76, 161
Nirvana, 159
Nivison, David S., 45
Nominalism, 51; default, 131
Nonattachment, 119
Non-being, 31, 69, 73, 137–38, 140, 145, 221; God beyond, 158–59; preceding or equal to the Great Ultimate, 143
Non-East Asian cultures, xxiii–xxv
Normative thinkers, 57
Normativeness, in reality, 167; of comparative philosophic claims, 115
Norms, xvii, 190
Northrop, F. S. C., 49
No-self doctrine, 70, 119, 170–71
Novelty, in creation, 137–38
Nuclear bombs, xxv
Nygren, Anders, 219

Obedience, 198
Objectivism, in ethics, 78, 127
Objectivity, 59
Objects, of signs, 131–33
Obligation, 6, 27, 118; in dysfunctional families, 198; to harmony, 190–91
Obsession, 85–86, 91
Ockham, William of, 131
Oedipus, 174–75, 184

One body with Heaven, Earth, and the myriad things, xvii, 88, 97, 157, 179–80, 188–89, 220
One, the, 140, 160; and many, 134–35, 145, 158
Ontogenesis, 75–76
Ontological context of mutual relevance, 136–39
Ontological ground of mutual contrasts, 149
Ontological question, 65–66
Ontology, 104, 136, 216; Chinese, 144; in Daoism, 31; defined, 130; and love, 96; science-tolerant, 217; of self, 157
Oppression, 74, 79–82; of women, xxiii
Order, 27–29, 155; conceptions of, 47–48; pockets of, 160
Ordinariness, 40
Organism, self as, 186–7
Orientation, 87–88, 169, 186–92; to cosmos, 81–82; defining the self, 70–74
Origination, 144
"Origination, flourish, advantage, definiteness," 184, 178–79
Orphans, 101, 196
Orthodoxy, 58
Otherness, 79–82, 89, 136–39; cultural, xxvi
Overlayment, of symbols, 120, 122
Own-being, 136
Oxtoby, Willard, 215

Paganism, 60
Pakistan, xxv
Parents, 182, 195–201; not all good, 101; teaching love, 99–102
Participation, in a tradition, 110–11
Pascal, B., 89
Patriarchy, in Confucianism, xxiii–xxv
Patterns, 48–49, 53–54, 149–50; cultural, shifting, 126
Paul, St., xix, 97, 99, 103, 161, 170–71, 176, 198, 200, 219
Peace, 196
Pears, stealing, 90
Peasants, in Moism, 32

Peirce, Charles S. xvi, 9, 11–15, 21, 29, 94–95, 213, 220
Pentecost, 196
People, small, 205
Perception, and self-deception, 174; in structure of self, 176–77; as conventions, 131
Perfection, 99; in Adam, 161–64; in Christianity and Confucianism, 200–01; of self and universe, 85–86; of virtue in the past, 200–01
Performance, 123
Performatives, 8–11, 45, 181, 213
Pericles, 4
Persia, 5
Person, 63, 169; God as, 159–61. *See also* Self
Personality, 169
Personification, of divinity, 27, 104, 126, 158–61
Peter, St., 219–20
Phaedrus, 98
Phenomena, checking theories, 78
Phenomenology, xxvii, 21, 60, 112, 216
Philia, 219
Philo, 134
Philosophy East and West, xxviii, 50
Philosophy, xiv, 90; academic, xxix, 41–43, 214–15; American, xxii; analytic, xxvii, 51, 215; background for, 128; Chinese, xxxv, 113, 149–51; as correlative, 48, and Western compared, 130–31, 151–52, 158–61; as world p., xxii; of culture, xiii–xiv, 125–26; curriculum of, 41–43; global, vi, 129, 193, 212; Greek, 134, 149; Hebrew, 134; Indian, 113, 127; Islamic, 135; legitimation of, 214–15; and religion, 57–62; of religion, 59; process, 217; as seeing, 131; systematic, 212; Western, not good on orientation, 189
Phonemes, of parental language, 204–05
Physicalism, in Wesley, 163
Physics, 187; and Confucian world view, 75

Physiology, and rituals, 123
Pietism, 59
Piety, Christian, 200; filial, xxii, xxiv, 4, 8–9, 13, 79, 91, 99–102, 105, 178, 194–201, 204–05; economics in, 99; four traits of, 195–96; as source of humaneness, 35; and ritual, 203
Pinyin, xxxii–xxxiii
Piquancy, in Augustine, 90
Plato, xxi, 4–5, 21, 43, 46, 51, 60, 89, 98, 130, 149, 161, 212; on dialectic, 221; as world philosopher, xxii
Platonism, xxii, xxix, xxvii, 2, 52, 206; on abstractions and the concrete, 49
Play, divine, 117, 140–41
Plenitude, 144
Pluralism, xvii, 79, 96, 127–29, 191, 203; in Christian churches, 198
Plurality, 136
Poetry, 187
Poise, xvii–xix, 169, 186–92; as harmonizing orientations, 81–82, 188–90
Poison, 163
Polarity, in Confucian conception of self, 175–79; in self, 186
Policy, 95
"Politically concerned," xiii
Politics, 5, 48, 72, 77, 92; world, xxix
Polo, Marco, 41
Polytheism, 158
Portability, of Confucianism outside East Asia, xxiii–xxv, 1–8, 193–94; of a world philosophy, 21
Positivism, 66–67, 71, 76, 92
Postmodernism, 59, 84, 213
Posture, as semiotic, 177–9
Poverty, 23
Power, and corruption, xxiii; exemplary, 35; among nations, xxv; political, 33
Practical Reason, xvii, 77–79
Practice, 52, 200–01; and beliefs, 59; of sageliness, 204; spiritual, 61–62, 207–09, 214

Pragmatism, xiv, 2, 9–15, 20–24, 29, 39, 50, 94–96, 104, 112, 181–83, 213, 216–17; and Confucianism, 68, 70–71; and semiotics in Confucianism, 179
Prakriti, 116
Praxis, xii–xv
Prayer, 63, 73, 208
Pre-Socratics, 134
Priest, xiv
Primal culture, 2, 6–7; of Boston and East Asia, xxiv–xxv
Primary process, in psychoanalysis, 173–74, 180
Principle (*li*, sometimes Heavenly Principle), xxiii–xxiv, 5, 27–29, 57, 68, 70, 76, 86, 90–92, 94, 103, 109, 147, 159, 171, 177–78, 191, 200, 216; in Cheng Hao and Cheng Yi, 155–57; as cool, 104; as explanatory, 147–51; compared to God, 165; in the heart, 88–91; as *ren*, 156; in Zhu Xi, 156–57
Principles, transcendent, two in China, 142–43
Privacy, 5–6, 120; as fault, 35; in philosophy, 127; and public, 80
Processes, 118, 122, 135; higher and lower, 31–33; in orientation, 188
Product, of creation, 137–38
Production and reproduction, 97
Profundity, competitive with clarity, 120–21
Progress, 39; economic, 32
Proletariat, authority of, 119
Prophet, xiv, 20, 34
Proportion, in exercise of ritual, 184
Propositions, 53
Propriety (often a translation of *li*), 15–21, 21, 25, 32, 36, 84, 154, 176–77, 199; in Tu Weiming, 83–88. *See also* Ritual *and* Ritual, propriety
Protestantism, 159
Proudfoot, Wayne, 216
Psychoanalysis, 173–75, 180
Psychocentrism, 126

Public, the, and the private, 80;
Intellectual, xiii–xiv; life, xxiv; for
philosophy, 127–28; service, 4
Purpose, 12, 14–15
Purusha, 116

Qi, material force, 27–29
Quiet-sitting, 156, 08
Qu'ran, 116

Racism, 16
Radhakrishnan, Sarvepalli, 117, 127,
139–40
Rahner, Karl, 150
Rajas, 116
Ramanuja, 119
Rationalism, 32; instrumental, 197
Realism, 108; moral, 76
Reality, 61, 68, 126, 130; as object of
orientations, 70–74; ultimate, 62–
69, 191–92
Reason, in Adam, 161–64; moral, 10
Reciprocity, xxiii–xxiv, 4
Reconciliation, 200
Reference, 84, 130–33, 216; in
comparison, 112–25; in engage-
ment, 131–33; semiotic, 71;
symbolic, 62; ultimate, 65–69
Regress, infinite, 75, 137
Regularity, in nature, 141
Reincarnation, 119, 168
Relation, 51, 191; defined, 136–39
Relations, 190; individuated in
humaneness, 98; interpersonal,
92–96, 168. *See also* Five Relations
Relatives, corrupt, 100
Relativism, 5, 131
Religion, 20; Chinese, 110; comparative, xvi; Confucianism as, 22, 83–
88; defined, 60–74; departments
of, 59; devotional versus philosophical, 159; natural, 59; and
philosophy, 57–62; popular versus
esoteric, 159; and spirituality, 63;
traditional, in late modernity, 201;
in West Asia, 159–61
Religiophilosophical thinkers, xxviii
Religious studies, 215; philosophy
in, 41

Ren, xii, xxv; meanings of, 220. *See
also* Humaneness, Humanity, *and*
Love
Renaissance, European, 72, 211
"Renovating the people," 6, 81
Repentence, 91
Representation, 53; in interpretation,
71; in Kant, 11
Resonance, 35, 120
Respects, of comparison, 111–15
Responsibility, xxii, 152; ruin of,
171; self-cultivated, 170; for sin,
91
Responsiveness, 82, 188; aesthetic,
153; in Mencius, 36
Retirement plans, 19
Revelation, 60, 203, 3
Rewards and punishments, explicit,
32
Rhetoric, 11, 129; spectrum of in
representations of the ultimate,
159–61
Rhythm, 30–31
Ricci, Matteo, 194, 214
Richardson, W. Mark, 217
Ridicule, 185
Righteousness, xii–xiii, 4, 25, 36–37,
75, 153–54, 176, 199
Rites controversy, 22
Ritual (often a translation of *li*, also
translated *ritual propriety* and
propriety, depending on context),
xxiv, 4, 45, 61, 80–82, 98, 104, 109,
116, 119, 122, 141–42, 152, 154,
177–78, 181, 183–84, 186–92, 201–
02, 214; and civilization, 34–38; in
culture, 29; as dance, 80; failures
of, 33–34; without humanity, 7,
205; in imagination, 123–25; takes
long to learn, 9; in orientation,
191; perfection of, 124; r. propriety (*li*), xii–xiv, xvi, xxv, 2, 4, 6,
8–21, 26–27, 194, 201–06, 213; for
multi-cultural society, 16–23; and
selfishness, 102–03; spectrum of,
123–25; in Tu Weiming, 83–88,
92–96; in Xunzi, 37–38
Robinet, Isabelle, 44
Roetz, Heiner, 203

Roles, social, 15–16
Romans, 198
Romanticism, 102
Rome, 126
Rootedness, of a philosophy, xxi–
    xxiv, xxvi
Rorty, Richard, 11, 47, 59, 84, 213
Rosen, Stanley, 134
Rule-centered civilizational motifs,
    126
Russia, xxv

Sacred Canopy, 58, 65–66, 68, 77
Sage, 4, 57, 61, 73, 75, 102–05, 156;
    legendary symbolic ancestor, 34,
    37, 199–200; Confucian (*zhunzi*),
    35–38; Daoist versus Confucian,
    31; in Neo-Confucianism, 38; way
    of, 91
Saints, for learning love, 198–99
Salvation versus holiness, 205
Samkhya, 116
Samsara, 32
Sanctification, 164–65, 204, 206
Sattva, 116
Saussure, Ferdinand, de, 12
Scale, human, relative to heavens,
    186
Scharlemann, Robert P., 215
Schematization, 115
Scholar-official, xiii–xiv, xxii, xxiv,
    22–23, 44, 50, 52, 156, 218
School of Names, 42
Schulkin, Jay, xxxiv
Science, xv, xvii, xxvi, 51, 53, 84,
    119, 126, 129, 135, 187, 189, 209,
    211, 215, 217; defining culture,
    74–79; explanation in, 48;
    hypothesis in, 72–73; and
    imagination, 122; and divine
    personification, 104; philosophy
    as, 214–15
Scientism, 38
Scotus, Duns, 60, 131, 138
Scripture, primary and secondary,
    3–8, 212
Searle, John, 45, 213
Secularity, 63; and Christianity,
    199

Selectivity, in perception, 174
Self, xiv, xxxi, 64–74, 82–83, 116–17;
    bifurcated, in St. Paul, 171;
    boundary of not fixed, 188–89;
    center of, 152–54; comparing
    theories of, 112; conceptions of, 5,
    70, 188; Confucian model of, 170,
    175–79, 212; Confucian and
    Western conceptions compared,
    167–91; s.-consciousness, 150–51,
    190; s.-criticism, 87–88, 180;
    s.-cultivation, xii, xiv, 88–91, 170;
    s.-deception, 168–70, 185–86, 190;
    and inadequate humanity, 179,
    183–85; psychological, 173–75,
    185; and inadequate signs, 179,
    181–83; and vague signs, 181–82;
    in Western conception of self,
    173–75; three dimensions of, 189–
    90; s.-examination, 208; Hegel on,
    120; inmost, 171; mature, 189;
    physical, psychological, and
    cognitive, 152–54, 173, 176–77;
    realization of, 92–93; in Axial Age
    religions, 147; Charles Taylor on,
    185–86; transcendence in, 152–54;
    Western conceptions of, 169–75,
    173–75
Selfishness, 5, 36, 87–88, 102–05,
    168, 170, 177, 205; in failing
    imitation of virtue, 200; in self-
    deception, 179–81; rationalized,
    180
Self-reference, 152, 169–75, 179, 185–
    86; in defining self, 169–70
Self-reflection, 53
Semerad, Marilyn, xxxiv
Semiotics, 10–15, 26–27, 29, 39, 70–
    73, 77, 94, 102–05, 111, 131–33,
    181–83; in Confucian conception
    of self, 177–79; European versus
    American, 12; of ethics, 38–40; as
    ritual, 123; and orientation, 187–
    88; pragmatic, 213; defining
    spirituality, 64–69
Sengzhao, 42
Sensibilities, training, 72; in Xunzi,
    27–29
Sentient beings, 32–33

Seriousness, Confucian, 209
Sex, 13, 67, 98, 171, 220
Shamanism, 22
Shame, 36–37, 153–54
Shang Di, 27, 69, 158–59
Shao Yung, 3, 42, 149–50, 188
Shenhui, 42
Shintoism, 22
"Short Happy Life of Boston
    Confucianism, The," xvi, xxi,
    xxiv–xxv, 1–23
"Short Happy Life of Francis
    Macomber, The," xxi
Shun, Kwong-Loi, 176
Significance, in ritual, 123
Signs, 22, 70–73, 94–96, 192, 202;
    cognitive, 178; in Confucian
    conception of self, 177–79; with
    interpretation, meaning, and
    reference, 220; natural and
    conventional, 12–14; pragmatic
    theory of, 213; systems of, 131–33
Sin, 89–91, 103, 161–65, 170–71, 203
Sincerity, 26, 35, 87, 153, 178–79,
    196
Singularity, of Jesus, 200
Sinology, xxviii; missing in some
    Western Confucians, 22
Skepticism, 59–62
Sky God, 158
Slavery, 171; to sin, 103
Smart, Ninian, religion defined by,
    61
Smith, John E., 12, 216
Snake, symbol of nature, 201–04
Social conventions, part of creation
    of the human, 201
Social disintegration, and Boston
    Confucian humaneness and ritual,
    96
Social sciences, making distributive
    justice possible, 79–82; defining
    religion, 61
Social services, and filiality, 195
"Socially engaged," xiii
Society, 129; in Confucian definition
    of self, 177–79; global, 79–82, 206,
    209, 218; mobility in, 203; scien-
    tific, 74–79

Sociology of knowledge, 68, 216
Socrates, 60
Solitariness, defining religion, 215
Son of God motifs, 126
Songs, 4
Sophistry, 5, 11
Soul, 65, 69–74, 115, 169; defined,
    70; s.-centered civilizational
    motifs, 126; symbols in, 193–94;
    transformation of, 192. *See also*
    Self
Source, of creation, 137–38
South Asia, xxvi, 127; dialectic of
    being in, 133; religious traditions
    of, 110–11
Space, 51, 136; created, 159; s.-time,
    77, imagination of, 121–22
Specification, of vague categories,
    112–15
Spectrum, of ideas of ultimate from
    personified to abstract, 152–54,
    158–61
Spence, Jonathan D., 214
Spinoza, B., 7, 138
Spirit, 63–69, 159, 169; of God, 164,
    172–73; motif of, 119. *See also* Self
Spirituality, xxx, 57–82, 191–93;
    defined by Ewert Cousins, 63;
    discipline in, xi; defining hypoth-
    eses of, 62–74; with multiple
    religious identity, 206–09; litera-
    ture on, 216; and religion, 63;
    practices of, 61–62; secular, 63
Spontaneity, 144, 162
Spring and Autumn Period, 33
Standing and walking, as culturally
    defined, 29, 123
State University of New York Press,
    xxviii
Status, recognition of, 183
Stewardship, of the earth, xix
Stoicism, 89
Stones and tiles, shattered, 179
Stories, 52–54
Streng, Frederick, 57, 60, 216
Sub-hypothesis, conditional,
    defining soul, 70; transformation,
    72; truth, 70; ultimate reality, 65;
    essential, about spirituality, 64–65

Subjectivity, in Luther and Wang Yangming, 156
Subject-object, 53–54
Submission, 48
Substance, philosophies of, 35
Substance-function distinction (*ti-yong*), 31, 86–87, 149
Subtlety, manifestation of, 181
Suchness, 70, 117, 159
Sumer, myths of, 116
Superficiality, in Confucianism, 167–68
Supernaturalism, 71
Superstition, 59
Symbolic reference, 62
Symbolism, 98, 181–83; and symbolic acts, 8–11; improved, 72; philosophic ideas as, 119–20; religious, 61–62, 64–65, 68, 192, 216; in systems, 132–33; transformation by, 72–73; ultimate engaged by, 207–08
Symmetry, 137–138
Symposium, 98
Synthesis, of Confucian and Western philosophies, 51–52; in imagination, 121
Systems, dynamic, 132–33; semiotic, 131–32, 181–82; and orientation, 187–88; of signs, 111; social, and conceptions of self, 167; of symbols, 120

Tablet, ancestral, in Confucian piety, 160
Tai Chen, 215
Taiwan, 52
Tamas, 116
Tan Situng, 42
Tangle, of civilizations, not clash, xxvi
Taylor, Charles, 40, 108, 185
Taylor, Rodney, L., xxiv, xxviii, 57, 211, 213
Technology, xxvi, 39, 51–52, 127, 129, 213
Ten thousand things, 5, 70, 82, 94, 152–53, 157, 175–77, 185
Thanksgiving, 116

The Platform Scripture of the Sixth Patriarch, 42
Theism, 86; and the infinite, 67–68
Theocentrism, 126
Theodicy, xix, 126
Theology, xiii, 59, 90–91, 159; apophatic, 61–62, 67–68, 208; Cappadocian, 172; negative, 61–62; Aristotelian, 199–200; Chinese, 41; Christian, xvi, 217; as cognitive, 59–60
Theonomy, 126
Theory, xvii, 77–79; scientific, 76
Theosis, 164
Thickness, of comparative categories, 112–15
Thinking, axiology of, 217
Thomism, 150, 220–21
"Three Schools Movement," xxx, 212
Tillich, Paul, 69, 89 104, 126, 158, 208, 214
Tillman, Hoyt Cleveland 3, 38, 43, 199, 211
Time, 51, 136; created, 159; and eternity, 134; modes of, 137
Tocqueville, Alexis de, 212
Togetherness, 136–39
Tong Lik Kuen, 47
Torah, 116
Totalization, 126
Totems, 122
Trade, xxv, 116
Tradition, 107–11; spirituality in, 63
Tragedy, 184–85, 190; and self-deception, 174–75
Tranquillity, 66, 75, 142–43
Transcendence, xviii, xxxi, 48–50, 62–69, 108; in Christianity and Confucianism compared, 164–65; in Confucianism, 68–74, 151–54; defined by Hall and Ames, 69, 147–51; properly defined, 151; of heaven, earth, and dao, 149; immanent, 57, 65–69, 216; motifs of, xvi, 147–65; in ritual, 124; of self, 191; in Tu Weiming, 85–86; in Wesley, 164–65; as separate from world, 68–69
Transcendent, the, immanent in self, 164–65

Transcendental argument, 11
Transformation, xviii–xix, 26, 61–62, 144; defined, 72–73; personal, 85–88, 168, 178, 206; religious, 63–73; ultimate, 57–58
Transitivity, of ancestral relations, 199
Translation, xii, xxx, 42–44, 113–15
Treatise on Jen, 144
Tree of Life, 163
Tree of the knowledge of good and evil, 201
Trinity, of heaven, earth, and the human, 14, 26, 76, 85, 141–42, 202, 213
True Self, motif of, 116–19
Trust, xii–xiii, 100
Truth, 48–49, 115, 120, 129, 177–79, 191–92; in engagement, 64–75; objective, 165; in philosophy of religion, 59
Tu Weiming, xxi, xxv, xxviii, xxx, xxxii–xxxiii, xxxv, 1–2, 9, 21, 35, 37, 43, 50, 52, 54, 57, 60, 68, 73, 79, 83–105, 107, 115, 150, 156, 168, 184, 189, 194–95, 211–12, 214–16, 218, 220–21
Tucker, Mary Evelyn, xxviii, xxxii, 213, 218
Turner, Victor, 216
Turning, to principle or God, 88–91
Twilight, none in Adam, 162

Ultimacy, 61–69, 143, 160, 191–92, 206–09, 216; of commitment, 86; defining spirituality, 73; transcendent, 167
Ultimate, the, xvii, 159; Category of, 221; concern, 22; of non-being, 66–67, 216; reality, defined, 65–69; embodying, 73; and modern science, 74–79; spectrum of representations of, 158–61; many ultimates, 208
Unconditioned, the, in Buddhism, 159
Unconscious, in Freud, 173–74
Underdog, rooting for, shoe-horned into by philosophy of culture, 109
Unification, 142
Uniqueness, personal, 176

United Nations, Secretary General of, as Confucian Ritual Master, 80
United States, xxv, 41–42, 44; philosophy in, 214–15
Unity of knowledge and action, xiii
Unity, anthropocosmic, 68
Universalism, in Confucian rhetoric, 159–61
Universality, 101
Universities, xxvii, 5, 107
University of Hawaii Press, xxviii
Univocity, 120
Upanisads, 110, 117
Us versus them, xxv–xxvii
Utilitarianism, 38

Vacuity, 7
Vagueness, in comparative categories, 112–15, 164–65; in signs, 181–82
Value, 5, 12–13, 51, 68, 70–73, 129, 217; grounding of, 75–76; spiritual, 92–93
Van der Leeuw, G., 216
Vaught, Carl G., 172, 219
Vedanta, 119; Advaita, 140, 171
Vedas, 110, 116, 139–40
Vietnam, xii, xv, xxx, 2
Virtue, 36, 157; of ancestors, 199–201; Confucian, 220; ethics, 22; transmission of, 199
Visvakarman, 139
Vulnerability, to correction, 78

Wade-Giles, xxxii–xxxiii, 42
Wang Anshi, 38, 211
Wang Bi, 31, 42, 125, 142–43, 145, 149
Wang Chung, 42
Wang Fuzhi, 3, 42
Wang Yangming, xiv, 3, 7, 42–43, 45–46, 50, 73, 83, 86–88, 152, 156–58, 161, 170, 178–80, 188–89, 21, 218, 220–21; compared with Wesley, 164
Water, motif of, 119; muddied, as model for selfishness, 168
Watson, Walter, 49
Way of Heaven, xviii, 97. *See also* Dao; of life, 58–62
Weather, 142

Weber, Max, 48
Weiss, Paul, 11, 213, 215
Weissman, David, 131
Wen, as high culture, 26
Wesley, John, 73, 148, 152, 161–65, 222; as Confucian sage, 207
West, the, xiv–xv, 129; contemporary Confucianism in, 41–54; culture of, 99–100; versus Chinese culture, 107–11; distinguishing philosophy from religion, 58–62; on the self, 169–75; dialectic in, 134–35, 142; philosophy of, 50–52, 109; in Asia, xxii, 38; learned and criticized by Confucians, xxvii–xxviii; connected to Confucianism by pragmatic semiotics, 94–95
Western Inscription, The, 105
Whitehead, Alfred North, xvi, 11, 42, 46, 51, 121, 126–27, 129, 139, 215, 221; religion defined by, 60–61
Wholeness, 48–49
Widows and orphans, 20, 101, 196
Wilderness, 81
Wildman, Wesley, xxxiv, 217
Will, 89, 149; decisive, 150; divided, 170–75; glorified, 96; heteronomous versus autonomous, 163; moral, in Adam, 161–64; to power, 76; transcendent, 150
Wisconsin, University of, 42
Wisdom, xii–xiii, 25, 36, 176, 199
Wittgenstein, 126
Wohlfart, Guenter, xxxii
Women, 16, 20
Word, motif of, 119
World, civilization, 1–8; conversation, 83; culture, xxvii–xxx; defined by Axial Age religions, 147; by determinateness, 135–36; w.-founding, 65–66, 69; philosophy, xxii–xxv, xxvii–xxxi, xxxv, 1–8, 20, 55; Confucianism as, xxi, 38–40, 50–52; and sacred canopy, 68; worldliness of, 65–66, 150
World Spirituality Series, 218; definition of spirituality in, 63–65

Worship, 198
Worth, discerned, in Confucianism, 177; of people and things, recognition of, 168
Wu Kuangming, xxxiii, 43–44, 46–47, 49–54, 218, 220

Xin (trust), xii
Xuanzang, 42
Xunzi, xiv, xvi–xvii, xxii, xxv, 3–9, 13, 26–29, 37, 42, 45, 80–81, 109–10, 118, 141, 143, 145, 154–55, 178, 180, 186, 188, 202–04, 214, 218; philosophy of culture in, 33–38; on ritual, 93–94; on selfishness, 102
Xunzi, 3–8

Yahweh, 116, 118, 158, 197, 202
Yale, system of Romanization of Chinese, xxxiii
Yang Xiong, 42
Yang. *See* Yin/yang
Yearley, Lee, H., xxviii, 46, 214–15, 220
Yen Yuan, 42
Yi (rightness, righteousness), xii
Yijing, 21, 42, 51, 117, 141, 212
Yin/yang, 48, 66–67, 117–19, 141, 149; motifs of, 117–19, 124–25; theory of, 144
Yin-Yang School, 42, 117
Yixuan, 42
Yoga, 72–73
Youth, culture, xiv; proper response to evil in, xviii–xix

Zhang Dunsun, 42
Zhang Zai, 3, 42, 66–69, 76, 105, 178, 188
Zhi (wisdom), xii
Zhizang, 42
Zhou Dunyi, 3, 7, 42, 66–67, 74–75, 83, 142–43, 145, 178, 216
Zhu Xi, xiv, 3, 38, 42–45, 96, 144, 152, 156–57, 177–80, 184, 215, 218
Zhuangzi, xxii, 30–31, 42, 44, 53–54, 118, 141, 220
Ziong Shili, 42
Zoroastrianism, 126